From Sinnership to Sonship
The Story of Becoming
Tom Anderson

Huios Publishing

Library of Congress Control Number: 2025914042
ISBN: 979-8-9928480-2-1

Book Cover Design by Sol Saez. (solsaez.design@gmail.com)

Published by Huios Publishing, Anderson, IN   w
ww.husiospublishing.com

Printed in the United States of America

Foreword

I have the privilege of teaching undergraduate and seminary students in courses related to the history of Christianity. Each year, I walk a new group of students through the story of God's Church, and each year, I come away with a deeper appreciation for the ways in which the community of believers has found ways to thrive amid tremendous societal change.

One particularly significant change was prompted by the rise of Humanism and the accompanying technological advent of the printing press. Some at the time, including a young German monk by the name of Luther, believed the end of the world was near. And yet the Church, thanks in no small part to that young German monk, found in the ground of societal upheaval fertile soil for renewal. The Reformation is just one example. Political and social changes in Europe and its colonies led to the First Great Awakening.

The Industrial Revolution introduced technological and cultural shifts that led to the Second Great Awakening, the World Missions Movement, and the emergence of the Holiness and Pentecostal movements. One can't help but notice a pattern (and it goes back long before the modern era): great technological and social change seems to prompt growth–both numerically and theologically–in the Church.

This growth, I tell my students, does not disrupt and restart the Church, nor does it lead to the abandonment of orthodoxy. On the contrary, we find through each of these eras of challenge a stronger Church emerging–one whose orthodoxy remained unchanged, yet also deepened.

My walk through the history of the Church this year left me convinced that we are now poised at the edge of another major cultural transition. Although as I write this, I am trying to resist the tendency to overestimate the challenges of the moment, I cannot help but conclude that this present shift might prove to be every bit as cataclysmic as the eras to which I just referred.

A growing number of writers and public thinkers have posited that we are in the early stages of a Third Industrial Revolution—this time built not by steam or electricity, but by information. Some have gone so far as to assert that our ability to leverage that information using artificial intelligence will someday be seen by future historians as the most significant of the three Industrial Revolutions.

Given the tenacious history of Christianity, my sense is that the question for Christians as they enter this transitional time is not whether the Church will adapt, but rather what form that adaptation will take. To be certain, a major challenge to our thinking and practice is coming. Will it bring with it renewal, as it has so many times before?

I believe the Holy Spirit is even now stirring up disciples for that very task. I don't pretend to know what the shape of the renewal will be, but something in my head and heart tells me that whatever is coming will 'rhyme' with the book you are about to enjoy. As I communicate with Christian leaders across various denominations and geographic locales, I have been hearing rumblings.

Luther's Reformation called the Church back to a truth that had been placed to the side: that we are–that each of us— is a sinner in need of the radical grace of God. And that our salvation was (and is) dependent on that grace alone. But now, some 500 years later, it occurs to me that this message has made its mark on the Church; the fact that we are sinners saved by grace has come to the front and center of our life and thought.

And it just might be that even as we have recovered this central Gospel message, another truth has found itself on the sideline. Romans 8:19 says that "the eagerly awaiting creation waits for the revealing of the sons and daughters of God." (NSAB) This is the message of Tom Anderson's book.

In the pages that follow, Tom Anderson makes a compelling case from Scripture that it is time for the Church to move forward from its default posture of "sinnership" into a newfound and God-ordained position of sonship. Both men and women who have been saved by grace through Jesus Christ have been invited–no, more than that, have been *called forward*–to step into the promise of the Father.

This mandate is not so that we can enjoy any sense of heightened individual spiritual achievement, or a sense of self-righteous satisfaction. We are being called forward into sonship because, to paraphrase our Lord in John 5:19, we want to do what we see the Father doing. We are entering a time of great societal turmoil where new (and age-old) questions are being asked. My sense is that our reclamation of sonship will feature prominently in the renewal that will come in response.

This book is provocative. It will make you uncomfortable at times. It is highly imaginative and incredibly rich. Read it. Sit with it. Process its challenge in small groups of other disciples, testing everything Tom writes against the witness of Scripture. I think you'll find the message of *From Sinnership to Sonship* both profound and highly edifying, even as you find it eerily relevant to the challenges of our age. I certainly have.

Dr. Jason Varner
Anderson University

Note to Reader

In the tradition of the author of Hebrews, who said "as it says somewhere in Scriptures", specific verse references will not be used with exception. Verses are easily googled if you want to find the reference. But all verses quoted are accurately. Unless noted, all Scripture quotations are from the ESV. TCA is my own rendering.

A large reason for this book is to foster thought, discussion, and hopefully a reexamination of the person of God and your own person. One of the hardest things to do is to stand outside of yourself to see yourself. With that in mind, questions will follow each chapter which are designed to engage both your own heart and the Spirit. You might even come up with better questions to ask (which I hope), so don't limit yourself to these because. as you ask yourself questions, answers will emerge.

Contents

The Journey Begins

O nce you have seen it, it cannot be unseen. This is one reason Paul prayed that the eyes of your heart would be opened. Whatever captured and motivated him, Paul wanted you to know. He discovered something both of God and himself that transformed him, which then became an unstoppable force that still transforms whatever it touches.

Paul discovered a God he could never have imagined, and his own person imagined before time. He came to know not only Christ on the throne, but the One who lived within, and, as he came to know Christ, Paul himself came into sharper focus. As his vision of God became clearer, Paul's sense of self grew, and, from that place, he lived.

He sang, "I am who He says I am", not because he wanted to believe it, but because he knew it. Otherwise, how do you explain his life? He knew himself to be a son of God in all its nuanced meanings.

Sonship is the cry of everyone because sonship means specialness. It is knowing that you are the center of one's attention just because you are. Sonship answers your deep-seated need to sense your own worth and significance and to feel safe. It does not create pride, but a healthy sense of self that is amazed and humbled and energized.

This awareness is found in only one place, that is, in a relationship with the Father, but both the world and the church are still seeking. The world looks for its uniqueness in a far-off country, while the church hopes to find it by working in the Father's field.

The world's gyrations are about trying to find their selves which Jesus encouraged. He said that the result of losing one's life is finding it, so the result is not the issue. He wants you to discover who you are along with your worth and significance. The issue is the way that this sense of specialness is sought and achieved.

The world offers those who are uncertain about their identity the choice to self-identify as this or that. Because they aren't aware of God's special call or love, they attempt to discard their sense of "I am not" and find that special sense of "I am" in things that will leave them flat or worse.

The church has its issues as well. You were created to sense God's high calling and live from that place of sonship. But while you are told that God loves you especially, you are also told not to feel too special. So, most Christians self-identify as a "sinner saved by grace." This mentality, however, drinks from the same "I am not" well that the world does.

Rather than going into a far-off country, many Christians remain in the Father's field, doing this or that in an attempt to find their worth and significance. As with the world, without hearing the Father's "You are my beloved," you too will do what you can to find your own specialness. This, however, will also leave you flat or worse.

"I am who He says I am" is another way to express Paul's "hope of His calling". Biblical hope means absolute assurance. Paul prayed that you would be absolutely certain, from the inside out, of His call of sonship because your calling is the same as his. Though it is expressed uniquely and differently, you too are called to live your life in an uncertain world with a quiet confidence that is rooted in the sense that you are "His beloved in whom He is well-pleased."

If you are honest, though, "absolute certainty" is probably not your daily experience. Otherwise, your life would look different. This book explores what that calling is and the process of going from "I wish it were so" to "I know it is so."

This book is also deeply personal. It describes my journey from sinnership to sonship, from "I am not" to "I am." You are not going to hear my story directly, however. Since my life is not that interesting, I will tell my story through the lives of some faulty, yet relatable Bible characters.

Their lives are more familiar and far more interesting. And you will soon discover that their lives are also pattern stories which were written to show the way God works to transform you into His likeness. So, what God purposed for and did in them is what He purposes for and desires to do in you. When He is done, it will just look like you and no one else.

I have been able to read my life in their stories and, because of that, have seen my life transformed. My hope is that, in reading this, you will be able to read yours in theirs as well, see yourself and God in a new light, and change. I pray that this book helps shift your thinking and bring it into alignment with God's.

Before I do, however, I need to address a few matters. The first is to define some terms. What the heck is sinnership? Never heard of that. And sonship? That seems to be a fuzzy concept and quite possibly an outdated, gender-ridden term which needs to be shelved. And is this an actual journey anyway?

After that, I need to lay out some principles which are woven throughout this book and which have informed my life. So, this chapter is a sort of an introduction to the introduction. After thoughts, like developmental darkness, how your perception of God impacts your sense of self, hope and calling, the concept of the meta-story, transliteration and self-interest are introduced, I will look at the lives of three individuals who explain your life. They are Adam, Peter, and Abraham.

Adam, pre-fall, is the glory from which you fell and the glory to which you have already been restored in Christ. Since pre-fall Adam is the type of the "you" whom God imagined, we will look at Adam and Eve from that place. I will examine the fall and its effect on your sense of self, but since you are more familiar with your post-fall version, I'm going to spend more time with the risen Adam than with the fallen one.

Then we will examine Simon Peter as detailed in the gospels. Peter is the story of every Christian because every Christian begins their Christian life with a false sense of who they are. It doesn't matter whether you have an inflated or deflated view of yourself, your version is wrong and doesn't come close to God's.

For three years, Peter lived with Jesus, but he was full of himself and didn't know it until his world imploded. Knowing God's breaking process will help you interpret the sometimes-crushing moments of your life.

Finally, we will look at the life of Abraham. His story is the story of becoming the person whom God imagined. You will relate to his life and embrace him as your father because he also walked with the Lord imperfectly, that is, first and for many years, as an unbelieving believer. Then he was an unhoping hopeful. Finally, on Moriah, James wrote that the saying, "it was accounted to him as righteousness" was fulfilled or made complete.

James knew that righteousness is much more than "being right with God". Righteousness is about growing into the awareness of your identity as a son.

Abraham was right with God when he encountered Him in Ur and believed who God said that He, God, was, but Abraham wasn't right with himself. He didn't believe God's estimation of himself until God brought him out under the stars at least a decade later. And so, it is with you.

At that point, his journey toward becoming the person God imagined began. Abraham became more and more right through a process that God established in his life until, on Moriah, he was willing to give up all external evidence of his fatherhood because he knew who he was. It's the same process you will discover as well because, as a son of Abraham, his story is yours.

This book will challenge some conventional thought, so you will need to read it with a wondering and worshipping heart. If you are predisposed to look for things that are wrong, this might not be for you because you will find things here that are outside of your box and that you haven't considered before. At times, you will be tempted to say, "Heresy." But if you knew what God really thinks about you and all of humanity, you would also accuse Him of that.

It is an understatement to say that your theology and mine are short-sighted and deficient. What you believe about God is your best attempt to encapsulate the infinite, so when you and I stand before the Lord, we will all have flat foreheads. (Slap your forehead and say, "Duh".) The best you can do is grope for a greater understanding, as Paul told the Athenians.

So, you are not going to find a neatly packaged theology here because I am still trying to figure it out. You will find, however, some boundaries pushed, some speculations, based on reading between the lines, made, and some assertions, of which you have never before thought, declared. When I do, though, I will tie them back to the Scriptures.

While these thoughts have been influenced by Trinitarian theologians, some of what I have written is uniquely mine, that is, thoughts that I have never read or heard before, and that should give you pause. It has me. But what the heck, these thoughts have also caused me to wonder and worship and have helped begin to answer David's "who am I?" question with "I am much more than I have ever thought."

So, I am willing to unpause and push the play button. You, however, will need at times to press your own pause button to question what you have read, question God, and examine your own thoughts. To that end, I created some questions designed to help you search your own heart. As you read and wonder, my prayer is that you come to discover the God you could never have imagined and the "you" imagined before time.

One more thing before you begin. You will find recurring themes woven throughout the book, and sometimes, phrasing that sounds like something you've already read. You might be tempted to think, "You've said that already.

Come on, you're repeating yourself. Let's get to the next point." (But if you are a Bible reader, you will know that I am in good company.)

If you find yourself thinking this way, examine how you are reading. While this book contains information, it's been written primarily to affect your heart, and, if you know anything about your own heart, hearing something once or twice is not enough.

As I wrote in *Ephesians and All that Jazz:*

"Grace creates such a disturbance and is so foreign that it takes time to figure out. Many grace bombs will need to drop on your head before it dawns on you. I hope that when I am done writing this, the shock of grace will become amazement and instead of retreating into your own meager efforts, you will be able to rest in His. My purpose in writing is to carpet bomb your mind and heart with one grace bomb after another."

So, my friends, are you ready to be bombarded with grace?

Questions

1. If you were asked to complete this sentence, what would you say? "I am a
_____." Did you have to think about it? Did nothing come to mind? *
Do you agree or disagree that you are "a sinner saved by grace"? Explain. * What
does that say about your relationship with God?

2. Do you agree or disagree that one large purpose for your life is to discover
who you are? Or is that unimportant? Explain. * If this is true, how do you
think God makes it discoverable?

3. How do you define righteousness? Take some time to think about your
definition because righteousness, being righteous, and growing in righteousness are major themes of the Bible, and quite possibly the greatest. Does your
definition get you excited about living day to day? Or should it?

4. When you think about specialness, how have you tried to find that, or
do you even think about that? * Do you agree or disagree that seeking a sense
of specialness is hardwired in everyone? Explain. * Do you think that you are
special, or do you think that thinking this way is prideful? Explain.

5. Is "sonship means specialness" a new concept for you? * How would
you define sonship, and do you think your life would be different if you knew
deep down that you are His beloved? * Is this difficult to believe for yourself?
Explain. * How might embracing the truth that "I am who God says I am"
change the way you navigate doubts or uncertainties in your daily life?

6. What theological assumptions or "tidy boxes" might you need to question
in order to open your heart to a grander vision of God and yourself, and how
can you approach this with humility and wonder?

Sonship

S innership and sonship are the beginning and ending points of your Christian journey. If the church had better definitions for unrighteousness and righteousness, I could have titled the book, *From Unrighteousness to Righteousness: The Story of Becoming*.

But since righteousness is defined both narrowly and objectively as "being right with God", this word has lost its meaning and its power to transform. This understanding of righteousness also keeps you feeling unrighteous, or not right, because you are more aware of your own failures and imperfections than of your identity in Christ.

On Sunday morning, you sing, "I am a child of God" with faith and conviction. On Monday, however, as you face the same circumstances with their accompanying feelings, the chorus of "I'm NOT a child of God" bubbles up from within. I know. I have heard that chorus.

The church doesn't help because it has encouraged this mentality by embracing a "sinner saved by grace" or a "righteous sinner" identity, leaving its adherents unsure and confused as to who they are. This results in flip-flopping from a righteous to a sinner's mentality, depending on which wave hits them in the moment.

Now, wait a minute. Didn't Paul embrace his sinful side because he called himself "the chief of sinners" near the end of his life? If that has popped into your mind at this point, I am going to ask you to hold your fire because Paul was not talking about identity. He was making a point by using himself as an example. Paul knew himself to be a son, not a sinner.

In writing to Timothy, Paul was putting an exclamation point behind the fact that God can save the most clueless and the worst by using himself as the best example of what God can do. If he still held to a "sinner saved by grace" mentality, then the Romans 8 treatise on sonship would never have been written with the Romans 7 "woe is me" struggle being the pinnacle of Christian living.

The question that needs to be addressed concerns identity. Are you a sinner or a saint? You cannot be both. While there are sinners who do good and saints who sin, your doings and how you navigate life are rooted in your identity. This is why Paul could press forward while everything pushed against him. He knew his own failings for sure, but more than that, he knew who he was in God's sight.

Most Christians, while being "righteous" live with a "not right" mentality because they trip over their behavior and cannot see how "the perfections and the beauty of holiness" applies to them. So, they identify as forgiven sinners, and not as embraced sons who thrill God.

The problem with this is something that the world has successfully addressed. It knows that behavior is an outgrowth of one's identity. Therefore, the world affirms identity, regardless of behavior, because it knows that a person who is affirmed in who he or she thinks they are will not only become more entrenched in that lifestyle but more of that behavior will occur. This is a self- and community-affirming cycle.

The church, however, is either confused about who they are or does not want to go down the perfection road. Therefore, a "sinner saved by grace" mentality feels right to many.

The church is also unclear about how God produces Christ-like disciples. So, while God affirms people into their destiny, the church focuses on behavior by either applauding or condemning it and then encourages practices which, of themselves, are good. It hopes that the graced sinners at whom they preach will somehow become saintly through various programs and meetings.

It is time for the church to be serious about addressing this. Paul embraced Christ as his life and identity and then gave himself to get others to see that very thing for themselves. Yes, he talked about behavior but, for him, behavior was the caboose (an important caboose, for sure), not the engine which powered the train.

And John, who self-identified as the one whom Jesus loved, had the same mission as Paul, which was to get the ones whom Jesus loved to know and believe the love of God for themselves. Both John and Paul had the same goal, which was to have their friends come to know their own selves in the same way that they did. And they knew themselves the same way Jesus did, as a son of

God. They realized that when God is known as your Father, sonship will begin to dawn on you.

This led me to coin the word, "sinnership" to get you thinking outside of your box. Sinnership is an identity term (as is sonship) and is that un-right state of mind which tells that you are not—not valued, not worthy, not significant, not safe, not resourced, not right, and without a secure and glorious future.

I'm sure that if you listen closely to yourself, you have probably heard that voice that can continually loop in your subconscious. It especially bubbles up when life jostles you. While you might have some certainty about God, you are less certain about yourself.

Let life happen and who you believe God and yourself to be spills over. Your reaction to life's slights, hurts, and failings reveals what you really believe about God and yourself. And it doesn't matter whether you have a healthy or an unhealthy self-image, a sinnership mentality is rooted in your own abilities and resources which are limited and will eventually fail you.

Sonship, however, is the gospel. It is the exceedingly good news about you—that you matter, and that you can become the person whom God imagined before time began. As it is said of Jesus, the word also can become flesh in you where you no longer try to be a Christian, whatever that is, but you know that you are loved for who you are, important in God's scheme of things, and safe enough to take risks.

And from that understanding, you live out God's call, whether it is saving the lost or sorting the laundry. It's you, living from a place of wholeness. In a word, righteous. Or in a couple of words, a son fully embracing his or her sonship and living life humbly and confidently.

This is the good news Jesus came to proclaim, and which Paul and John took pains to explain. That message is a redeemed you, vitally connected to other redeemed ones and to the Triune.

Paul's message was "you in Christ" and "Christ in you", that is, you, no longer animating your own life, but sharing in the righteousness, peace, and joy of Jesus' life. His message was you, continually growing into the awareness of a beloved son of the Father. And since God has only one type of Son, which is the Jesus type, you are as loved and as secure as He is, more significant than your most far-flung thoughts, and safe.

Sonship is not a concept tinged with gender. As I will discuss in the next chapter, sonship is the upward call of God in Christ Jesus which applies to all, regardless of gender, and, as such, must be defined by the life of Jesus. As revealed in Jesus, who is the the Son, sonship is a relationship, as it relates to the Father, and a position of authority in the cosmos.

Sonship, as revealed through Paul and John, can only be embraced from a Trinitarian understanding of God. Without exploring the delightful relationship enjoyed by the Father and the Son, and without realizing that you have been invited into and included in their relationship, sonship will seem heretical. A most Holy, sovereign, self-sufficient, and transcendent God might like you, but He would never share His glory or throne or bridal chamber with you.

But to these things, you have been called. Everyone, regardless of gender, is called to participate in the relationship of the Father and Son and, from that place, make their mark on their world, like Jesus did. This is the reason He came and the reason you exist.

1 Corinthians 1:9 states that you have been called into "THE fellowship of the Son." With whom has Jesus been interacting and forever enjoying, but the Father? It is into their close friendship that you have been invited and actually brought. It's time that the church begins to declare this truth and to start believing it.

John also wrote that when you came to be, Jesus sparked something of Himself within you, that is, an amazing uniqueness which He purposed to be fully expressed. "Jesus", John wrote, "is the true light who enlightens everyone who comes into the world."

When you came to be, He lit you up and put something of Himself in you that He longs to come to life. God gave you the most precious gift that He could ever give when you were born, which is your sense of self. How do I know that this is true? You spend your entire life projecting and protecting it.

The Fall did not snuff out your need to be valued, to feel safe, and significant. You still have the God-given desire to amount to something. You still want to accomplish something and be recognized for it. This is God's imprint on each person, calling each to discover the glory from which they fell.

The Fall threw a monkey wrench into the works. It left you frustrated and chasing your tail, that is, trying to fulfill by yourself what is only satisfied in a joint venture with God. In fact, because humanity's plug was removed from the Source, your sense of vulnerability heightened.

The mentality that tells you that you don't measure up remains even after conversion. Your brokenness and how that was expressed before conversion, as you have hopefully come to learn, is not magically mended. It takes time and a believing in the finished work of Christ. The church uses the word, sanctification, to describe this mending process.

Sonship is the place where you come to know that you do measure up, and in that knowing, find yourself beginning to. This sense does not produce pride, but a humble acknowledgement of who you are in Christ. It is where you are no longer controlled either by your own personality and opinions, or by your strengths and giftings, but are led by the Spirit, which, according to Paul, is the definition of sonship. He wrote, "For all who are led by the Spirit of God are sons of God."

Since the rest of this book is given to expand the meaning of sonship and describe your journey into its experience, I will leave it there for now. But I do need to take a chapter to discuss something I'd rather not. Since sonship, on the surface, sounds male, the concept has been largely skirted around by the church, and not celebrated, because it sounds exclusionary and offensive. This, however, can be no further from the truth as you will see in the next chapter.

Questions

1. How does viewing righteousness as an awareness of your sonship identity, rather than just being "right with God," challenge or reshape your understanding of your relationship with God? * How might this shift help you move away from a "not right" mentality?

2. The chapter describes sinnership as a mindset that tells you you're not valued, worthy, or significant. When have you experienced this mindset, and what triggers these feelings in your life? * How can embracing your sonship identity—knowing you are loved, significant, and secure in Christ—counter these negative thoughts?

3. The author calls sonship the "exceedingly good news about you." Do you find it easy or difficult to accept this gospel, and why? * What doubts or objections arise when you consider yourself as a beloved son or daughter of God. * How can you open your heart to this truth, perhaps through prayer, reflection, or community, to let it transform your sense of self?

4. Reflect on a recent moment when life "jostled" you—perhaps a conflict, disappointment, or failure. What beliefs about yourself or God surfaced in that moment? * What practices can you adopt to consistently remind yourself of this identity when circumstances challenge it?

5. The chapter emphasizes that sonship is rooted in a Trinitarian understanding of God, where you're invited into the Father and Son's fellowship. How does this vision of God as a relational, inclusive Trinity differ from your previous perceptions? * How can you cultivate a deeper awareness of this fellowship in your daily spiritual practices?

Sonship and Gender

In this gender-crazed world, the concept of sonship has been marginalized, even by Bible translators, and has come to mean something less than it does. To keep from offending, the church has ceded its place of naming and defining to the prevailing culture. Since they think that sonship marginalizes women, sonship is out and the more neutral "children" is in.

This current culture has a touchy-feely, exclusive-inclusive lens through which it looks. Sonship is then interpreted as a term of gender and privilege that comes from patriarchy and, therefore, must be shelved. But sonship is the most inviting and inclusive word that you will ever hear, regardless of gender, because this word comes from the most inviting and inclusive Person in the universe.

Jesus is forever known as the Son and therefore is its definition. Sonship describes Jesus' relationship to the Father and His position in the cosmos. Relationship and position define sonship, not gender. Both Scriptures and the Spirit call you a son, regardless of gender. Paul wrote, "And BECAUSE you are sons," so everything hinges on sonship. Without embracing sonship, whether you are a male or female, you won't get off the starting line.

What applies to the One applies to all. Jesus intimated this when He declared, in the prodigal son's story, that the Father has only two sons. So, there are only three options for everyone—a son in a far country, a son in the Father's field, or one in His arms. All humanity, that is, every gender, every race, everyone, with either screwed-up or screwed-down thinking, is sons, whether they know it or not. What is required are open eyes.

So, I hope that you don't have a pronoun fixation because you will trip over them and miss the message. But know this—Jesus, the firstborn of many sons (both men and women), is the rock of offense and the stone of stumbling. If you walk with Him for any length of time, something is going to offend you because He wants your thinking to rise to His. He will not lower His to yours.

Sonship is not a gender term. It is neither exclusive nor resulting from some sort of male perspective. Genesis clearly states that "Male and female, He created THEM." "Them" are sons, not "hims." God has never pitted men against women. That occurred because of the fall.

The two were to become one in such a way that together they would become greater than if they journeyed alone. Adam and Eve, together, would accomplish more than Adam could do in his original creation. In God's thinking, it has always been man-and-woman, spoken in one breath. They were to reflect the Godhead—a unity in diversity, a delightful collaboration, and not a competition.

Paul said that God erased the gender, socio-economic, educational, and racial differences in Christ. If any exists, it's on us. It is not God's fault. And while I am on my soapbox, let me take this a step further.

As it relates to females specifically, they have a greater place in the kingdom than has been traditionally thought. While the Church has embraced a kinder heart toward women than the hard edge of Islam, it still has pigeon-holed them and has been exclusionary. But when God pulled man apart, like taffy, to make Adam practically whole, He called the one who faced Adam, "Ezer-right-in-front-of-him."

Most Bibles interpret these two Hebrew words as a "suitable helper", implying that women are great tag-alongs. And yes, I would agree that this interpretation smacks of patriarchy and has been interpreted by men through the lens of Adam's fall. But "Ezer" is a name of God and means helper.

This word is scattered throughout the Scriptures, including the Psalms, which declares that God is our helper. "Helper" then finds its fullest meaning in Jesus' upper room talk. Jesus said that the Helper has come and is with you to lead and teach you. The Holy Spirit is always the behind-the-scenes leader. He is the saint-whisperer.

God determined to have such a whisperer in the man's life because, alone, he can easily fall off the rails. So, God formed a life-sized representation of Himself to stand in His place. Since God wasn't going to be physically present with Adam 24/7, He made Eve, so He could.

Yes, I know that didn't work out. But that doesn't negate God's original intent, which leads me to ask the following question. "Who is greater? The helper or the help-ee?" Hmmm?

Much of our biblical perspective has been colored by Adam's fall and not by Christ's rising. As this relates to females, Paul worked with and praised fellow female apostles and deacons. Luke and Paul both recognized the leadership, teaching, and pastoral gifts of Priscilla and acknowledged her primacy in her relationship with her husband and church by putting her name before Aquila's. They recognized that gifting and calling take precedence over current cultural norms.

Yes, Paul addressed specific situations concerning women and gave guidelines, as he did on many things, and sometimes in conflicting manners. In 1 Corinthians 12, he encouraged ALL to prophesy in church, confirming Peter's Pentecost message that your sons AND daughters will prophesy. He encouraged both men and women to be sensitive to God's spirit and speak as God gave them words for the moment. But right after that, Paul instructed women to be quiet in church. Puzzling.

At that time, their gatherings reflected the Jewish custom where men would worship on one side with women and children on the other. So, Paul wanted to make sure that the flow of the meeting would not be disrupted by ladies who would either ask their husbands questions from across the aisle, which could have been discussed at home, or possibly would talk among themselves.

They were to hold their peace, as men were expected to do as well. The flow of the meeting was the imperative. Since women, at times, are a little freer to express themselves in the moment, Paul felt the need to address this.

And of course, women are not to take authority over a man. That wasn't the Genesis, pre-fall order. They were to have authority WITH the man, and the man was to have authority WITH the woman. It was never an either/or proposition. They were to acknowledge each other's strengths and work together.

Additionally, in light of Jesus' resurrection, do you really think that male domination is the only consequence and curse which was not overturned? What harmful decisions could have been, and can be, avoided if godly women attend elders' meetings with godly men?

I could go on. Read the last chapter of Job and ask yourself what stands out. The only practical result I see from Job's trial is how he highlighted and elevated women as Jesus did. The last chapter does not list the names of Job's sons, but his daughters are named and given an equal share of the inheritance.

Could the practical result of all that Job went through be having his eyes opened to the importance of the female gender? Seeing God as Job did might have opened his awareness to the totality of God's personality and then have him rightly esteem and elevate women. And could this also be what will happen in the church when we collectively see God with fresh eyes?

The Old Testament history is replete with examples of both men AND women in positions of leadership and influence. God is not exercised over gender. He looks for willing vessels who have meek and quiet spirits (including men) to accomplish His work. In fact, Iran's church, which is one of the fastest-growing churches in the world today, is led primarily by women.

Now you can believe what you want to believe, and I hope we can still be friends, but I don't believe that God splits hairs. He weaves both genders together into a cohesive, amazing, and beautiful whole. As the church understands and embraces sonship, both men and women will lean on each other and stand toe to toe, while the kingdom comes.

Men and women are both called into sonship. Romans 8, which is considered by many to be the pinnacle of the New Testament, is about sonship. He wrote, "For you did not receive the spirit of slavery to fall back into fear, but you have received the Spirit of adoption as sons, by whom we cry, 'Abba! Father!'"

He followed that up with "for the creation waits with eager longing for the revealing of the sons of God." You can almost see creation straining and aching, as it waits for you and me to get it. Paul's implication is that once sonship dawns on the church, and as it celebrates that relationship, not only will the children of God be free, but the universe will also be released from its bondage.

Questions

1. The author has defined sonship as "a relationship with the Father and a position of authority in the world." Does this definition bring clarity to how you might view yourself and gender? Describe the relationship you have with God. Describe those positions of authority, that is, where has God placed you to bring in His kingdom?

2. The chapter critiques the church's tendency to adopt neutral terms like "children" to avoid offending, ceding ground to cultural definitions. Have you encountered resistance to the term "sonship" in your church or personal beliefs due to gender associations? * How does the author's perspective—that sonship is the most inclusive term because it reflects Jesus' identity—challenge or align with your views?

3. The author reinterprets "Ezer" as a powerful representation of God's helper, akin to the Holy Spirit, elevating women's roles. How does this perspective shift your understanding of women's value and contributions in the church and society? * Are there areas in your life or church where women's gifts are underutilized, and how can you advocate for their inclusion? * How might men embracing a "meek and quiet spirit," like women, foster mutual respect and collaboration?

4. Paul's instructions for women to prophesy yet remain silent in certain contexts seem contradictory. How do you approach these scriptural nuances, considering cultural and contextual factors? * Do you view biblical teachings on gender roles as flexible or fixed, and why? * Reflect on a time when you wrestled with a seemingly contradictory biblical passage—how did you seek clarity, and how can this process inform your understanding of sonship and gender?

The Trinity and Your Sense of Self

B ecoming who you behold is a truth found from psychobiology to the Scriptures. Just ask a duck. Imprinting is a real thing, both naturally and spiritually. If this is true, then your image of God is paramount. Your theology matters because it affects your anthropology as well, or that "Who am I?" question that determines how you do life.

If your god is no god, then you are, and you will have to determine your identity on your own. This often leads to your own confusion and hurt. If your God is the Great Sovereign, both Separate and Transcendent, this too affects how you see yourself and engage life. It puts you in your place, at a distance, and on your toes. However, if your image of God is the One who dances with anyone who takes His outstretched hand, the possibility of being swept off your feet and into delightful adventures is huge.

So, here are three different people with three different images of God. I am going to assume that you would agree that God is not the issue here. Whatever and whoever He might be, He is who He is.

The difference is the filters or the glasses that you have on. These filters not only affect your theology, as I have said, they affect everything, which includes your self-image, how you interact with others, and how you perceive your circumstances.

A.W. Tozer knew this. He wrote in *The Knowledge of the Holy*, "What comes into mind when we think about God is the most important thing about us." He also wrote that "the history of humankind will probably show that no people have risen above its religion." He knew that conscious living is an outgrowth of unconscious beliefs. J.I. Packer said it more succinctly. He wrote in *Knowing God*, "We can never know who or what we are till we know at least something of what God is."

C.S. Lewis also knew this. In *The Last Battle*, all sat around the same banquet table, eating the same food. One group was overjoyed and sated. The other spit out hay, and it wasn't the seasoning. It was their taste buds.

Jesus also intimated this when He said, "According to YOUR faith, be it done to you." Scary words, these. Not "according to who God is or what God can do", but according to your belief or interpretation, or according to how you perceive Him.

So, what is your image of God? This question should be a wake-up call. It should make you cry out to God and begin to grapple with the faith that was once delivered to the saints. What is the faith that was once delivered? What does that faith say about God? What does it say about you?

It, at least, should make you realize that while God does not change, your understanding of Him should and must. As I wrote in *Ephesians and All that Jazz*, "If your theology is not evolving, it's a fossil."

John, in his first epistle, talks about evolving theology when he addressed little children, young men, and fathers. John knew that the perspective of a little child is vastly different than that of a father. A baby's knowledge of his or her father is based on "oohs" and "ahhs", and not on in-depth conversations over a beer. Being a father also adds a layer of knowing that an adolescent can never have.

So, while you might say that your theology is Bible-based, it is, and it isn't. It is based on the Bible, for sure, but it is also combined with your spiritual stage, your personality, and your life experiences.

For example, if you grew up with a critical, stand-offish father, the image you have created of God and of yourself will be vastly different than one who grew up with an engaged and affirming dad. Both could and do justify their theology from the Scriptures. And then, if you are churched, throw into the mix a good measure of systematic theology that further colors that image.

That being said, you may have your theological talking points down pat, but your real theology, that is, how you perceive God and yourself, is more felt than telt. It is revealed in the trenches. It pops out in your close relationships.

How do you respond or react when you are disrespected or ignored? How do you hold up under stress? How do you act when no one is looking? What do you tell yourself daily about yourself, your circumstances, and your future? This is your real theology. This is what you really believe about God and about yourself.

If theology evolves then, what should it be evolving into? Wouldn't this be good to know so you can begin to instruct your heart and persuade it before Him? Well, it might be good to listen to two individuals who were set apart for this very reason. Both were taken above the fog into heaven and clearly saw the One whom we confess to know. Their image of God and its corollary, their sense of self, still sends shock waves wherever their message is preached, even in the corridors of the church.

John and Paul are these two individuals. Both began their theology "in the beginning". John used these very words, while Paul wrote about being known and chosen before the world began. Both exalted Jesus but also said some heretical things about you and me because they clearly perceived that you and Jesus are now inextricably linked. I'm talking about the "I in you" and the "you in Me" thing. And how they lived matched their theology.

John, in his little children, adolescent, and father progression assumes that you, the reader, would agree that a father's perception of both God and self, along with their understanding of life, would be more mature and more aligned with God's than a little child's or an adolescent's, even though these are important developmental stages.

A little child, according to John, is aware of his or her missteps and the amount of time spent falling on their keister. This life stage rightly focuses on the child's "missing the mark" and God's forgiveness and help. Man's imperfections and God's perfections take center stage. Learning to control bodily functions, hopefully seeing God's smile and outstretched arms, and connecting need (sin, by the way, is a subset of need) with His provision are all parts of this stage.

But if you were to codify your theology at this point, what would it look like? To me, it looks a lot like the "Lord, be merciful to me, a sinner" mantra of mainstream denominations and the "sinner saved by grace" confession of many Evangelical churches where God's holiness and perfection and man's sin and imperfections take center stage with repentance, justification, and sanctification being their primary teachings.

Now, don't hear what I am not saying. Repentance, justification, and sanctification are important, but as the writer of Hebrews said, these are just the starting points that lead to his real point of going on to perfection or to a more perfect understanding of spiritual realities.

A little child's theology, rooted in the fall, centers on sin and its remedy. God's holiness is often misinterpreted as Him distancing Himself from sin-

20

ners due to His hatred of unholiness. This understanding fosters a sense of unworthiness and the 'sinner saved by grace' mentality, which exalts God while diminishing humanity, and putting them in their place.

The Triune redefined holiness in the Incarnation because they debunked the distancing, the holding of their nose, and the "you repent first" sort of God that is assumed from reading the Old Testament. When all Three showed up in person, Jesus, who always does what He sees the Father doing and who was anointed by the Spirit, washed feet and let sinners wash his. The ground didn't open up to swallow rebels either. It opened up to swallow Him. (Yes, yes, repentance is important.)

On one level, however, a little child's understanding creates an appreciation for God's greatness and mercy, but relating to God primarily because of need is only foundational. It is not the superstructure. And since you will never rise above your religion, as Tozer said, you will continue to live with a sinner's unworthy state of mind, no matter how graced you are.

A sinner's mentality, as I have said, is that little voice within that tells you that you are not right in your relationship with God, not right with yourself, and not right with your world. You hear that voice in the bumps and grinds of life when circumstances, either real or imagined, spark all sorts of emotions. Emotions, such as anxiety or depression, fear, anger, or resignation, are the effects. Your inner voice, not your circumstances, is the cause.

Yes, you readily acknowledge that God is the "I am", but you fail to make the connection that you are an "I am" as well because being in Christ, too often, is just a talking point. So, "not valued", "not important", and "not safe" can tend to be the spaces in which you live.

But John wrote, "As He is, so are we also in the world". Please note that John used the present tense. He did not say that someday, in heaven, you will be as He is, even though you will be revealed in full measure. John wrote that you are now.

You are as loved as Jesus is. You are significant, just like Him, and more important than you think. You are as safe as He is. And His righteousness, or that inner, quieting sense of being right while the rug is pulled out from under you, and your righteousness has the same source. You are as righteous as Jesus because there is only one type of righteousness.

Jesus is readily acknowledged as the image of God, but the light has not yet dawned on you that Jesus, as the Second Man, is also the image of you.

Traditional theology, while rightly emphasizing God, downplays mankind, and that can easily obscure your identity in Christ.

There is also a young adult's understanding of God and self that precedes the fall. It is called dominion theology, and many Pentecostal-type churches embrace this. Christian nationalism, Zionism, et al, swim in this stream. This type of thinking perfectly describes a young man who is "strong and has overcome the evil one".

He can and must take on the world and make it bend to God's will. Since he knows that he was created to "subdue and rule" and to be the head and not the tail, anything that looks like it needs subduing becomes the target.

Whereas traditional theology is deeply influenced by Genesis 3, dominion theology finds its justification in Genesis 1. The first mandate for humanity was to put things in order and rule and, as I will write in a future chapter, to do it forcibly. So, there is a Scriptural basis for this type of thinking, and as the Preacher wrote, "for everything, there is a season and a time for every matter under heaven."

Dominion theology emphasizes man's part in the work, and, it seems to me, can put man on a little higher pedestal than God because they are the instrument by whom the kingdom comes. It is THEIR faith, THEIR declaring and claiming, THEIR prophesying and praying which moves the hand of God, moves out the devil, and brings in the kingdom.

Young adult movements have changed the direction of history. Sometimes, the results have been destructive, sometimes questionable, and, once in a while, they've been good. From Mao Zedong's Red Guard to the Vietnam protests to the Jesus movement, youth, full of vim and vigor, have taken on the established order and have disrupted the status quo. But I am sure that if you have lived for at least three or four decades, your youthful bluster has turned into middle-aged circumspection.

Since the adolescent stage has its own blind spots, they will also "miss the mark". But unlike a small child, they often don't know it. Young children are very aware of their limitations when they do what they do best, which is to fall down.

Adolescents, however, are less aware because they are strong and are sure that they can carve out their own space. But adolescents with overblown estimations of themselves, and some authority, can be problematic and become bullies. Yes, there are Christian bullies, and you might even be able to name a few.

An adolescent knows what he knows, but he doesn't know what he doesn't know, which can become his fatal flaw. Presumption, pride, and self-effort can become substitutes for wisdom, humility, and walking in the spirit. God can also be used to justify their aggressive stance with "In His name" used as a bludgeon, and "In Jesus' name" really being "In our name" in disguise.

But if John was indicating stages of a growing understanding of God and of one's self, then the father's stage is the final and ultimate stage. As a father of adult children, both my children and I are well aware of our failures in their parent-rearing and my child-rearing years. But what is central for us now is the relaxed relationship that has grown out of these previous relational stages. Our understanding of each other has changed over time, and rightly so.

Now, neither of us try to change the other. When they were young, I was in charge and exerted pressure on them. They took charge and put pressure on me (to my chagrin) when they became teenagers. But now, we enjoy an ease of relationship, which means that we can pick up the phone and talk for a bit as equals who enjoy each other's company and who share concerns and life together.

John declares that there is another theology and anthropology which precedes Genesis 1. "Fathers, you know him who is from the beginning." There is an understanding of God and self which goes beyond the fall and creation, and beyond the veil into eternity. It is rooted in the Trinitarian relationship.

So, it is important not to settle or camp out in either a little child's or a young person's theology. These are stages to be passed through and embodied as you continue toward a more perfect understanding of God and yourself.

Before I take a little time discussing this last stage, you might be saying, "This is interesting, but speculative. I am not buying it." Ok, I agree that it might be, but the Scriptures say, "Out of the mouth of two or three witnesses, let every word be established." Since this "establishing" verse is quoted both in the New and Old Testament, let me show you the same progression that John writes about in the New Testament, in the Old.

The tabernacle was comprised of three spaces: the outer court, the holy place, and the Holy of Holies. The tabernacle speaks of many things. It is a type of Christ. It is a picture of tri-part man. There have been volumes written on the tabernacle with pages even devoted to the discussion of the meaning of a specific color of a thread.

But what is most instructive here is the progressive approach it reveals about salvation or one's journey into wholeness. Wholeness is dependent upon your understanding of God because your understanding of God affects your understanding of self.

Your entrance into the reality of God first goes through the gate, then into the courts with its brazen altar and laver, and then into the holy place where you minister to God. Finally, you enter into the presence of God Himself, where you come to know Him without veils, and in that knowing, know yourself.

While you should and must linger and ponder in each place, you are not to camp out in the first two. You are to "go on to perfection", as the writer to the Hebrews said. But if you did camp out, what would your understanding of God be like? Since each space has a different emphasis, it paints a different picture of God and His relationship to man. Each space, like John's stages, has its own theology and anthropology.

The outer court's focus is on sins committed, the sin nature, and God's remedy, which is the gate of repentance, the justifying brazen altar, and the sanctifying laver. This space is where your sins find forgiveness and your walk finds cleansing. It is the place of God's great mercy because it is where He ministers to you and provides the remedy for your brokenness. Your place, in the outer courts, is to believe and receive, to submit, and to keep your nose clean.

If you camped out here, your understanding of yourself and of God would center around your sin, His holiness and provision, and the distance between. Repentance, justification, and sanctification would keep your focus on your own efforts. So, while you might say that your eyes are on God alone, they are really on the tightrope, and on your steps and missteps.

There would still be internal curtains of your own making, keeping you from walking in the "freedom of the sons of God". A "sinner saved by grace" mentality would be celebrated, and, in so doing, would keep God at a distance, just like the elder son distanced himself from his father. He stayed in the field because he perceived his father as an accountant and himself as a commodity.

While forgiven, you would still journey back and forth from the gate of repentance to the altar to the laver, and then back to the gate. The altar calls you back to the realization that you don't measure up. The writer of Hebrews spoke to this when he said not to keep laying the foundation of repentance from dead works and of faith toward God, but to go on into the Holy place.

The Holy place, which is the second space that you are to inhabit, is not concerned with sin. Its focus is on keeping the bread warm, the lights on, and the room smelling fresh. The priest would know his own importance because it was on him to make and keep things right in the world because if there was no bread on the table, it was on him. If the candles went out, it was also on him. If there was no incense? Yep, again on him.

While God was the active agent in the outer courts, the priest was the prime mover in the Holy place. Whereas God ministers to you in the outer court, you minister to Him there. You stand in His presence because you are strong and have overcome the residue of evil and the sinner's mentality, which has kept you from moving in that space. Your understanding of yourself would be vastly different within that enclosed, intimate space than in the outer court, where you would be exposed to the elements.

But just as a little child's and a young adult's understanding hopefully gives way to a father's understanding, so the outer court and Holy place are but stopping-off places on the way to engaging the One who no longer resides behind the veil. The God of the Bible is now unveiled because that veil was torn in two when Jesus died.

So, the Who and the what that was behind the veil, according to John and Paul, have now been revealed. The Who has revealed the what to be "the light of the knowledge of the glory of God in the face of Jesus Christ".

Doesn't this thought pique your interest and create a desire to know Him from that most Holy, and previously restricted place? Doesn't this question reveal that you might have a way to go in your understanding of God and yourself?

Hopefully, at this point, you are not putting up some theological roadblock to this unbelievably good news. The veil has now been removed, but if you are still primarily circumventing the outer court or attending to the altar, your understanding of God and of who you are, is still out of focus.

Both Paul and John declare that there are two things which fill the Holy of Holies. (They have a father's understanding of this spiritual reality.) The first is the relationship of relationships—the Father and the Son in the envelope of the Spirit. And the second is you, and all of redeemed humanity, who are included in this relationship.

Paul wrote that we, which means you, are the "fullness of Him who fills all in all". Try to get your mind around that! The One who is the fills everything is filled up to the brim by you and me. You, completing Him, as He completes you.

How can this be? This doesn't mesh with "a God who doesn't need any-thing" or a "self-sufficient God" theology. This sort of understanding of God resides in the outer court, and not within the Holy of Holies, and is a little child's assumption. By definition, a person in a relationship is less without the other and needs the other. Relationships also add to each and are designed to bring each into a greater sense of being.

Additionally, a relationship, in itself, is a growing and unique entity. It has a life of its own. God is in relationship with God, and the implications of this are huge. (God cannot become more, or can He? We will have an eternity to find out.) Paul also realized that God included humanity in this equation, which adds another layer of complexity and mystery.

Only a Trinitarian understanding of the Godhead can begin to imagine this sort of God and this sort of love because it certainly does not fit into a theological framework of a Sovereign, Holy, and Transcendent God who needs nothing. That God, while beneficent, is still a bit stand-offish and exacting. And that sort of God would never give a thought of marrying the likes of you because you could add nothing to Him.

Only a God, whom you could never have imagined, would say that without you, He would be emptier. Doesn't saying, "I do" mean "I need and want" and "you complete me"? The implications of "the marriage of the Lamb has come, and His bride has made herself ready" are huge, if you dare to follow its breadcrumbs. These seemingly heretical thoughts, though, can shock the Church's heart, which has been out of rhythm for a long time and can get it back in synch with God's.

The relationship and friendship of the Father and the Son took center stage in Paul's thinking. His teachings sprang from an eternal perspective and from a Trinitarian viewpoint. Every letter he wrote, whether to a church or group of churches, whether to close friends or acquaintances, began by acknowledging the relationship of the Father and the Son who have forever existed in the atmosphere of the Spirit.

It was this relationship that instructed him. God's holiness or uniqueness was less moral (though deeply moral) and more relational. The perfect, sinless beings who cry, "Holy!", are amazed at the "otherness" of God's relational, inclusive, humble, and self-giving nature, not His moral and separate perfection. And in heaven, the saints who have been made holy are not crying, "Holy!" They are exclaiming, "Worthy!", because they too are amazed at the unrivaled, unequaled, and incomparable love of God.

The love of God, shed abroad, has its roots and finds its life in His own relationship. And since God's love has always been self-giving and other-honoring, it then followed for Paul that if God inhabits His people, they too will exhibit this "agape" type of love.

John also plainly declared that the Son became incarnate to reveal the Father, and that the Father glorifies or shines the spotlight back on the Son. There has always been mutuality in their relationship. They have always worshipped or worth-shipped each other.

Isn't this the hallmark of a healthy relationship? God's glory becomes more glorious as they glorify each other. And how could they not be overcome by the other's beauty and, because of that, lay down their lives for the other?

John also wrote, in the prologue to his gospel, that the Son has always been "with" the Father and that they were One. As he wrote about this "in the beginning" relationship, John twice mentioned that "the Word was *pros* or with God". The Greek word, *pros*, means so much more than being "with" in a cooperative sense.

It means "face to face". It means invading one's space and always getting closer. It means not being able to get enough of the other. There is an ease in their relationship which invites closeness, and the fullness of their relationship is the eternity which He has put in your heart.

Your desire to be known and loved, along with your desire to know and love, has its roots in the Father and the Son who know and love each other. John must have seen this early on because he was the one who leaned on the chest of the One who has been forever leaning on the bosom of the Father. He somehow perceived that he was included in this lover/beloved relationship. This affected his perception of self because he self-identified as the one Jesus loved. How would your life be different if this were how you perceived yourself as well?

"Face to face" means a relaxed relationship between friends (*phileo*). It means the love and respect a father has for a son who is taking over his business and the son's admiration for and deference to his father (*storge*). It means the passionate desire that two lovers have for each other (*eros*).

This *agape* love of God creates the everlasting and all-consuming fire that consumes anything it touches and anyone who touches it. This is the God who was behind the veil and who has fully made Himself known in Christ. This God is also the one whom both Paul and John were constrained to proclaim.

It was also the gospel which the Judaizers of their day poo-pooed because it resided in the Holy of Holies and not the outer court or the Holy Place. For them, the Holy of Holies was too holy for mere man to trespass. Grace, for them, had to be tempered with the law. Union had to be governed by rules. And so, it is today.

But as I wrote in *Ephesians and All that Jazz:*

This makes what Christ did even more remarkable. In essence, God tore up the old agreement on the cross and re-enacted the one He had in His heart all along. No rules—just the Creator, creating; the Giver, giving, the Uniter, uniting.

Paul and John clearly saw that you were created for and included in this relationship, and that this should inform your sense of self. "In Christ" for Paul, and "abiding in the vine" for John, meant your intimate inclusion in their relationship. This was hidden behind the veil for millennia, but now with the veil rent, the Voice that spoke from heaven is no longer muffled. Jesus' sonship declares your own. You too are "His beloved in whom He is well-pleased".

Paul's overarching theme is an identity or sense of self that is deeply rooted in the Father/Son relationship. Over 140 times, Paul used the phrase "in Christ" to describe who you are. He proclaimed Christ, for sure, but didn't put a period behind His name. For him, there was a big AND between Jesus and you, which means that the circle of the Trinitarian relationship just got bigger.

John agreed when he recalled Jesus' intimate talk with his disciples as he faced Calvary. "In that day you will know that I am in my Father, and you in me, and I in you." Try to unravel that tangled mess! Only this mess is too wonderful and can't be undone.

Isn't this the sort of God whom you desire to know? Well, He is. Reread the first chapter of Ephesians and tell me that it ain't so. The message of Christ, for Paul, was not just Christ, but a restored humanity who is no longer in the timeline of Adam but in the shared life of Christ.

John saw the same thing but often spoke poetically. He wrote about branches and vines and about abiding in Him as He abides in you. He talked about being begotten by the Only Begotten of the Father. He describes a bride preparing herself for her wedding night.

And He remembered Jesus's prayer in the upper room where Jesus discussed with His Father their up-to-that-point, exclusive glory. Isaiah proclaimed, "I am the LORD; that is my name; my glory I give to no other." But Jesus rebutted this in His High Priestly prayer. "The glory, which You said we would give to no one else, give to them because they are not other." (TCA)

We will explore and develop these thoughts through these pages, but for now, this is the shockingly good news Jesus came to unveil. God has forever been dancing and has come out from behind the curtain to graciously and excitedly extend His hand toward you.

Your sense of self, which is both the motor that powers the car and the steering wheel, should be rooted in THIS relationship and not in systematic theology. You can outline any sort of objective theology you might want, but how do you bullet point a dance? You will never get to know your partner by studying film. You have to take their hand and dance. That's it, you just have to dance.

And in the inclusive relationship of the Trinitarian God, your sense of self is just right. It is not too little, as reformed and traditional theology implies. Nor is it too big as dominion theology would lead you to believe. A Trinitarian understanding of the Godhead produces a sense of self that is bathed in a love that is both humbling and expansive.

It creates in you the desire and the ability to be as self-giving and other-honoring as the One who gives Himself to you. Like a healthy marriage, you discover that it is not about you, though your heart swells as your relationship thrives. It is about us. You stand out for sure, but you know that you would be nothing without the other.

This is the mystery that was hidden behind the veil. A Trinitarian understanding of God will change both your image of God and your sense of self, which, when joined together, is the truth that sets you free.

Questions

1. What, in this chapter, has challenged your thoughts? * Has this chapter deepened or challenged your perception of God and yourself? If so, in what ways? *Based on John's stages (little child, adolescent, father), where do you see your current understanding of God and yourself, and why?

2. The chapter describes two realities behind the rent veil: the Trinitarian relationship (Father, Son, and Spirit) and your inclusion in it alongside redeemed humanity. How does this revelation challenge or reshape your view of God's nature and your identity? * What emotions or questions does this stir in you?

3. The chapter suggests that your image of God shapes your sense of self and how you navigate life's challenges. Reflect on a time when your perception of God influenced your response to a difficult situation. * How might embracing the 'face-to-face' relational love of the Trinity change your approach in the future?

4. The text describes God's love as a 'face-to-face' relationship that invites you into the Trinitarian dance. How does this imagery make you feel about your relationship with God? * What is one practical way you could respond to this invitation in your daily spiritual practice?

5. The chapter argues that a Trinitarian understanding of God fosters a balanced sense of self—neither too small (as in traditional theology) nor too big (as in dominion theology). How does this perspective challenge your current view of yourself? * How might it influence the way you love and serve others in your relationships?

Developmental Darkness

Darkness and light are foundational themes in the Scriptures. The world began in darkness and will end by being enlightened by the glory of the Lord, with its light source being the Lamb. Between the beginning and the end, light and dark have jockeyed for position. An age has even been named for darkness with an age of enlightenment following.

Darkness, however, as is its counterpart, is one of those terms which have a nebulous meaning. You can have a sense of what it is and point to specific things that epitomize darkness. But since darkness is an environment in which one lives, it is hard to stand outside of it to identify darkness or recognize the effect it may or may not have. By definition, darkness keeps you in the dark.

There is without a doubt a supernatural component to darkness. The devil is called the prince of darkness and rules over its domain. This sort of darkness is aggressive, destructive, and evil. Like a black hole, it grows by making things smaller as it sucks them into its abyss.

Its genius is to have those who are being pulled in, unaware, or to think that they aren't affected, or that nothing can be done to pull them out. This darkness is a moral darkness because a moral choice or lapse brought it on the cosmos.

So, the Light of the world came both to reveal its nature and the way out. Paul's personal testimony included that his mission was "to open their eyes, so that they may turn from darkness to light and from the power of Satan to God." He later wrote that "the god of this world has blinded the minds of the unbelievers, to keep them from seeing the light of the gospel of the glory of Christ, who is the image of God."

This moral darkness was dispelled on the cross where it seemed that the Light of the world was being snuffed out by the darkness, all the while the glory of God was being revealed in all of His luminosity IN the darkness. The cross, on which hung the Image of God, is the true revelation of God, shining forth and playing out in real-time.

The veil of a distant, judgmental, vindictive, quid-pro-quo God was torn asunder. It revealed a self-giving, forgiving, self-effacing, and self-sacrificing God, whose vibrant life force has pulsated from the beginning.. From the smitten Rock flows, that is, from the very depths of God, grace and truth, redemption and forgiveness, righteousness and sanctification and glorification.

Paul said a simple turning to the Lord opens one's heart in order "to give the light of the knowledge of the glory of God in the face of Jesus Christ." For those who turn, they are no longer children of darkness but children of light.

However, if you and I had an opportunity to chat, I think we would agree that while a veil has been lifted, a cloud of unknowing remains. You and I, as Christians, still experience darkness, but not the darkness resulting from sin, because that was dispelled at the cross and exposed at conversion.

This darkness is different. It preceded the fall and is not an effect of sin. In fact, it is a darkness by design. This darkness is embedded in the life of every creature. It is neither supernatural, destructive, nor evil. It is entirely natural, positive, and good.

I call it "developmental darkness" because it is the same darkness that a seed experiences as it grows. There are epochal moments in the life of a seed when, with the right conditions, it becomes something other than a seed but in the same breath, seedier.

A new awareness of self emerges each time it interacts with its environment. From root to stalk to blossom and fruit, the seed slowly reveals its hidden glory to the end that it fulfills Adam's mandate to become fruitful, multiply, and fill the earth.

Its perception of the world and the world's perception of it also changes. The seed becomes the full expression of itself and, as it is transformed, transforms the world around it.

This is the same darkness that a PhD in mathematics experiences as a 3-year-old. The best she could do is count apples. Her mind has not yet developed to where she can grasp anything but 1+1.

But then there is a moment when she realizes that she has an affinity toward numbers and sees the relationship of pi to how much water is in her glass. And then she writes her doctoral thesis on the number 1. (Yes, that thesis has been written.) Little by little, numerical darkness is dispelled.

Since the natural is a shadow of the real, this applies even more to spiritual development. The apostle John recognized this progression in his epistle by acknowledging the different developmental stages of little children, young men, and fathers. Each might be in the same space, looking at the same thing, but their takeaways and the way they interact are entirely different. Yet each has a correct perspective.

We will also see, in the life of Abraham, how the stages of faith, hope, and love played out, and how they marked changes in Abraham's understanding. These stages will also be seen in the Parable of the Sower, which describes the challenges a seed faces to becoming fruitful.

Your well-worn suppositions about who you are, about who God is, about grace, righteousness, etc., can keep the truth, which sets free, from germinating. The rocks of unfulfilled expectations, and the "why is this happening to me?" question can cause that thing you once believed to wither and die.

And attachments to things, even Godly things, can suck the life out of you. But if you protect the seed through thick and thin, through rain and drought, fruitfulness results. As you see this worked out later in Abraham's life, hopefully, you will be able to interpret your own life in his and blossom.

If the Scriptures are to be believed, both Adam and Jesus came into the world perfect but not complete. They were to blossom and become, in every aspect, who they were—the son of God, perfectly imaging the Father's nature. (The difference is that Jesus is the Eternal Son of God and therefore, THE Image of God, where you and I are made in His image. But it is the same image.)

Luke recorded that Jesus grew in wisdom and maturity, and since Adam was a type of Him who was to come, he also was planted in the garden, not only to attend to it, but to grow and become. Isaiah said that you are the planting of the Lord, that is, God's specific seed which is to grow into a fully mature plant for His glory.

Paul also wrote that you are His tilled field. This implies that your soul is the perfect medium in which God can plant the seed of His word and enjoy increase. Wherever you look in the Scriptures, you find allusions to seeds, to gardens, to fruit, to farmer's fields. Jesus brought this to its fulfillment when He identified Himself both as the Sower and the Seed, and you as His garden.

The assumption is (and must be) that Jesus, as the Second Man, came into the world exactly like you, a seed full of potential. While the eternal Son of God, He was born with a zygote understanding of His personhood. It took years of listening to His parents telling him who He was, discovering Himself in the

Scriptures, being sensitive to the Spirit's witness, choosing to submit Himself to authority and obey, and discovering the spiritual in the mundane in order for Him to fully embrace His Father's "You are my beloved Son" sense of self.

Jesus' sense of self was then immediately tested when the Spirit drove Him into the wilderness. The test came to confirm His Father's assessment because, in the wilderness, there was little to confirm the Father's declaration. No food, no applause, no external blessing. More darkness than light. All that He had were the words that His Father spoke and planted inside of Him. And when the test came, He asserted His Sonship when the devil questioned it. "IF you are the Son of God" was answered with a resounding, "Yes, I am."

Adam, the first man, had the same opportunity. Because he was the type of the One to come, Adam heard through many sources that he was the beloved son of God. The garden unlocked its secrets to him. The animals gladly embraced their Adam-given names. God often discussed with Adam, in the cool of the day, their relationship, which included Adam's sonship. All of this was confirmed in the eyes of his spouse.

But revelation without testing is a puff of smoke. The test came for both Adam and Jesus, as it comes to you. Each was tested by the devil concerning their identity. To Adam and Eve, the serpent said that they could BE like God, if they would only do one thing.

However, they already were like God. What does "made in His image" mean, but that? Though Adam and Eve heard it, it didn't register. (Does that sound familiar?) Since it hadn't dawned on them, they didn't embrace their sonship or realize its staggering implications.

Adam was already in His image but needed to grow into His likeness, which was a large reason for the testing. So, while he heard "in His image", he neither believed or understood it, nor did he know it experientially because this word hadn't penetrated his heart. Adam and Eve were living in developmental darkness.

The test came expressly to refine Adam and Eve's understanding of their selves and to bring them into a new awareness of their identity. The devil offered Adam and Eve a shortcut to be like the One they loved. Since they were in the dark about who they were, that is, they didn't feel that they measured up, what the devil said resonated with them, and they took the bait.

Satan offered Jesus the same shortcut when challenging Jesus on His identity. "IF you are the Son of God." Whereas Adam and Eve failed the test by taking the bait. Jesus didn't. "If, if?" I am the Son of God, so I don't need to do a darn thing."

Jesus came out of the test in the power of the Spirit, fully embracing His Sonship. Adam and Eve, however, left under their own power and lost any sense of who they were. And we have grasped for straws ever since.

Part of developing is being tested. Isn't this your expectation with any area of competency, whether it's getting your PhD or becoming a cashier? So, how can it not be true, spiritually? The test comes to confirm, both to you and to all, your true self.

Unlike Adam, though, you can take the test again and again. God's intent is never to have you fail, but even in your failing, progress is made because a baby will fall many times before she walks. To walk well, you must learn to fall well because falling is part of the process.

We will see this play out in the life of Abraham. He fell on his butt many times. God's gentle attitude toward Abraham's missteps will also be instructive. God didn't call him out for the many times he missed the mark. He called Abraham into more and more light because the darkness in which Abraham lived was developmental.

It was not due to a moral lapse, even though he had moral lapses. And as Abraham responded, his understanding of himself and God grew. And as you walk in his steps, you will discover this as well.

Questions

1. How does the chapter's distinction between 'moral darkness' (resulting from sin) and 'developmental darkness' (a natural part of growth) reshape your understanding of struggles or uncertainties in your spiritual life? * Reflect on a current or past challenge that might be 'developmental darkness' and how viewing it as part of God's growth process could change your perspective.

2. How does the chapter's distinction between 'moral darkness' (resulting from sin) and 'developmental darkness' (a natural part of growth) reshape your understanding of struggles or uncertainties in your spiritual life? * Reflect on a current or past challenge that might be 'developmental darkness' and how viewing it as part of God's growth process could change your perspective.

3. The chapter describes both Adam and Jesus as 'perfect but not complete,' needing to grow into their identity as God's beloved sons through testing. Reflect on a time when your sense of worth or identity was tested (e.g., through failure or doubt). * How might embracing your identity as one made in God's image, as Jesus did in the wilderness, empower you to face similar tests in the future?

4. The chapter suggests that both Adam and Jesus faced tests to confirm their identity as God's beloved sons. Recall a moment when your sense of identity or worth was challenged. How might embracing your identity as God's image-bearer, as described in the chapter, help you respond differently to such challenges in the future?"

5. The chapter portrays Jesus as a seed who grew into His Sonship through listening, obedience, and testing, becoming the full expression of God's image. Imagine yourself as a 'seed' planted by God with potential to reflect His image. What practical step (e.g., prayer, scripture reading, or trusting God in uncertainty) could you take to nurture your growth toward your God-given identity and purpose?

Transliteration

Transliter-what? Transliteration is the difference between the light going on and you remaining in the dark, that is, you either living with a quiet confidence within or with noisy uncertainty. Regardless of the darkness, whether it is the darkness of an unregenerate soul or of a growing Christian, the Light that continually shines in the dark must somehow penetrate the room-darkening shades of your soul. C.S. Lewis called these shades "watchful dragons", which keep out any thought foreign to your limited understanding.

You and I have an internal dictionary written in its own language. This dictionary contains well-worn patterns of thought, that is, years of thinking certain ways about things, coupled with experience. It is your belief system.

These beliefs determine how you do life. They create your comfort zone, forming an almost impenetrable crust over your imagination and understanding. This crust can block the inner sight and belief that propel you on a faith adventure.

Jesus talked about this in the first soil of the parable of the Sower. The well-worn path is the pattern of thought that creates the hardened soil. Instead of producing tomatoes, the word sown becomes birdseed.

Pathway Christians aren't aware that some thoughts, which are outside their box, are of God. Neither do they know that their unplowed, encrusted hearts resist God's good news about them, as much as a unbeliever resists the gospel, only in different ways.

For Christians, believing and receiving the good news of God about you, is the first obstacle to be aware of. While it is easy to read that this soil applies to others, especially unbelievers, what if it applies to your unbelieving heart as well?

How many transformational seeds that house your destiny, that is, seeds which have the potential to produce the fruit of the Spirit in abundance, and restore relationships, have lain dormant in your mind and have not penetrated your heart? It is probably best that you don't know. But, if I am reading this parable correctly, the Sower is continually sowing an abundance of life-producing seed on the soil of your heart, waiting for germination.

Let's take a moment to do a test to see whether some seed has penetrated the crust of your heart. I will give you a word and you give me your immediate reaction. Righteousness. What is it? Hmmm?

Did you give me a book definition? Did you stammer and stutter? Were you a deer caught in the headlights? Luther said when he preached grace, it seemed to him that his congregants looked like cows who had just encountered a new gate and didn't know what to do.

Or did you describe how righteousness has transformed your life and relationships? Can you define righteousness in palpable terms and describe how it has changed your perception of God and yourself? Has righteousness healed the wounds of your heart or are you still nursing them? Has righteousness become your new identity or are you still confused about who you are?

If righteousness still causes your eyes to glaze over or if its definition hasn't changed over the years or changed you, you have an objective book definition. It has not been transliterated or found meaning in your internal dictionary.

Should I take another word? What about the simple word, "grace"? I was in a small group once where the leader in commenting on a verse said, "Well, we all know what grace is." I said, "Whoa! I don't know what grace is. I want to know."

I understand that he was talking about the dictionary definition of grace, which most Christians can recite, while I was talking about my experience of it. The difference between the book definition and experiential knowledge is transliteration. Many Christian-ese words have recitable definitions which remain foreign concepts because, while having a definition, they have little to no meaning.

Doctrinal positions can be established with these words. They can also be hidden behind or wielded as swords, but walls and swords have little nutritional value. For the Bible to have meaning, light must penetrate your heart.

Transliteration is different than translation. In translating any manuscript, one hopes that there is a one-for-one correlation in both languages. Beauty in Spanish is *belleza*. In German, it is *schönheit*. Though there might be cultural differences in how this word is perceived (beauty IS in the eye of the beholder), everyone has an idea what beauty is.

But what about a word that has no equivalent in the other language? When the Bible was translated into English, there were some words with nothing comparable in English. Passover was one of them. The festival was understandable, but there was no single word in English to define it, so Tyndale transliterated that word from Hebrew.

To take this to another level, what about a word that has absolutely no meaning or reference point in the other language? Take, for example, the word thermodynamics. How do you communicate that to an Aboriginal culture? You would have to create a word, lay out a scientific foundation in order to attach meaning to it, and then hope that the tribe somehow gets it. In most cases, it is an impossible task.

This is the difficulty that the Holy Spirit has in communicating spiritual concepts to you. God thinks so differently and speaks in a different language. Paul wrote that "no eye has seen, nor ear heard, nor the heart of man imagined what God has prepared" and also prayed that spiritual realities would get around your watchful dragons. Jesus said, as well, "IF you have ears to hear," implying that while you hear the words spoken, you might not catch the meaning.

Jesus' words are spirit and life, so they can't be understood just by trying to figure them out. Try as you might, His words remain shrouded and become theological mumbo-jumbo. For you to get it, they must be transliterated. And when you do get it, it really is a miracle.

The best story that I know that speaks to this is the story of Helen Keller. Born in the late 1800s, Helen succumbed to an illness at the age of two, which rendered her blind and deaf. With no way of comprehending or effectively communicating with the outside world, Helen lived in her own little world, and her world was a world of darkness. She bumped into life, yet did not know what she was bumping into.

Writing in her autobiography, *The Story of My Life*, Keller recalled the moment when life was transliterated. Prior to this, she encountered the physical world but couldn't understand it because she had no internal reference to define it. Life was speaking in an unknown tongue. Then, while Anne Sullivan poured water on one hand and spelled "water" on the other, Helen writes:

"I stood still. My whole attention fixed upon the motions of her fingers. Suddenly I felt a misty consciousness as of something forgotten — a thrill of returning thought; and somehow the mystery of language was revealed to me. I knew then that w-a-t-e-r meant the wonderful cool something that was flowing over my hand. The living word awakened my soul, gave it light, hope, set it free!"

From that moment of awakening, not only did the world change for Helen, but Helen went on to change the world.

There is a Living Word that awakens your soul, gives both light and hope, and sets you free. And how your heart longs for this! But too often, you can remain in the dark, accepting what you know as all that there is.

Not knowing is one thing, but when you assume that you do, as Jesus told the Pharisees, you don't. This also was the blind spot of the Laodicean church. The Laodiceans were unaware of their condition but thought that they had it all together. Not only did they think that they were correct in their worldview, they also thought that they possessed the resources to navigate life and accomplish what God wanted.

They had their version of Christianity down pat, but it was wrong. What the gospel was proclaiming, they were not hearing. Jesus was outside of their party, and they were unaware of His.

Being clueless is a scary place to be and, unless confronted by Jesus, is a place where you can comfortably reside. Jesus' knock, like the one on the Laodicean's door, alerts you that, regardless of your Bible knowledge, you haven't got it yet, or Him. This alone should drive you to your knees.

Without the sense that you are clueless in whatever knowledge you think you might have, coupled with crying out to God for wisdom and understanding, the little light that you have will be your only light and, as Jesus told the Pharisees, will be your darkness.

So, how are things of the Spirit transliterated or defined internally? When something is transliterated in you, as it was with Helen, there comes a settled and quieting, yet excited sense which buoys you. You know that you know, without feeling the need to explain or defend.

Transliteration begins with an awareness of lack or need. Felt need, I believe, is one of the greatest gifts God can give anyone because need is heaven's currency. Need is what you have in your pocket to purchase what God has in His. Jesus' knock brings with it an awareness of need.

It tells you that there is something more, something outside of your experience, desiring to come in. His knock is the reframing of Isaiah 55:1, where the prophet wrote, "Come, everyone who thirsts, come to the waters; and he who has no money, come, buy and eat!"

It seems that one of the most difficult things to do is to deeply acknowledge need. You are tempted to think that neediness makes you less. But God, by design, created you with holes. While He created the angels with no seeming need, He created you with ALL need.

The Psalmist wrote that angels excel in strength. They also walk by sight. You, however, were created to excel in weakness and, in your weakness, walk by faith. As you embrace your design, you will discover the joy and the secret of rejoicing in your need as Paul did.

Your felt need is heaven's currency with which you can purchase gold for your pockets, ointment for your eyes, and clothes for your body. Your need, coupled with a crying out, is the doorway into the unseen realm. This cry is the doorway from "I am not" to "I am", from sinnership to sonship. It's the cry to have what is real in God to be made real in you. It is the cry for transliteration.

There are a couple of Biblical words that describe the concept of transliteration. These words are "mystery" and "revelation", without which there is no spiritual awareness or growth. Jesus told Peter, "Flesh and blood has not revealed this to you" because God, Himself, does. So, chasing prophets or following the latest and greatest is not going to help much.

Words, like righteousness and grace, are such big, hard-to-grasp words, though, that they can often be left alone or left for the perceived spiritual giants to explain. Even worse, in some quarters, personal revelation is frowned upon because the written word is deemed enough. Obedience is all that is required.

But the freedom Jesus declared, and the one which Paul proclaimed and taught ("for freedom, Christ has set you free") is something different than keeping rules and keeping everyone in line. Freedom disrupts the status quo and can be a scary thing.

Paul prayed that the eyes of your heart be opened so that you would have "aha moments". He also assumed that what he was laying down, you would grasp. Paul wrote to the Ephesians that one reason he wrote his letter was that the mystery of the revelation which God gave Paul would be transliterated in you. These are the words he used: "When you read this, you can perceive my insight into the mystery of Christ." Paul wanted you to know experientially what he knew.

Mysteries abound in God, and Paul knew a lot of them. Because of that, you can waste much time trying to go down different rabbit holes in an attempt to figure them out. They can, if you are not aware, keep you engaged but not engaged in the things that are transformative. From how the world started to how it ends, from Biblical numerology to the Nephilim, much time and energy can be wasted on things that will puff you up and let you down.

The revelation that God is invested in, however, is the unveiling of Himself to you, and the unveiling of you to you, This is the reason Paul took pains to proclaim and explain, with the hope of it being unveiled to your heart, "you in Christ" and "Christ in you". These are the greatest and most wonderful mysteries because God is the final frontier, with you being a close second.

Paul put it succinctly in Colossians, "To them, God chose to make known how great among (literally, in) the Gentiles are the riches of the glory of this mystery, which is Christ in you, the hope of glory." The greatest mystery, and the one worth giving your life to pursue, is "Christ in YOU", (or for the purists out there, "CHRIST in you"), the absolute assurance of glory. Maybe it is just CHRIST in YOU. Either way, Christ plus you equals glory.

The wonder of Christ AND the wonder of you is a wonder squared exponentially. Paul wrote that the whole universe is on its tiptoes, waiting and longing to see the unveiling of the sons of God. It has already acknowledged Christ's unveiling and now awaits yours. When the church begins to cry out for the revelation of "Christ in you" and wait for that very thing to be transliterated, we will be a step closer to aligning ourselves with God and seeing His glory and kingdom come.

Questions

1. The chapter describes 'watchful dragons' as internal belief systems that block new spiritual truths, such as the 'unbelievably amazing you' in Christ. Reflect on a belief or assumption (e.g., about God, yourself, or faith) that might be a 'watchful dragon' in your life. How could inviting the Holy Spirit to challenge this belief help you embrace a deeper understanding of your identity in Christ?

2. The chapter uses Helen Keller's breakthrough with 'water' to illustrate transliteration, where a spiritual truth becomes a lived reality. Recall a moment when a biblical concept (e.g., grace, righteousness, or love) moved from head knowledge to heart experience, transforming your life or relationships. * If you haven't had such a moment, what truth do you long to experience more deeply, and how might you seek it?

3. The chapter portrays need as 'heaven's currency,' a gift that opens the door to spiritual revelation. Reflect on a time when acknowledging a personal or spiritual need (e.g., weakness, doubt, or lack) led to a deeper encounter with God. * How might embracing your neediness, as Paul did, help you exchange it for God's 'gold, ointment, and clothes' in your current season?

4. The chapter highlights the Laodicean church's blind spot, where they were unaware of their spiritual poverty despite thinking they 'had it all together.' Have you ever realized you were 'clueless' about a spiritual truth, as the Laodiceans were? * How did God's 'knock' (e.g., through a challenge or revelation) awaken you, and what might you do to invite His knock in areas where you feel self-sufficient?

5. The chapter emphasizes 'Christ in you' as the greatest mystery, worth pursuing above all else. How does this truth challenge your current spiritual priorities (e.g., Bible study, prayer, or community)? * What is one practical step you could take this week to pursue a deeper revelation of 'Christ in you,' allowing it to reshape your sense of purpose and confidence?

Hope and Calling

H ope and calling both anticipate the future. Hope attaches itself to the future with calling, being your future lived out in the present. They invite you from your past and present to an expected end. They also assume that what you have seen or heard is not tangibly apparent but that it resonates within because Paul wrote that "hope that is seen, is not hope."

Paul, in writing to the Ephesians, and after trying to express the greatness of what the Father did in Christ, prayed. He knew that what he began to write to the Ephesians was not only too much to take in, but that it was also written in a foreign language. So, he tried to encapsulate his thoughts by praying.

He also felt compelled to stop writing and pray because he wanted his friends to get what he was throwing down—that the reality in which he lived would engulf them as well, so they too would walk confidently toward a certain future. "Having the eyes of your hearts enlightened, that you may KNOW what is the hope to which he has called you."

Hope is often framed in these terms, however. God knows what He is doing and whatever He does is good and the best for you, so even though you don't have a clue, you can hope that life and whatever you are presently going through will turn out ok. And even if it doesn't work out here, you can still hope that some good might be realized in heaven.

While this is a component of trust, that is, relying on God's character and ability, this sort of hope is not Biblical hope because Biblical hope is always attached to a vision and a call. Biblical hope is not fuzzy. It is not reactionary. It is both visionary and proactive, and it cooperates in the process.

To navigate life successfully, Paul knew that you had to be certain of both your life's direction and its outcome because life is often a smoke screen, and sometimes it's a battlefield. Being uncertain of the outcome makes you uncertain of the process and will cause you to blink. Uncertainty will keep you from moving forward because you, becoming the person God imagined, is a joint venture. It has always been by grace (God's initiative) through faith (your baby steps).

The ability to wait expectantly, to press on when everything seems to be pressing against you, to be joyful in the journey and kind under stress, and to participate in the process are all functions of Biblical hope because hope steadies the present by interacting with the future. Hopelessness, however, looks at the snapshot of a dismal present, overlaid on the disappointments of the past, and creates an even more dismal video of the future. Hopefulness interprets the present by looking at a glorious end and then putting the present snapshot into its proper frame.

Abraham's story also gives an important insight into hope. Paul writes, "who against hope believed in hope." Here, he contrasts two types of hope. The first is when all the stars align, you see a clear path, and you walk confidently into your future. This type of hope is always wonderful until it isn't.

For Abraham, though, against the backdrop of the impossibility of fatherhood, that is, confronted with his own impotence along with the circumstances that were lined up against him (Sarah's barrenness), his faith grew stronger because his hope was not based on what he saw naturally, but on a clear vision of a hope-infused promise which the God of hope spoke.

Paul put this "hoping against hope" another way when he wrote to the Ephesians. He started his letter by stating that you live in two places at the same time—in Ephesus and in Christ. You are called to synthesize these two often incongruous realities—the limiting and depleting day-to-day grind with the expansive, unseen realm. Paul helped by first painting a grandiose, hope-filled picture of you in Ephesians 1 before he got into the weeds.

The hope of your calling, by the way, is so over the top that it has "heresy" written all over it. Sonship is both your call and hope and can be perceived as heretical when viewed from your perspective. I would venture a guess that "amazing" is not one of your self-descriptors. (Unless you are amazed at your own stupidity and ability to mess things up.)

But "amazing" is God's estimation of you. While you might be more comfortable with a "graced sinner" mentality because you are aware of your own stumbling and limitations, God will have none of that because He knows you as a beloved son.

This is the quintessential struggle you and I face: the one between "in Ephesus" and "in Christ", that is, between a sinnership or lacking-mentality and a sufficient, sonship mentality. Lacking and "in Ephesus" seems more immediate and real, while sufficient and "in Christ", not so much. In truth, both are true, but "in Christ" must be your default position, even as you acknowledge your lack.

This is why there needs to be an enlightening, or an "aha" moment, or in Biblical terms, a revelation, where in a moment of time, light from heaven breaks into your consciousness and you begin to see yourself as He does. Otherwise, you will remain asleep in the light and not know it because only when you wake up do you know that you have been asleep.

For Abraham, the hope of his calling was bigger than extravagant. It was a greatness beyond his wildest dreams. It was as big as God. "Count every particle of sand that you can find. This does not approximate your greatness, Abraham. Now start counting the stars and keep counting. You will never fully grasp My vision for you." (TCA)

This same thing is spoken to you because you are blessed, not just in Abraham's blessedness, but in Christ's. What do you think the implications of "in Christ" are? How big, do you think, is the space that He inhabits? How resourced is He? How loved and honored is He?

This is the same space that you inhabit. So, what does this hold for you? How you answer this question determines the amount of land that has been promised to you, you will actually possess. Isn't this the story of the children of Israel? They only conquered and possessed about 25% of the land God promised them.

Abraham's call was a reframing of Adam's "be fruitful, become great and fill". It also foreshadowed Christ's call to fill all things. And Christ's call is also your high calling. Paul declared that you have been included in Abraham's and Christ's sphere, and he tried to encapsulate it in his letters.

"Blessed with every spiritual blessing" is the high call of God in Christ Jesus for you. This is the hope or certainty which buoys the present and steadies your future.

Head-scratching and hard to believe? Yep, but that does not negate the call. It confirms it. It is so big that it has to be God because God never calls to the water's edge. He has called you out to the deep, that is, to know experientially the length and width and the height and depth of His love. And doesn't your heart long for this?

As it was for Abraham, God's call to you is not just for the "by and by" (though heaven, where all things are renewed, is our blessed hope). Abraham was to become the one God imagined here. He was to fill his space, as much as possible, while he lived, knowing that when he was finished, God would take over. The seed, which was God's word of promise sown into Abraham, developed and grew and is still growing. This is what God holds out for you as well.

The Greek word for "call" or "calling" is *kaleo*, which has two basic meanings. The first is to name or declare. Naming, in the Scriptures, is significant. It indicates both ownership and an intimate knowledge of that thing's essence. It requires two entities that accept their place. One is god-like, who names, and the other is creature-like, who is named.

When Adam named each animal, there was no conflict. Adam was, to the animals, as God was to stars, who named them. The lion did not quibble with Adam when Adam named it "leader", nor did the lamb rename itself when he called it "led".

And it wasn't in their naming that they became that thing. Rather, each animal was recognized as who they were. The naming confirmed to each creature their nature and purpose and gave them the freedom to be.

The concept of someone else naming you might be difficult to accept today, with the current bent to choose your own pronouns and gender, but naming yourself also brings confusion, uncertainty, and anger. You are not your own god, so you name yourself to your own hurt.

Since God has called you into existence, He has the right to name you. He also reserves the right to rename, as he did with Jacob and Simon. But either way, because of creation and redemption, He has called or named you, and as you embrace that identity, you will find the freedom and confidence to become. And the name He has called you is "son".

This, then, puts the onus on you to discover and accept that call, that naming, or identity. As we shall see in the lives of Adam, Abraham, and Peter, the call is first to a relationship, called sonship, before it was a call to action.

While you can sense a specific call on your life (though most don't initially) through various means, whether it's a predisposition, a strong impression, someone recognizing God's hand on your life, or even a prophecy, unless it is rooted in this Father/son relationship, that calling will become a burden that you will carry and eventually wear you out. But if the specifics of your life are an outflow of this relationship, that call will carry you.

The second meaning of *kaleo* is to invite. You are invited from and to, just like a parent would call their child from whatever he or she is doing, to supper.

The child would need to respond. A better example, though, would be inviting a friend to meet you for lunch because you would not want to force a decision.

This is the nature of being called for most. There are a few, like Abraham and Paul, who are confronted with the reality of God in such a way that nothing can be done but surrender. They are those whom Jesus described as chosen.

But for the many (which means the rest of us), God's way to reach you is to invite consistently and subtly and then wait. He awaits your response, that is, for you to follow the trail of breadcrumbs scattered in front of you.

If the many are called and if God is calling all the time, it would then be important to recognize what that call practically looks like. Though circumstances thunder from time to time, God seldom uses lightning strikes.

His call is more elegant because it is disguised in the longings of your heart, in your dreams, and in your brokenness. He calls through your roadblocks. So, the times when hope arises or when unease, uncertainty, brokenness, or lack seeps through your consciousness, you are hearing the call of God.

It can even be the effect that songs, like Sheeran's "Perfect", or Whitney's "I will always love you", have on your heart. It is why movies like "Reacher" or "Braveheart" suck some in.

Don't tell me that God doesn't speak through secular songs or movies. The Proverbs declares that "Wisdom cries aloud in the street, in the markets she raises her voice." So, it's not that God is not calling, it's you, not being able to recognize His voice.

As circumstances call you out, pointing out your lacks or giving voice to your dreams, He is calling you from the narrowing mentality of "I am not" to the ever-expanding "I am". "He who is calling you believes in His ability, in the process, and in your potential, and will not give up on you until He has finished the work that He has already begun in you." Philippians 1:6 (TCA) His call is to the best version of yourself, to wholeness, to clarity, and to significance and worth.

His call bounces off the walls of your heart and continually echoes. Your lack, and even your uncertainty, is God's call which invites you into the fullness and certainty of God.

You can ignore it. You can misinterpret it. You can spend your life trying to fill that void yourself, but, as Augustine wrote, "the heart is restless until it finds its rest in God." Or you can respond with Abraham's, "Here am I", when your life is disrupted.

God has placed the enormity of eternity in your heart. The difference you sense between your dreams and their unfulfillment is His call. The desire to be recognized, to be loved, the longing for more is deep calling unto deep—if only you can hear His voice through the noise of life.

Too often, however, you are told that these thoughts are evidence of selfishness. As I will write in the next chapter, they might be acted upon wrongly, but these desires are the residue of a glory that the fall cannot drown out. The fall cannot silence them because God has put these desires in your heart.

The call to worth and significance was first heard in the garden, then reiterated to Abraham, and finally, clearly and emphatically stated to all of humanity in Christ.—"You are my beloved. I am so excited about you and pleased. Go get 'em." (TCA) "Be fruitful, become great, and fill your space with you" (TCA) is God's call on your life, and knowing this will release you to pursue His call. This is the good news that you are called to embrace.

This call is your hope. It is your blessed assurance. As with Abraham, you will need to hope against hope while His voice penetrates the dark recesses of your psyche to dispel the "I am nots" which still hide there. But in time, as you keep believing the God who makes alive the dead (you have to be dead in order to be raised) and calls those things which don't exist into existence, the One who raised His Only Begotten Son from among the dead, will raise you into an awareness of your sonship, which is both your present reality and your future hope.

Questions

1. How does your personal understanding of hope compare to the chapter's view of biblical hope as a clear, visionary force rooted in God's calling? * Reflect on a time when you felt uncertain about your future. How could embracing your identity as God's beloved child reshape your perspective on that moment and guide your next steps?

2. The chapter describes God's calling as naming you His beloved child and inviting you to live out His purpose. How does this understanding of 'calling' resonate with your sense of who you are? * How might fully accepting your identity as God's child influence your approach to a specific responsibility, such as work or family, or a long-term dream?

3. The chapter suggests God speaks through subtle calls, such as heart longings, dreams, or even secular songs and movies. Recall a moment when a song, movie, or deep desire stirred your heart, or consider a current longing if no specific moment comes to mind. How might this be God's invitation to a greater purpose? * What practical step could you take to better discern His voice in these moments?

4. The chapter contrasts the struggles of living 'in Ephesus' (daily challenges) with the reality of being 'in Christ' (God's glorious vision for you). What are some current challenges that make you feel limited or lacking? * How could focusing on the 'glorious end' of your calling as God's beloved son help you reframe these struggles and move forward with hope?

5. Abraham's hope persevered against impossible odds because it was anchored in God's promise of greatness. Think of a time when you faced a significant obstacle. How might rooting your hope in God's vision of you as His beloved child, as Abraham did, empower you to keep going? * What specific action could you take this week to strengthen this hope?

Self-Interest

I f you have read this far, you might be wondering why there seems to be too much "me" and not enough Jesus. Didn't John the Baptist say, "He must increase, but I must decrease"? Therefore, isn't the goal of the Christian life to glorify Jesus and not yourself? Isn't it to die to self so that others see Jesus and not you?

Well, yes to glorifying Jesus and not yourself, but a "not so fast" to that last question. You are a big part of, and the reason for, the good news. Jesus came to redeem YOU and glorify YOU. (This "glorifying you" statement might not sit well with you at this point, but it will become clearer as you continue.)

In every gospel, however, some version of Jesus' admonition about losing or not loving one's life (psyche, soul, or persona in the Greek) is found. To have this recorded in every gospel is significant. The self seems to be the obstacle that gets in the way and is often spoken of in a negative light. Phrases like denying self and even the command to commit self-acide are scattered throughout the Scriptures, and for good reason.

We are all born with a self-destructive, self-centered nature that is bent toward me first, me last, and me always. Becoming a Christian does not end its reign automatically (as you have hopefully discovered) because it's hard to acclimate to a new center. By default, you are the center of your universe, asking both consciously and unconsciously, 'What about me?' and 'What's in it for me?' You then make decisions based on how you would benefit.

Philosophers, like Plato, Sarte, and Hobbes, described this as a perennial and bewildering longing of the human soul and called it glory-seeking. They looked for ways to either justify it or make it socially acceptable. Within Christian circles, it is often called self-centeredness and pride, and your antenna is raised to detect it in others. (But certainly not in yourself.)

But, according to Jesus, the "What's in it for me?" question is not wrong in itself because the result of denying oneself is not the obliteration of self. It is quite the opposite. It is putting you in God's spotlight where you discover why you were created and the glory that is meant for you. "Those who lose their life will find it" is how Jesus put it, or to put it in 21st-century jargon, you will discover your "authentic self".

That you were made for glory and were created to be glorified, that is, to have the spotlight shine on you, is both subtly and plainly declared in the Scriptures. It began in the garden where the cosmos honored and deferred to Adam and was reestablished in Jesus, the Second Man, who is the first fruits of glorified humanity and the prototype and fountainhead of who you are.

Jesus also asked His Father, in His High Priestly prayer, to give you and me the glory that was His. Paul then wrote that seeking glory was more than ok. He said that glory-seeking is a primary motivation and will encourage you to persistently and consistently do good. "To those who by patience in well-doing seek for glory and honor and immortality, he will give eternal life." Glory is both the goal and the gospel.

Paul also wrote that it was God's glory, the glory that radiates from God and reflects back to Him, from which Adam fell and is the very glory that Jesus has restored to humanity. Paul even goes so far as to say that you have already been glorified.

But what does the word "glory" mean? To be sure, in its rawest form, glory would stagger you. In the presence of God's glory, some fell down as dead, some cried that they were "undone", and others stammered and stuttered as they tried their best to describe it. And until we stand before Him in bodies that match His, we will only have wisps and whispers.

But a good place to start is with the Hebrew and Greek. In Hebrew, the word is *kavod*. It indicates a worth and value which results in praise. *Doxa*, the Greek word for glory, is similar. It means a brilliance or splendor that also results in the acknowledgement or the praise of others. It is a spotlight locked onto an individual who has just amazed the crowd, eliciting shouts and praise, which reverberates and shakes the theater.

To be sure, those whose motivation is to receive the praise of man and not acknowledge the God of glory have ended badly. Hollywood is replete with examples of stars who shined brightly for a moment before burning out. Herod, being extolled by the masses as God, was eaten by worms because he didn't credit God for the position given to him. But these examples do not negate the truth that you were made for glory.

Most Christians acknowledge that God deserves all the glory, and some will also concede that a David or Mother Teresa-type also needs to be spotlighted without thinking that it diminishes God's glory. Some denominations have even created a special category of believers, called saints, to venerate and then use them to either motivate or put you in your place. There is an acknowledgment that, at least, some people deserve to be highlighted or glorified.

But most have a hard time putting glory and themselves in the same sentence because we all know our own foibles, and many think that wanting, at minimum, to be acknowledged is selfish. It's as if glory is mutually exclusive—God gets 100% and you get zero.

If this is your concept of God, your God is more Allah-ish than Yahweh-ish. God gets 100%, for sure, because no one will be able to take their eyes off Him. But the beautiful thing in God's economy is that the Triune shares all that He is and has freely.

This is the God we serve. He shares the spotlight. So, when the bride walks down the aisle, all eyes will be on her to the delight of the Groom. He loves to show us off and be glorified in the work of His hands. This does not diminish His glory. It increases it.

Why wouldn't He want to show off His handiwork and His bride and the people He spent all that He had to purchase and restore? So, while you give Him all the glory, He turns the spotlight around on you and glorifies you because this is His nature. This is the nature of love.

You get 100% of His attention, as well as a good measure of affirmation from others, hopefully. God, by the way, affirms you into your destiny, not by pointing out your shortcomings. Life does a good enough job of that, so you needn't help the devil by beating yourself or others up.

How your heart swells when you are praised, and how it shrivels, or reacts, when your deficiencies are pointed out. If you are honest, you know that your issues often revolve around either seeking the spotlight or not being recognized. You are hard-wired with the need and desire to be noticed and praised, and that wiring happened the moment Adam met God for the first time, as you will see in the chapter on "Blessed".

But only praise from God will fully satisfy. On that day, "Well done" will be enough. But until that day, hearing, "You are my beloved, in whom I am well pleased", will cause you to cease your striving. And, in that moment, everything will begin to change for you.

Let me reiterate that self-interest is neither sin nor selfishness. Rather, it is God-implanted and a primary motivation in life. Jesus said the result of losing is finding. He wants you to find yourself, that is, discover who you are, be fully you, and shine. Doing the hard work of disregarding your life to such an extent that others take precedence over your own interests puts you on the stage with Him because this is exactly who He is and what He does.

The issue has never been about you expressing your own special uniqueness as God's prized possession and expecting a return. It has rather been how you have gone about trying to achieve it. Life often blows up, and ulcers occur when you pursue these God-given desires for worth and significance in the wrong way.

Agape love, which is the highest form of love, is often thought to be selfless. Verses like "there is no greater love than this" and "God so loved the world that He gave" seem to say that His love is totally other-centered and without a smidgen of self-interest.

But that would negate the many verses which say that God does everything for His own glory. God is jealous of His name and wants His name to be known. So, *agape* love is not selfless. His love, while sacrificial, is a self-giving love that is infused with self-interest.

This is an important distinction which houses a truth that can set you free from a pride that clothes itself with a pseudo-humility. While it is not about you, it is all about you. You were created with self-interest, accompanied by a desire to have gain because you were made in His image.

But for now, this is both a blessing and a curse. It's a blessing because the desire for glory is the echo of the call first heard in the garden. Adam was honored, highlighted, and then told to fill his ever-increasing space with who he was. He was also put in charge of the cosmos which is not insignificant. He sensed his worth and his significance, felt safe, and acted from that place.

It's a curse because this desire for the glory that preceded the fall did not leave after the fall. The glory, which gave a right sense of self, left and left you with a gnawing, empty hole meant for glory, which you have tried to fill without success from the moment you were born. Understanding that God planted in you the seed of "glory-seeking" will help you to humble yourself, align yourself with God, and keep you on your journey toward wholeness.

Before Adam fell, he lived in an unconscious awareness of the glory of God. He was clothed with it. It filled his heart. His sense of self was derived from the look he saw in God's eyes. God was delighted with him, and Adam knew it.

And there was nothing in him or in the world that told him otherwise. (Until the serpent, that is.)

What Adam experienced was the adoration that the Father has for the Son, and the thrill the Son has for the Father. Adam was caught up in the Trinitarian relationship. Their relationship spilled over on Adam, and it was glorious.

The moment he fell, however, he realized that he was naked. The glory, which covered him and gave him his sense of self, evaporated. And so began the lifelong attempt to reclaim and regain that sense of self, and he did it initially by hiding behind fig leaves. And ever since, the world has retailed fancier fig leaves to entice you to do things that make yourself look presentable. Have you identified what you are wearing and hiding behind yet?

Discovering glory, by the way, is the reason that we are going to devote many chapters to Adam, pre-fall, and also look at Jesus, who is as much a type of Adam as Adam was a type of Christ. Their stories reveal the glory meant for you because that glory from which you fell is the same glory to which you have been freely restored. Glory was your starting point, and then as you go from glory to glory, you will come to realize that glory is also your destination. Adam's sense of self will also give you clues as to what living in the sphere of God's glory and admiration looks like.

Adam, post-fall, will also be instructive because he reveals what you do to recapture that lost sense. All your attempts to get ahead, to be noticed, to be heard, and to express yourself are your best efforts to recapture that for which you were made.

So, glory-seeking is not wrong. It is the high calling of God. But as you learn to walk as Jesus did, the light of His glory will shine on you, and you won't need to seek your own glory because you will live in the sense of His.

Questions

1. How does the chapter's view that self-interest is a God-given drive, rather than sinful, challenge your understanding of ambition and humility? * Can you recall a time when you pursued a personal goal or recognition? * Did it feel selfish, or can you now see it as part of God's design for you to seek worth? * How might this perspective shape your future pursuits?

2. What 'fig leaves'—such as achievements, roles, or behaviors—do you use to hide feelings of inadequacy or gain approval? * How might embracing God's affirmation of you as His beloved, as described in the chapter, help you let go of these facades? * What would living more authentically look like in your daily life?

3. How does imagining God delighting in you and sharing His spotlight, as the chapter suggests, make you feel—comforted, excited, or uneasy? * Why do you think you feel this way? * How could resting in God's affirmation, like Adam did pre-fall, influence your confidence in pursuing your purpose?

4. The chapter describes glory-seeking as a natural desire that can lead to pride if misdirected. Think of a time when your pursuit of recognition or success went astray, perhaps causing stress or conflict. What drove that pursuit? * How might aligning your desire for glory with God's perspective, as seen in Jesus' self-giving love, transform your approach in the future?

5. What thoughts or emotions arise when you consider that God's glory and your glory are intertwined, as the chapter claims? * Does this idea feel liberating or challenging? * How might this perspective shift the way you view your worth in everyday situations, such as at work or in relationships?

Meta-Story

Much of the Bible is stories. In fact, 43% of the Bible is narrative. While you might be more comfortable with bullet points, God, in His wisdom, decided to make you uncomfortable by telling stories so that you and I might enter another's and, as you listen to theirs, hear His voice.

Commands are the easiest to understand and follow, or not. While "not" may be your bent, your druthers are still to have clear, concise directions to follow. "Just tell me what to do!"

Commands, however, are only a small part of the smallest part of the Scriptural genre, which is discourse. Discourse comprises 24% of the Bible. Within this 24% are also found speeches, prophecy, and parables. Parables push you a little further out of the objective, rote mode because they cause you to think and ask questions.

Then comes the head-scratching and, hopefully, heart-searching genre of poetry, which comprises 33% of the Bible. Poetry is a veil of words behind which one can be drawn into another's experience and perspective.

With poetry, the meaning is subject to interpretation. What the poet tries to express might not be the meaning you get. This is the scary part for literalists and systematic theologians because the question that is asked is, "Whose interpretation is it?" If the poet has a tough time putting into words the fuzzy reality he or she sees, how can anyone put that thing in a box?

While we need our boxes, poetry invites you to venture out and have your heart touched. You become part of the poem because you are between the shadow and the light—the shadow being the natural phenomenon and the light being the spiritual reality. Since you are its interpreter, what it means depends on your past, your makeup, and your present situation because the filter it goes through is you. This is one reason your understanding of the Scriptures grows as the years go by.

For the most part, poetry takes snapshots, capturing the essence of specific moments in time. With exception, they don't tell extended stories, which is one reason you won't find a book of poetry on the bestseller list.

Everyone loves, however, a good story, whether it is read, viewed, or told. Storytelling is an art form, but there is also a science behind storytelling and story-receiving. The brain gets excited and engaged on many levels when it encounters a good one.

Another thing we like about stories is that they have a beginning, a middle, and an end. Whether a romance, a mystery, or a biography, they resolve a tension, and somewhere in the recesses of our soul, we identify with the hero. That is why the ones we like best either have a "happily ever after" or a "justice required/justice served" ending.

Stories also have a way of sneaking past the guards, or the "watchful dragons" as C.S. Lewis would say, that protect your set of beliefs and your sense of self. Watchful dragons breathe fire when any thought, either good or bad, presents itself and threatens your set of beliefs or sense of self. But they don't know what to do with a story.

Stories can evoke thoughts or feelings that you didn't realize were there. At times, they can reveal your aspirations and, at other times, your disappointments because your dreams haven't come to fruition.

Have you ever had your emotions surprise you while watching a movie, or reading a book? For me, it's been the Susan Boyle video where the plain wrapper is unwrapped on stage to reveal someone who amazes the crowd. For others, it might be Braveheart, leading the charge. "Arrrrg!" Stories can also inspire, warn, teach, and give examples. Most stories, though, are just that—stories of someone else's life from which you can glean.

However, some Bible stories have a larger purpose. These stories not only have the power to read you and uncover hurts and needs, along with your desires and unfulfilled dreams, they also are Rosetta Stones by which you can interpret the often-puzzling parts of your life and find meaning.

They answer the "Who am I?" and the "What am I about?" questions, as well as the "What in the world is going on?" question, which can hang like a mist around you. Some stories are meta-stories by which you can read your own life.

A meta-story is an overarching story which can be overlaid on another's life. For example, Jesus knew that the story of Jonah, for Him, was a meta-story. "Just as Jonah was three days and three nights in the belly of the great fish, so will the Son of Man be three days and three nights in the heart of the earth," Jesus proclaimed.

Think of the insight and comfort, the vision and courage, and the hope and purpose given to Jesus as He considered this story. Jesus was able to interpret His life and its events, accept the seeming injustice done to him, and press through because He saw both the end from the beginning and the process He needed to endure.

But Jonah's story cannot be overlaid on everyone's life. It was certainly written for your learning, but I think that it was specifically written for Jesus' own comfort and encouragement. Jonah's story can give you a greater appreciation for what the Lord willingly endured, as well as needed attitude adjustments for yourself. So, while you can learn from his story, as well as David's and Esther's, et al, these are not meta-stories or stories by which you can determine your destiny and the path you must follow.

But there are stories in the Bible that tell your story, and everyone's. So, you can, like Jesus, find the same insight and comfort, the same vision and courage, and the same hope and purpose in them. They answer the "Who am I?", the "What am I about?", and the "How do I become the person God imagined?" questions which hide in the recesses of everyone's soul.

Wouldn't you like to know the person you were created to be? Wouldn't you like to know your purpose? And wouldn't it be great to have a roadmap to refer to when confronted with obstacles? This sort of understanding seldom happens by chance or with a sudden flash of insight. And it certainly doesn't come through the do's and don'ts of the Bible. You come to understand yourself and how you fit into the cosmos through a meta-story that will light up your imagination.

There are three individuals specifically in the Scriptures whose stories are meta-stories. They are archetypes or prototypes, which those who follow are patterned, without exception. Each of these individuals is the loins from which you came. They are seeds that have already blossomed and have produced more seeds that look like you. So, you also have the same destiny and will go through the same process that they did.

The problem is that, while you have believed truths about God, about the nature of man and redemption, and have even met the Jesus of the Bible, you haven't yet met yourself in the Bible. You still don't see yourself written into the story, so you wonder about life and hope that you will amount to something.

You are still not sure from whence you came or your destiny, and therefore, flounder and live your life on a much lower plane than God intends.

This is why God has woven these stories into the Scriptures. While I believe that these are not just stories, but historical accounts, it doesn't matter. They were written down so you can discover the "you" imagined before time began. These three individuals are Adam, Peter, and Abraham. Each one of them can say to you, "I am your father."

Adam is everyone's father because everyone has been made in the same pre-fall image, and everyone has acquired the same post-fall nature. Peter is next because Jesus referred to him as the rock on which the Church is built. (Yes, the rock refers to the revelation of Jesus and Peter's confession, but Catholics are not wrong in their understanding either.)

All who follow will not only discover Jesus the same way that Peter did but will also be exposed as the fraud that Peter was. And Paul was very clear that Abraham is the father of all those who would walk in faith. So, each of these stories applies specifically to you.

Adam, pre-fall, speaks to everyone's high calling and paints the picture of the glorious "you" whom God imagined before time began. Adam and Eve, together, are the prototypes of glorified humanity. What was spoken to them was spoken to all of their progeny.

I will also touch on the fall, but the glory from which you fell is your high call of God in Christ Jesus and was Adam's before he sinned. This glory remained yours, and has been restored, because "the gifts and calling of God are irrevocable".

Post-fall, his story speaks to the human condition and is what Jesus came to redeem. Every person is in a cage fight with themselves, trapped with the desire for worth and significance in one corner and the emptiness and restlessness of feeling unworthy in the other. And the winner is?

Simon Peter picks up where Adam left off, outside the garden. He is the poster child for every Christian on whom the residue of pride and self-righteousness still sticks. Throughout the gospels, Simon Peter had flashes of brilliance, but for the most part, he was "too much Simon", who was full of himself. He had a strong personality that unknowingly controlled him. Pride has a way of blinding you, even as a born-again Christian.

Now, Peter was taught by the best of them and was even rebuked to no avail. God had to burst his self-righteous bubble. To do that, Peter had to have a flash of self-awareness before he could be used. Peter is the story of whole-hearted

Christians who want to please God but have blind spots, just like you, and then try to do Christianity in their own way. Again, just like you.

The process Peter went through, which is chronicled in the gospels, is the same one you will also go through. You might not think of yourself as Peter because you might be introverted, but make no mistake, your personality controls you as it did Peter. Reading your life in Peter's can keep you from completely giving up on your walk with the Lord when you crash and burn.

Abraham's story is written for many reasons. From the founding of the Hebrew nation to the foreshadowing of Christ and His work on the cross, a lifetime can be spent mining it without depleting the treasures hidden there. But there is a reading of Abraham's story which is more immediate and personal because you are called his child and are also called to become.

Abraham was called "the father of many nations" in Haran. But it was 25-plus years later before he became that father, and over a decade after that before God said, "Now, you ARE". Between the time when the seed was planted and its flowering, the process of becoming is detailed in Genesis. This is the same process that you will go through to become the fully actualized seed that God planted.

Abraham is the father of faith. So, whatever the journey of faith is, it is found in Abraham's story, and if you are to walk in faith, it would be good to know what that looks like. He is also your dad, which means you will look like him and have his significance when God is done with you.

Abraham, when all was said and done, looked just like the Father who was willing to give up His own Son on His own Moriah. Like the Father whom Paul disclosed in Ephesians 1, Abraham was blessed and a blessing. Like Jesus, Abraham has had an ever-increasing influence and has possessed the gates of his enemies.

Abraham's call echoed the first words spoken to Adam, which were to be fruitful, become great, and fill. These words were then fully sounded in the second Man, and they now reverberate in you. The gospel according to Paul is that you are blessed with Abraham's blessing.

The map for your life is found in these meta-stories. You cannot discover God's will for your life, nor can you discover who you are, in the dos and don'ts of the Scriptures. Moses, who wrote the dos and don'ts, got bit by them just like Israel did. Commands are just the beginning signposts designed to get you moving in the right direction. But if you continue living in them you will go in circles and not far, just like the children of Israel.

As already stated, there is a reason that the Scriptures are 43% narrative. Your story is embedded in these stories. Your journey from brokenness to wholeness, from uncertainty to certainty, from sinnership to sonship, from faith to faith, and from glory to glory waits to be unfolded there. As Paul wrote, these stories are written that you might have hope, and not just hope as an encouragement to go on when life is dark, but a hope that is a clear and certain vision of who you are to become, so that you can walk confidently through times of darkness and end your life, shining more than a billion stars.

Questions

1. How does the chapter's emphasis on the Bible's 43% narrative content, compared to commands, change your view of how God reveals your identity and purpose? * Can you recall a time when a story—biblical, literary, or cinematic—touched you more deeply than a direct instruction? * What did it reveal about your desires or struggles, and how might engaging with the meta-stories of Adam, Peter, or Abraham further illuminate your path?

2. The chapter describes meta-stories of Adam, Peter, and Abraham as keys to answering "Who am I?" and "What am I about?" Have you ever felt a biblical story resonate with your personal journey? * How might seeing yourself in one of these meta-stories provide clarity or courage for becoming the person God created you to be?

3. How do you connect with C.S. Lewis's concept of 'watchful dragons' guarding your beliefs and sense of self? * Can you think of a time when a story—biblical or otherwise—bypassed these defenses to reveal new insights about your fears, aspirations, or identity? * How might approaching the meta-stories of Adam, Peter, or Abraham with openness help you grow in self-awareness?

4. Peter's journey from 'too much Simon' to a humbled disciple reflects a process of overcoming pride and blind spots. Can you identify a personal trait or tendency, like pride or self-reliance, that might hinder your faith? * How does Peter's meta-story offer hope for your transformation? * What practical step could you take to invite God's work in this area?

5. Abraham's story highlights a long process of becoming, from a call to a fulfilled destiny over decades. Reflect on a time in your life when you've had to wait or endure uncertainty to grow into a calling or purpose. * How does Abraham's meta-story inspire you to trust God's timing and process in shaping you into someone significant and fruitful?

Outline by Isaiah

T he prophet Isaiah wrote the outline of this book over 2,500 years ago. The prophet declared, "Listen to me, you who pursue righteousness, you who seek the LORD. Look to the rock from which you were hewn, and to the pit from which you were dug. Look to Abraham your father and to Sarah who bore you; for he was but one when I called him, that I might bless him and multiply him." Isaiah 51:1-2

Isaiah wrote to a people who were seeking the Lord and wanting to please Him, but were at a standstill and uncertain about the next steps. I also assume that some of my readers are in the same place as Isaiah's audience, not knowing who they are, what they are about, and wondering what to do next. So, "Listen to me!" or better, "Listen to the voice of the Spirit."

Isaiah begins with an appeal to faith. "Look! Look! Look!", he called out, not "Do! Do! Do!" "Look" is not a "pull yourselves up by the bootstraps", try-harder sort of word. It's not about more Bible studies, though Bible studies are good. It is about a new way of thinking, that is, thinking with your heart. It is about a new faith sight.

"Look" is code for "believe". It is the same word that God spoke when He brought Abraham out under the stars. "Look at the stars. Do you now believe?"

Believe is a tricky word, however. It can be, and certainly is, used in psychology. But the "I believe I can fly," the "I think I can, I think I can" or the "imagine it and it will happen" sort of faith that the world offers is not the faith that is given to you by hearing a word, or sensing something, from God.

"Faith comes," Paul wrote in Romans 10:17. It is not worked up. It comes as a response to God impressing you with a thought, a sense, or a feeling. At times, a phrase or a verse of the Scriptures will stand out to you. This Romans 10:17 word for "word", in the Greek, is *rhema*, which means "the now word of God" or a word that is witnessed within. It is contrasted (or really joined) with *logos*, which means the entirety of God's revealed thought.

This is the Spirit part of the Scriptures. While ALL Scripture is profitable for all, God has specifically set aside a desk for you because, while He desires ALL to be saved, the "saved version" of you is vastly different than anyone else. Since you and your calling are unique, God knows that you also need one-on-one attention. So while the *logos* lectures, the *rhema* sits next to you.

Out of the volume of God's written word, the Spirit will speak something specific to you, and in that hearing, faith is sparked in your heart. From the ocean of God's expressive heart, a teaspoon, specifically filled for you, is poured onto your heart, and you will have a sense that these thoughts came from outside of your own thinking and will cause you to stop and consider. This will begin a journey into the experience of it.

Moses did not continue on his way after he encountered the burning bush. Rather, he took time to consider the "strange sight" long enough for God to clearly speak. This is why, hopefully, you have already paused and will continue to wonder along the way to question the strange sightings that you encounter because, as you wait and wonder, you will get greater clarity. If not, much of what has been written will just be debatable information.

But back to the outline. Isaiah tells you to look at three things, with the first being, "the rock from which you were hewn." In Hebrew, this word for rock refers to the face of a cliff. I think that we can all catch Isaiah's allusion and agree that we are to look to Jesus.

There are a couple of Hebrew words that are translated "rock" in the Old Testament. One means a boulder, or a big rock sitting on the ground. This word, however, means the elevated face of a cliff that forces you to look up. While both allude to Christ, Isaiah directs your faith toward the risen One who sits enthroned and who overcame the taint of sin, and not toward the boulder, smitten for and by you.

You are to look to Jesus, ascended, and seated on the throne. This is Christianity 101. But Isaiah isn't talking about Jesus alone because he doesn't tell you only to believe in the Rock. He adds the little phrase, "from which you were hewn", which has astounding implications.

You are to look to the rock in order to know yourself. The picture, painted by Isaiah, is that of a mason hanging from the face of a cliff with a chisel in hand, carving out a piece of granite. So, when you hold the piece of granite, you know that the only difference between it and the cliff is that this piece of granite now has an existence apart from the cliff. The piece of granite and the rock's face are, in essence, the same. Paul clearly saw this because he wrote that you are OF Him.

You are firstly to know from whence you came and the stuff of which you are made. Most Christians don't have a problem extolling Christ and His perfections, and your faith must start and remain there. But most have a harder time seeing themselves in the light of His perfections.

You were not hewn from a sinner, nor were you born from below, so a "sinner saved by grace" mentality is suspect and not conducive for a growing, healthy individual or for healthy relationships. While most will recognize that this rock is a type of Christ, they don't realize that Christ is a type of you.

You are a chip out of the Eternal Block. Equals with a small "e" or sons of the Jesus type. This might be heady stuff for an introduction, but it will unfold to your heart as you continue to read. I plan to arm wrestle you until you cry uncle and say, "No more 'sinner saved by grace' for me because 'I am a son of His love'".

If only some mere man or woman made these declarations of God-likeness, then they could be dismissed as heresy. But Paul and John echoed and restated Genesis' "made in His image" and Jesus' words, "In that day you will know that I am in my Father, and you in me, and I in you."

If you are in Christ, then you are in the Trinitarian stew. And what part of the pot is not stew? How can you remove the seasoning once it has been added? The stew is the stew, whether it is in a pot, in a bowl, or in a spoon.

So, the first section of the book, which will be the longest, will look at Adam, pre-fall. Pre-fall Adam is the glory from which you fell and the glory to which you have already been freely and fully restored. And that glory, Paul declares, is the glory of God.

God made Adam in His own image, which includes His glory or essence. Every other creature was created to produce after its kind. Their own unique essence or glory would fill the earth as they propagated. With mankind, however, God purposed to produce more of Himself, so He created you after HIS kind and in His image.

He desires sons whom He could engage and enjoy, who would represent Him in the world, and who would be kings over their own domain and under His Lordship—sons, sharing in and reflecting His glory.

Isaiah knew that the first step for you becoming in real-time a son is to first embrace your sonship, regardless of the sin-residue that still sticks to you. So, he said, "Look to the rock from which you were chiseled."

But a sin-consciousness still sticks to you. The confident, joyful pre-fall Adam gave way to an uncertain, striving, and anxious post-fall one. You and I must contend with this post-fall Adam, as you try to reconcile that nature, with its old way of doing and thinking, with the new nature that God gave at conversion.

Your old way of thinking and living passed through conversion unscathed. While Jesus makes all things new, a large part of this newness is having to relearn everything. A large part of this newness is uncovering the treasure within because the new nature is still buried under your old way of thinking and doing life, and there are layers to dig through.

The treasure, in fact, can be covered with so many layers that you can easily delude yourself. On one hand, gifted Christians can assume that they are alright because of the effectiveness of their gift. But just have them go through a dry season or have what is dear to them threatened and see what happens.

Some dig in their heels and become unbearable. Some give up. Some lose it, and some are lost. I know of one who took his own life, and others who long for the past because their identity was wrapped up in a position they no longer fill.

On the other hand, this new nature can be buried under so much dirt that you cannot even lift your head because all you see is the dirt. I know because this was my experience. Either way, the "you" imagined by God can be encased by the "you" whom you have imagined, whether you know it or not.

This is the reason that Isaiah says that the next step is to honestly assess your life and acknowledge how you have protected and projected yourself. So, he wrote, "Look to the pit from which you were dug."

The word for pit is also used to describe a dark and damp dungeon in which you are trapped. You are not only chiseled, in all of your glory, from the face of a cliff, you were also pick-axed, in all of your gory, out of a pit. This is Peter's story, and Paul's.

Both began their Christian life, full of themselves. The Spirit had to prick their self-righteous bubble. You might disagree at this point with my inclusion of Paul in this scenario because most feel that he came out of the spiritual womb, a dynamo. But this principle of being dug out of a pit has no exceptions, as you will see.

Simon Peter's story is the story of every Christian who has set his or her mind and heart to follow Jesus. And it doesn't matter whether you have a healthy self-image, like Peter, with gifts coming out of your ears or someone who hides and is unsure of your worth or contributions.

Either way, you will have moments of self-awareness when you realize that you are not who you think you are, and that how you are trying to be a Christian or do Christian ministry is nothing more than self-effort. For Peter, the moment in which he was exposed was the darkest moment of his life. Jesus, however, saw light beginning to dawn.

Moments of self-awareness are holy, necessary, yet painful times because your ugly side is exposed. You can be rebuked by the best of them, like Peter, and told that what you are dealing ain't worth buying. But until, like Peter, you sense God's knowing look and have a moment of self-awareness, you will remain unchanged.

God has arranged for moments in your life when you will be exposed and know it. As painful as this is, looking to the pit is an important step in your spiritual journey. So, I will look at the pit from which you were dug through the stories of Peter and Paul. I will also include mine, with the hope that you can truthfully look at yours. Self-awareness is part of the truth that sets free.

So here you are, stuck between the perfections of Christ and the mess that is you. But how do you get unstuck? Isaiah says, "Look to Abraham your father and to Sarah who bore you; for he was but one when I called him, that I might bless him and multiply him."

The story of Abraham can be read in many ways, but here Isaiah says that you are to understand your own story in his. He is the father of faith and faith's journey. His is the story of the way out and up.

Abraham was "but one" when he began his walk with God. Abraham would not have even been a blip in Ur's history if God hadn't stepped into his life. But God called him when he was insignificant, almost a less than nothing, so that HE could make Abraham great.

And this is God's heart and nature—He wants to make everything the full expression of itself, and great. Angels, by the way, were created complete, so what you see is what you get. You, however. . . who knows what God's intent is for you to become?

Abraham's story is the story of becoming and details the process he went through to become the person God imagined. Abraham is the Rosetta Stone by which you can interpret your life. So, after looking at Adam pre-fall, and Adam and Peter post-fall, we will then examine the life of Abraham.

What you will discover is a lifelong journey from sinnership to sonship. Abram, when he encountered God in Ur, believed in God, and that is without question. He left his comfort zone. He worshipped God. He did exploits. But Abraham did not believe what God told him about himself. He was an unbelieving believer.

He believed who God was, but didn't believe who he was. He believed the exceedingly good news about God but not the exceedingly good news about himself. It took over a decade before God provoked Abram, in Genesis 15, to confess his unbelief.

Only then, under the stars, did Abram begin to believe God's assessment of himself. Not believing the good news about yourself is also where many Christians find themselves. But the good news is that this was not only Abraham's starting point but yours. We all begin NOT BELIEVING. We all are unbelieving believers.

This is the faith stage where, while Abraham believed in God, yet didn't believe in God's assessment of himself. But there came a time for Abraham when the "faith comes" moment came. And, in the moment of believing, God considered it done and declared him, and his faith, righteous. Abraham now, not only had a right view of God, he also had a righteous or correct view of himself. He believed himself to be a father of many nations.

But while Abraham was that, in faith, he wasn't yet holding a baby. So, he entered the hope stage. When God plants a seed in you, the sun will come out and you will wonder why what God declared hasn't happened already, and why this good news doesn't feel that good.

It was also during this time that Abraham tried to help God out. He initially used, like we all do, his natural wisdom and strength to accomplish what God purposed to do in Himself. So, Abram and Sarai, out of a good heart, did what they could to "obey" God and fulfill His will. And the reward for their efforts? Ishmael.

When God then appeared to Abram, in Genesis 17, to tell him that he was now going to be a father, Abram dismissed God out of hand because he already had proof of his fatherhood. Besides, at this time, it was impossible for him and Sarai to have a child. Abram was an unhoping hopeful.

The temptation to produce on your own what God plans to do in His time is great for you as well. God's timing always starts when time runs out. To be kind, Abraham and Sarah didn't know the "how". They only knew the "what" of God's will and found a way to accomplish it.

But when that was finally sorted out, Abraham hoped against hope that he might become the person God imagined, and that person looked an awful lot like God Himself, who is the real Father of many nations. And so, Isaac was born.

Having Isaac, however, was not the end of Abraham's journey out of sinnership into sonship. His righteousness was not yet fulfilled. His identity as a son, who was like the Father, had not yet been fully tested. Abraham had successfully passed the faith and hope stages. One more stage remained, which is the love stage.

Circling back to the beginning, both sinnership and sonship are identity terms. Sinnership is that inner sense that says, because there is no external evidence and because you don't feel it, you are not who God says you are. Sonship, however, is embracing your identity, regardless of your feelings or circumstances.

This was fully realized and expressed on the cross, where all that Jesus had was his faith in His Father and in His own personhood. The sense of his Father's presence was gone. His own people had rejected his claim of Sonship. The devil put into the mouths of those gawking at him, derision and accusations. It was on the cross, though, where the faith of the Son of God, which Paul claimed to live by, was evident.

Jesus, when stripped of all external evidence of His Sonship, declared it until the end. "FATHER," the Son said, "into Your hands, I commit my spirit." This is the love stage, where you will also be stripped of the externals that have defined you.

For Abraham, the external was Isaac, whom he loved dearly. His identity as a father was rightly sensed and evidenced in Isaac. But one thing remained. Would Abraham still know who he was when that thing which defined him was asked to be given back?

His answer was an emphatic "yes". He willingly gave up all external evidence of being a father because he knew who he was. So, James said, "it was FULFILLED that it was accounted to him as righteousness."

I know when this happened in my life and will briefly tell that story later. I know who I am, and from that place, I live. Abraham's story is yours as well because it is a meta-story.

You might be an unbelieving believer or an unhoping hopeful. It might be that God has not yet asked you to give back that thing that has defined your life. But know this, He has called you to greatness. Your journey will take you from being aware of your insignificance to being blessed in Abraham's blessing because it is God's glory to glorify you.

"Now, I will SURELY bless you, and I will SURELY multiply your offspring as the stars of heaven and as the sand that is on the seashore. And your offspring shall possess the gate of his enemies, and in your offspring shall all the nations of the earth be blessed."

Paul was clear that this pronouncement not only pointed to Jesus but also to you because you are blessed in both Abraham's blessing and in Christ's. Their narratives are one and the same, and both point to you. Paul wrote, "The words 'it was counted to him' were not written for his sake alone, but for ours also."

So, there you go. The book in a nutshell. I will take time to expand and drive these points home with the hope that you will become a believing believer, a hoping hopeful, and someone who needs nothing but the inner witness of the Spirit to step confidently into the future.

Questions

1. How does the concept of "looking" to the rock from which you were hewn (Jesus) challenge or reshape your view of your own identity? * Reflect on a time when you struggled to see yourself as more than a "sinner saved by grace"—how might embracing the idea that you are a "chip out of the Eternal Block" influence your sense of worth and purpose?

2. Do you find yourself in Isaiah's audience, wanting what God wants but not knowing how? * How does the idea of "looking" instead of "doing" feel when you think about your own spiritual struggles—does it ease the pressure or stir uncertainty? What does "looking" look like for you?

3. What do you think about the statement that you were "not born from below" or "hewn from a sinner"? * Does this shift your view of your worth compared to what you usually tell yourself?

4. The idea of rhema—a personal, Spirit-spoken word sparking faith—suggests God speaks uniquely to you. Have you ever experienced a moment when a scripture, thought, or feeling stood out as a "now word" from God? * How did it guide or encourage you, and how might you cultivate openness to such moments in your current spiritual walk?

5. Of the chapters that you have already read, which one(s) resonated with you the most? Explain. * The book began by stating it would be dropping "grace bombs" on your heart and mind. Have they found their target? Did you find yourself resisting some parts of this introduction? If so, why? * Or are you beginning to open yourself up to the unbelievably good new of you?

Adam-The Image

T hen God said, "Let us make man in our image, after our likeness. . . So, God created man in his own image, in the image of God he created him; male and female he created them." Genesis 1:26-27

"In our image, after our likeness." Let's try to unpack these words because they are the very first breadcrumbs that describe you, and that the Holy Spirit has scattered for you to follow. As you do, you will begin to answer David's question, which is, "When I think about all the wonders of the perceptible universe, what is it about man, about me, that You can't get out of Your mind?" (TCA)

These six words, used in God's internal dialogue, are two Hebrew words, *tselem* and *damuth*. *Tselem* means a fixed image, like a photograph or a statue. The closest representation today might be 3D projections. The problem with a photograph or statue is that they are static and do not possess life. Neither can you engage a hologram with any sort of heartfelt conversation because it can't do anything outside of its programming.

Damuth means to be like something. It has a little fuzzier meaning because that picture has now come alive and has become a moving target. Ezekiel used this word as he grasped for words to describe his visions of the unseen world. "It was like this. It was like that."

Tselem and *damuth*, together, indicate a perfect resemblance, a mirror-like representation that comes into greater focus as time goes by. Image and likeness point to a greater reality and wonder than either David's physical universe or Ezekiel's spiritual one because these words declare that you image God.

You are a picture of God. This may jar your senses (and I hope it does), but what else can it mean? A "sinner saved by grace" mentality will dilute this, and explain it away. But the gospel is the heretically good news about you. And I can't think of anything better than being a living picture of God, whom He can't take His eyes off.

73

It seems that God made the photo of Himself come alive when He made Adam. And by giving Adam and Eve the ability to produce after their kind (which is really after His kind), He intended to fill the earth with little versions of Himself—mini-Hims, as it were. God created a species that possessed His DNA, embodied His essence, and having His capabilities and passions, while still possessing their own separate life and identity.

That life had the ability to make choices, even the choice of rejecting the image and not becoming like God. The likeness, however, would become clearer as Adam and Eve chose to embrace it and stay connected to the One whom they were becoming like.

"In His image and INTO His likeness", I think, is a better way to look at God's words. It's as if the blueprint was spread out at the construction site at creation, but what God envisioned for humanity never got off the ground.

Because God's project failed, "in His image and into His likeness" became both the hope of humanity and the explanation for all the hurt and hurting in the world. His implanted image created the desires for beauty, goodness, and justice. But because these desires have not been fulfilled, frustration, striving, and disappointment are all that's left us.

Righteousness is rooted "in His image" and therefore deeply rooted in all. From Rambo to Reacher, justice-served satisfies. It doesn't matter which side of the aisle you are on, you want the bad guy, however that's defined, to get what's his.

You were also created to love and be loved. Why do you think Harlequin novels are the top-selling paperbacks? Harlequin novels account for 1 of 6 paperback books sold because love-found resonates and happy endings sell. This is your deep-seated hope.

"Into His likeness", though, houses the hurt because humanity is not right and doesn't act a bit like God. Do I even need to explain this because you know that life has fallen woefully short of heaven? Broken relationships. Injustice. The world is a mess, looking more like hell than heaven at times.

Hurtful and hurting are apt descriptions. Unrest within and conflict without. The bad guys, winning. Discouragement, disappointment, and depression rather than an inexpressible joy that is glory-filled—all because of these words, "In His Image and into His likeness".

The first thing that came to God's mind when He considered you was His image and likeness. What God did not say was, "Let us make man in their OWN image" as He did with the geese and the rest of the animals.

For them, He said, "Let us make geese after THEIR own image and let them produce after THEIR kind." But for you and me, He said, "Let us make them in OURS." "Let us make (<u>put your name here</u>) in Our image."

Geese were made in their own image, with their own DNA and instincts. So, when it comes time to migrate, they don't need to be told. They just refer to their implanted image, and their instincts are always right. They also don't need to gather for a lecture on aerodynamics before they form a V because they are hardwired to conserve energy when they fly. They are geese, for goodness' sake.

But it's possible for a baby goose to grow up and not act like a goose, even though it will honk, eat grass, and molt. If you remove a baby goose from its natural family, its life will turn out vastly different because of a thing called imprinting. While possessing the physical attributes of a goose, it will not act like a goose. There is a difference between image and likeness.

A baby goose has an internal image of what it is, but it won't be a goose in full measure without imprinting. Without being present with its mother and other geese where goose stuff can be observed and followed, and without acting on the image within, that goose will never be like the other geese and do the things geese do. It won't even know that it can fly.

Geese, in fact, are great pets and even more loyal than dogs because, if you are the one they initially follow, imprinting takes over. You are not their mama, but they will think that you are. It will identify with you as its species, and the only migrating, that it will do, is to waddle from your armchair to your bed before jumping into it.

Genesis agrees with this because it describes "in his image and into his like-ness" a few chapters later by using the same language for human procreation. Adam fathered Seth in his image and, in time, Seth grew into his likeness. Seth had his dad's DNA when he was born and came to look more and more like his dad as he grew, not only in his physical features, but also in his mannerisms, tastes, and perspective because of their closeness.

Adam, who had God's DNA, was to become more like God as he followed Him. Where Adam failed, however, Jesus did not. God came more and more into focus as Jesus walked with His Father toward the cross. And on the cross, the Image shown brightest.

In Jesus, both God's image and His likeness sync, and because of that, sonship is defined. Sonship is being like the Father, and that doesn't mean just having His schnoz. Sonship is reflecting, in real-time, the Image by allowing what's on the inside to shine through.

When Adam failed, God's image was defaced. You and I are made in God's image, for sure. A masterpiece. But that painting has been scribbled over. You can see, if you look hard enough, glimpses of what the Artist had in mind before graffiti covered the painting. Francis Schaeffer describes you as a "glorious ruin", which explains Jesus' reclamation and restoration mission.

Jesus didn't fail because, before Jesus breathed His last breath, He said, "Tetelestai", which means "it has been accomplished." What He came to do was finished. A significant part of that mission was the restoration of His Image in mankind with the potential for His likeness to shine forth in each and every one.

Sins forgiven means that the graffiti has been erased, and the image of God, the glorious you, now has the potential to emerge. But while the graffiti has been permanently removed, you and I still struggle because its memory still affects your consciousness.

Your internal digital recorder, that tells you who you are, still loops "I am not", "I have not", and "I don't measure up", or it might trick you into thinking that you are when you are not. Giftedness can be problematic and misinterpreted. The gospel of a glorious you IS hard to believe, however, knowing what you know about yourself.

The residual effect of the fall makes discerning the image difficult and, without a clear picture in your mind of whom God has made, you will never become the person who God imagined. This is one reason the Scriptures tell you to look unto Jesus because as you behold Him, the reflection that you see in the mirror is you.

There is an internal image of yourself that has been burned upon your consciousness and which you unconsciously follow. Past experiences and various choices strengthen that image. This internal image of yourself becomes the guidance system that keeps you on your trajectory for better or worse.

Proverbs rightly says, "As he thinks in his heart, so is he." (NKJV) Jesus also said, "Out of the abundance of the heart, the mouth speaks." What is on the inside spills out, whether you like it or not. Since your outside reflects your inside, the changing of your inside changes everything.

Now, while it might be futile to try to figure yourself out, it is not futile to assume that the image which you have created of yourself is faulty and a new one needs to be reformulated. This is the starting point. Repentance, which is your true beginning, has more to do with the image than with your actions because your actions follow your image or how you perceive yourself.

Paul put this into words in Colossians when he wrote, "you are being renewed in knowledge after the image of its creator. Here there is not Greek and Jew, circumcised and uncircumcised, barbarian, Scythian, slave, free; but Christ is all, and in all." Paul writes that there is no material distinction between you and me, or between you and Christ, because Christ is all and in all, and transformation is dependent upon knowing what that Image is.

While Christ, who is the image of God, has done His part in restoring His image in you, you still have a small part to play in becoming like Him and, that is, to believe this heretical gospel. The smudges that still blur His image and the spray paint that you have added are what Paul describes as the old self or old man. This is the residual image that you have strengthened as you have tried to defend yourself, make up your own deficits, and make yourself look good.

The first step, then, is to acknowledge both your messed-up thinking and the part that you've played in it. Paul writes that we are to take that tired, old façade and put on the fresh, new image of Christ, who is the image of God. You CAN put on the image of God by faith because the old is gone and the new has come.

When Jesus cried out, "It is finished", He had this and you in mind. That old way of thinking, that is, the way you have protected and projected yourself and the self which has kept you diminished and afraid, has been exposed as empty and as a fraud. God obliterated that self in His death, burial, and resurrection.

By faith, you can put on the fresh, never-seen-before image of a self that is as beautiful and expansive as Christ. Regardless of your ethnicity or gender, your social status, your religious framework, or intellectual capacity, you are made and can become like the person God imagined when He created you, that is, a son of His love.

"Being renewed" means that the new image, while true and real, must be, over time and repeatedly, refreshed. Just like the old had its practices, so the new has its. And, as you daily look at Jesus, then at yourself, and say, "This is me," you are doing your small part.

This is why looking at creation and at Adam, pre-fall, is so important because, before he fell, Adam was on track and was taking baby steps into that Image. Before Adam did one thing, God breathed His image into him and then put him in the perfect environment so he could grow into it.

So, we will now examine the words that God spoke to Adam because these words describe God's motivation in creating you and what He envisioned for you to look like. The following chapters will look at each word spoken because each word expands the image and makes it clearer. Then we will examine the garden where His image was to come alive, with the hope that you can identify your garden and come alive yourself.

But for now, you are made in His image with a depth that cannot be fathomed. I hope that you grapple with this amazing pronouncement and not just read over it because the implications are staggering.

"In His image and into His likeness" is the gospel in a nutshell. You are of the same species as God according to your essence, and you are a child of God who can become more and more like a son, who looks just like the Father. "But to all who did receive him, who believed in his name, he gave the right AND the ability (the Greek word, *exousia,* combines both thoughts) to become children of God." Your part now is to grow into His likeness, and, if you have received Him, you can because God has not only opened the door, He is also giving you a push.

Let's take time to allow the image of Adam, pre-fall, to reorder your thoughts and imagination. Pause and wonder as you read about Adam, pre-fall, because who he was before he fell, is who you are NOW, because Jesus' resurrection resurrected and restored God's image in all of mankind, and that means, you.

Questions

1. The chapter describes being made "in God's image and into his likeness" as a dynamic process of growing into a reflection of God's essence. How does this perspective challenge or reshape your understanding of your identity? * Can you identify moments in your life where you've sensed a glimpse of this divine image within you, and how might embracing this truth influence your daily choices or self-perception?

2. The author suggests that negative self-messages like "I am not" or "I don't measure up" stem from the residual effects of the Fall. What specific negative messages do you hear in your own "internal digital recorder"? * How might focusing on Jesus, as the restored image of God, help you replace these messages with the truth of being a "glorious you"?

3. The author uses the goose analogy to illustrate that, like a goose separated from its kind, you possess God's image but fail to grow into His likeness without a connection to Him and other "geese". How does this analogy resonate with your own experience of feeling disconnected from God or His people and then struggling to live out your divine identity? * What steps have you taken to foster that connection?

4. The chapter emphasizes that repentance involves rethinking your self-image rather than just changing behavior. Can you recall a time when you recognized a faulty or limiting self-image (e.g., seeing yourself as unworthy or inadequate)? * How might actively choosing to "put on the fresh, new image of Christ" by faith change the way you approach challenges or relationships?

5. The author describes Jesus' declaration of "Tetelestai" (it is finished) as encompassing the restoration of God's image in you. How does this idea—that the work of restoring your divine image is complete—resonate with you? * Reflect on a current struggle or doubt about your worth—how might believing that Jesus had you in mind when he said "it is finished" bring hope or freedom to that area of your life?

Adam-Blessed

T he Triune God is a blessed and a blessing God. Blessing can only be understood from within the framework of a relationship because it takes a bless-er and a bless-ee for blessing to work. From eternity, within the interplay of the Father and the Son, blessing abounds. The Father blesses the Son while the Son blesses the Father, and the Spirit enjoys the overflow, because He is the breath that carries the praise, adoration, and worth-ship that each has for the other, back and forth.

Creation gave God the ability to perfectly replicate this spiritual reality, tangibly. Creation, like God, dances around itself and with itself, holding itself in a delightful embrace. More specifically, God created a living person, whom He could bless and receive blessing. God breathed His spirit into Adam, and Adam responded by exhaling. Blessing in. Blessing out. Essence in. Essence out.

We need to examine this word because it is not only one of those Christian words that are hard to define, but more importantly, is a word that helps define you. "I'm blessed" means what exactly? Its fuzziness needs to be demystified because, if it isn't, you will have a fuzzy sense about yourself, about God, and life.

You will not be able to stand, and having done all to stand, if "blessed" doesn't become an internal reality. And without a growing sense that you ARE blessed, you will spend your life looking for it in all the wrong places.

It is also an important word because "blessing" was the very first thing Adam experienced when he awoke, and the last thing the disciples sensed in Jesus' physical presence when He ascended. One could argue, as well, that Abraham's life was about God reinserting blessing into the story of humanity. And it goes without saying that Jesus' ministry can be summed up in this one word.

From God's perspective, regardless of your experience, this word defines you because He declared it. God is both blessed and the blesser, with humanity being both the recipient and the instrument of blessing. With that, let's try to flesh out this word.

There are a couple of words, in Hebrew and Greek, which are translated as "to bless" or "to be blessed". One is the verb or act of blessing, and the other is the state of being blessed. For this chapter, we will look at the act of blessing because that defines the state.

When God blessed Adam, He *barak*-ed him. When Jesus lifted His hands as he ascended, He *eulogeó*-ed them. God also used this word when he told Abraham, "With *barak*, I will *barak* you and make you a *barak*. When this verse concerning Abraham is quoted in the New Testament, the word used is *eulogeó*.

Both have similar meanings. *Barak* means to honor by kneeling before. *Eulogeó* means to speak well of. The implication is that you are, that humanity is, praise-worthy. When this dawns on you, it will shake you to your very foundation because these are words of worship.

The very first thing God did when He saw this dust-formed, Spirit-infused creature was to kneel before Adam. The wonder of what He just made overwhelmed Him. Minimally, God knelt before Adam, but "minimum", I trust that you know, does not describe God or anything that God does or feels.

Barak was much more than an outward act. God's knees buckled and His breath was taken away because He saw before Him, a perfect representation of Himself. Kneeling before and honoring is the essence of worship. Whether you know it or not, this has forever changed the trajectory of humanity for, at that moment, you were put in the center of Another's attention.

For better or worse, deep down, you know that you were made for this, that is, to be blessed, that is, told in so many ways that you matter, that who you are and what you have is special, and that you were made for the spotlight. If you are honest with yourself, you know that this is so and that your life revolves around seeking the blessing Adam lost.

You were made to sense your own specialness and to have eyes focused on you. Now, this will only work if you don't seek your own glory but give your life to bless the Lord and others, but it is true, nonetheless. You can beat this desire down, try to deny it, or convince yourself that this desire is just pride.

But try as you might, these feelings keep seeping up from within because, in the moment that God blessed Adam, the longing for blessing was also planted deep within. Or you can go the other way and use people or things, hard work or charisma, to get your "center of attention" fix, even if it is only in your own mind.

Isn't this the story of the two sons? Both sought the satisfaction that appreciation and attention give. Blessing makes one alive. The younger son expended his resources to be the life of the party, and while he had them, he was, until the day that he discovered that the only ones who would party with him were the pigs. The elder son buried himself in work, even his father's work, to get some props. It is obvious from his response to his father's entreaties that he harbored resentment about not feeling appreciated.

Both were looking for blessing's touch, which Adam lost. The father's hands of blessing, however, were within reach for both. The oldest hopefully came to realize that he did not need to work for it. The youngest discovered the very thing he sought was in his dad's embrace, not in a far-off land. "You are my beloved. I am so thrilled with you" (TCA) are the words we all long to hear, and these are words of blessing and worth-ship.

Now, I know that the thought that God worships you might seem heretical and has been the basis for heresy. Aren't you told that you are to worship God and Him alone? This is absolutely true. You were created to worship God and are most centered and fulfilled when you do.

The Bible, in many ways, says that worshipping God is best. "I will *barak* the Lord at all times. His praise shall continually be in my lips." "*Barak* the Lord, oh my soul, and let all that is in me set His name apart." "*Eulogeó*-ed is He who comes in the name of the Lord." "And they were continually in the temple, *eulogeó*-ing and praising God." "*Eulogeó*-ed be the God and Father of our Lord Jesus Christ."

But Paul said in the same breath, "And *eulogeó*-ed are you." On your part, you are to *barak* and *eulogeó* God, but that does not stop God from doing what He does best, which is to bless. He is, after all, the Worshipper-in-Chief. So, while praise is unidirectional, there is a mutuality in worship.

Unidirectional worship would be true if your God were Allah or the Allah version of the Christian God who sits at a distance and apart, self-sufficient, and dispensing blessing or judgment as He sees fit. It would also be true if you are setting up a hierarchical, religious system that allows unworthy worms to somehow worm their way into God's good graces through rules and rituals.

But God is the God of all grace, not the God of all restrictions and impediments and distance. The Triune does with His creation what He has been doing within His own relationship forever. The Father and the Son, in the atmosphere of the Spirit, worship each other, which means that they have centered their lives around the other and have given themselves to honor, in every way possible, their best friend. Worship is the language of friendship and love.

All of creation, and you specifically, have been included in this relationship of the blessed and blessing Triune. God, in Christ, has set you free, freely sharing His glory and including you in everything, God. As within the Godhead, the Father initiates all things with all of heaven and earth responding. This is the essence of worship—God calls, and you respond. Then you call, and He responds. Some call this a dance; some, divine play. Some call it a relationship. I call it worship.

The reason that you can worship Him is that He first worships you. When you know, deep within, that you are His focus and that He isn't just enamored with you, but likes you, you are set free from the "what about me?" pull that plagues humanity, and because of that, can freely worth-ship others by serving them.

Barak and *eulogeó* are intimate words of mutuality. These words are the whisperings of the marriage bed. "With my body, I thee worship" is still repeated at wedding ceremonies and is practically expressed later that night.

Barak and *eulogeó* are words that are found in healthy families where the child IS the center of attention for a time and where children are encouraged to discover both who they are and their place in the world because they are special and significant. The blessing of the father and mother over a prolonged period of time, through both the successes and struggles of the child, is essential for a successful launch into adulthood.

I did not have such a launch. My dad seldom had a good word for me, and my mom was not expressive. It took decades for me, as a Christian, to believe what God thought about me and my life. The hole I found myself in was real and deep, and the results of the decisions I made early in life, out of fear and unbelief, still have a residual effect today. This book is the product of being oriented to the love of God.

One large purpose of adulthood is to overcome one's childhood. This also includes those who have had a great childhood in which they were affirmed and disciplined because, regardless of your upbringing, the image of yourself, formed in your childhood, neither goes deep enough nor far enough. Your sense of self needs to overwhelm you as you are overwhelmed by the grace of God.

Yes, there are times when the sense of God will reveal an ugliness within, of which you are possibly unaware. Isaiah, when he saw God, became aware of how undone he was and how woefully short all his words and efforts were. At that time, though, Isaiah was not a slouch. He was at the top of his game, an established prophet, and a counselor in the king's court.

So, Isaiah might have felt that he had it all together. His sense of self might have been a little too self-assured. So, God needed to undo him to right him. For Isaiah, the unveiling of God might have revealed a pride he harbored about being a good Jew and prophet.

While this breaking, as we will see in Peter's life, is necessary and a result of being aware of God's knowing look, the result of beholding God in His perfections and beauty has the opposite effect. It makes you aware of your beauty and perfections.

You become like Him by beholding Him. "And we all, with unveiled face, beholding the glory of the Lord, are being transformed into the same image from one degree of glory to another." Something is released within when you realize that you are praise-worthy and that God is the One shouting, "Atta boy!" or "You go, girl!".

When you see the Father, you come to realize that you are a son. When you behold Jesus, you see yourself because He, who is the Image of God, is the image of you. Knowing that God is love comes with the corresponding sense that you are the beloved.

When you embrace the Deliverer, you begin to walk in freedom. You become aware of your great worth when you know Him as your Redeemer. Your sense of God (that is, your theology) defines you, and without a revelation of a God whom you could never have imagined, you will be weighed down by your own version.

Now if this is true, that a primary and driving force within is to sense that you are blessed, valued, and significant and be acknowledged for it, and that God has put this in you, then the question is, "How do you find and live in the blessing which Adam lost, Abraham found, and Jesus reinstated?" This process will be discovered in the story of Abraham.

But the place to start is to acknowledge that your inner person longs for blessing and that it's ok that you do. This longing has had a direct effect on your attitudes, your actions, and interactions with others. Most don't think about this because the bulk of their energy is used to swim against life's current to get upstream. But the connection between your inner and outer person is real, and it is critical that you stop for a bit, hold your inner person up to the light, and turn it around to examine it.

You can have every external blessing and still feel empty. Or worse, you can be full of yourself. If you feel empty, you will beat yourself up, but if you are full of yourself, you will beat up others. And woe to those who come into contact with people who feel empty but are still full of themselves.

If your life is neither expansive nor growing (which is the ripple effect of a God-blessed inner life), if the thought of getting up in the morning doesn't excite you, or if you don't sense a purpose that keeps you going each day, you need to check your blessing meter. Then you need to create space and carve out time and do what the prodigal did. He came to the realization that his pursuit of blessing came to nothing. He then turned around and came, just as he was, to the father. All he could do was present himself to his father. He had nothing else to offer.

He acknowledged a greater truth than his feelings and logic told him—that his father would, at minimum, listen to him. Little did he know, in fact, he didn't know, that the father's love hadn't changed, that His hand of blessing had never been withdrawn.

You are already in His embrace because He has never let go, so keep coming back to that place, staying there, waiting. Regardless of what you think or feel, even while your mind and heart are being assaulted with the devil's lies, confess the truth of God's word.

The word "confess" means to say the same thing. God says, "You are my beloved", but what are you saying? You are not creating any new reality by speaking the truth. You are allowing God to make real in you what is real in Him. You are making a highway for your God.

The Christian life is one of faith, so feelings and logic must be secondary. Faith says that what God wants to do and wants to produce is already done. Your part is to keep saying, "Amen", until what is true in your spirit bubbles up into your day-to-day consciousness, that is, until the God-blessed part of you takes over and you know that you are His beloved and can navigate life as a son of God.

You will discover that this is a journey and that most of your time on earth will be given to holding on to those few moments when you have sensed His pleasure. You are, as Jude said, to KEEP yourself in the love of God.

You will see this traced out as you continue to read and discover your little part. But let this settle in your heart. You are blessed, God-honored, and adored.

You are the center of His attention, so stop trying to have others recognize you or prop you up. Prop them up.

If you still don't believe this is scriptural, carefully read Psalm 139 and think about David's sense of self compared with yours. His wasn't an empty, hopeful bravado. David's assessment of himself in the light of God was expansive, and, if he were alive today, David would be called a heretic in some circles. In fact, if he weren't the king, he would have been stoned. As I wrote in *Ephesians and all that Jazz:*

"David prioritized and cultivated the presence of the Lord wherever he was, and in whatever situation he found himself. His desire for the Presence overpowered propriety.

Whether taking food which belonged only to priests, dancing foolishly before the masses with hardly anything on, or taking the ark of God's presence from behind the veil home with him, David did not accept the Old Covenant proscriptions. While others thought God mouthed "no," David heard one big, "yes!"

What barriers? The veils which kept everyone else away were entry points for David. Nothing was going to keep David from the intimacy he desired, even if he needed to live in the New Testament while everyone else lived in the Old. Regardless the rules and regulations, David saw the heart of God because he walked by faith and not by sight. And he worshipped. Oh, how he worshipped."

His sense of self was not pride, but the outflow of a humble life pursuing the Presence that pursued him. Is this your sense of self? Your sense of self is rooted in and reflects your sense of God. How you respond to life, and all it throws at you, reveals who you believe yourself to be, along with its corollary, which is who you believe God to be because God-awareness and self-awareness are coincidental.

David was truly an Old Covenant Christian who lived in the blessing of the New Covenant. Let's not then be New Testament Christians who live under the Old. You are no longer under its curse, but under the hand of the God who blesses.

Questions

1. The chapter suggests that God's act of blessing (barak and eulogeó) involves kneeling before you in worship, overwhelmed by your worth as his beloved son. Does this excite or disturb you? * How does this idea challenge your view of God and your own value? * Can you recall a moment when you felt truly valued or significant—how might recognizing God as the source of that blessing deepen your sense of self?

2. The parable of the two sons illustrates the universal longing for blessing, sought in misguided ways. Have you ever found yourself chasing affirmation or attention through external achievements or relationships, like the prodigal or elder son? * What might it look like to turn toward God's embrace instead, trusting that his blessing is already yours?

3. The author emphasizes that your longing to be blessed is God-given, not prideful, but can lead to striving if misdirected. Where in your life do you notice this longing for recognition or significance influencing your actions or emotions? * How could acknowledging this desire as part of God's design help you redirect it toward worshiping him and blessing others?

4. David's expansive sense of self in Psalm 139 is rooted in his awareness of God's affectionate focus on him. How does your current sense of self compare to David's, and what barriers (e.g., negative self-perceptions, past experiences) might be preventing you from embracing God's blessing? * What small step, like meditating on Psalm 139, could you take to cultivate a deeper awareness of God's presence?

5. The chapter describes the Christian life as a journey of holding onto moments when you sense God's pleasure, confessing his truth despite feelings or circumstances. Can you identify a time when you sensed God's love or approval, even briefly? * How might practicing confession—saying "I am your beloved" in faith—help you live more fully as a blessed son or daughter of God?

Adam-Be Fruitful

The first words that God spoke to Adam were "Be fruitful." On the surface, the command seems to make reproducing a top priority to ensure that humanity, like the other species, would survive and thrive. If that is all it means, however, it is a strange command because, even without these words, the "doing" of fruitfulness that produces the "being" needn't be a command because the doing is quite pleasurable. It's like commanding a hungry person to eat the medium-rare ribeye sitting in front of him. "Well, if I must . . ."

No, there must be something else going on. If you consider the end result and the genius of humanity, you will get a better understanding of God's thinking. One thing that stands out from other species is mankind's creativity, the desire to express it, and an appreciation for its expression in others. Within each has been planted the desire and ability both to express their own unique essence in front of others and to be the audience for others. YouTube's success proves it.

For some, this might be expressed through their singing, in others, through building, in others, their cooking, and in others, well, you know what I mean. You have been given a lifetime to develop your gift and become the full expression of the "you" imagined by God. And regardless of the talent, there is an audience for every artistic expression under heaven because even the most mediocre of talents have groupies.

So, the words "be fruitful" did more than give you a nudge toward the bedroom. He has planted within you an expansiveness in seed form. You can trace the reason for you, the reason for your hopes and dreams, and for your frustrations and struggles back to God and His original intent.

In blessing Adam and speaking these few creative words into him, your future was programmed because these words have hard-wired all of humanity. "Be fruitful" has not only created your deep-seated desire for worth and significance, they have also become the call of God, calling you to find your voice.

Fruitfulness, along with becoming great and filling your space, has to do with your worth, that is, sensing your specialness and growing into that person. This is the "being" part of your life.

You have a "being" and a "doing" part of your life. While you cannot separate the two, it is important to be able to step outside of yourself to determine which part is driving you. God has created you both to be and do, and ultimately to have both work together.

But if you are only aware of the "doing" part, then your life will just be a to-do list that will drain you. You will feel the pressure of making things happen with its accompanying anxiety, yet without the resources to accomplish them. You were made first to be and then to do, though you begin your Christian journey by doing. The concept of "being" usually doesn't come until after you realize that your doing doesn't work.

Doing, by the way, is Old Covenant thinking, where the pressure is on you to perform. Three times, God asked the children of Israel, "Will you keep your end up?" To which they said, "But of course. We can, and we will." The lesson that I hope you are learning is that you can't do God's will, that is, at least in your own strength.

This is the brilliance of the New Covenant. Paul wrote, "For neither circumcision (which is doing) counts for anything, nor uncircumcision (which is not doing), but a new creation (which is being)." Your life is no longer caught up in doing this or that, but in a new creation where you find yourself acting out of a new nature.

If you walk with the Lord long enough, you will discover that the Christian life, that is, the life into which God is calling you, is not difficult. It's impossible. Only one Person has ever lived that life or can live it, and He lives in you. Somehow, you must learn how to live an exchanged life, that is, learn to have Him live His life out in you.

The good news that Paul proclaimed was that Jesus died as your substitute and now lives as your replacement. So, as it is said of Jesus, God's hope is that the word, or that which God has planted within you, becomes flesh. By that, I mean, you become it. What a difference it makes when you go from trying to be Christ-like to being Christ-like.

Paul knew this from experience, which is why the one who worked harder than any wrote, "It is no longer I who live, but Christ who lives in me." For Paul, all of his doing came from this place, which he identified as his spirit. He lived from the inside out, and as I wrote in *Ephesians and All that Jazz*, "When the concept of being grabs you, oh, the doing you will do".

An example that shows the difference between being and doing is trying to be a family member. Imagine yourself walking into a stranger's home (even if you were invited) and trying to be a relative, whether a son or daughter, brother or sister, or an aunt or uncle. You would be tripping over yourself from the moment you entered their home.

Now contrast that with getting together with your family. Even with strained relationships, you know the lay of the land and don't have to be anything other than who you are. You ARE a brother or sister, an aunt or uncle, and you act out that relationship.

"Subduing and ruling" and "tending and keeping", which we will address in a bit, refer to the "doing" part of your life and determine your significance. The amount of territory you have under your control speaks to your significance. Just ask Caesar or Genghis Khan. The difference is that they subdued and ruled by force. You, however, are to control your world by drawing others into your orbit, and, like the sun, holding them there.

You intuitively know that you were created to express yourself and be fulfilled in the things you set your hands to. This is both your hope and your struggle. If God didn't plant this in you, you would not struggle, nor would you get discouraged, worked up, or depressed.

Even without the sin wounds that need to be healed, though, becoming and filling the shoes that God made for you is difficult because obstacles abound. For one, as I wrote in the chapter on developmental darkness, and as John wrote, "what you will be, has not yet appeared".

So, the picture of your future "you" is fuzzy at best, and it's hard to determine the path if the destination is not clear. It's even harder if you don't know that there is a destination.

Neither a seed nor a caterpillar has a clue what they will become and could become confused when things happen for no apparent reason. I would think that the seed and caterpillar, in their limited consciousness, would have to think, as you do, "What the heck is going on?" when things begin to change.

So quite possibly, the command to be fruitful was given with this looming challenge in mind because it is easy to give up when the road becomes confusing or hard. Knowing that God has determined for you to go through a process to fully blossom should keep you from giving up too soon because, at times, neither the seed nor the caterpillar, nor you as well, have a clue what's going on. So, what you experience can feel a lot like death.

But Jesus made it clear that the path to life includes, and even requires, death, yet not a death brought on by sin. Jesus said that His future was tied to death. "Unless a grain of wheat falls into the earth and dies, it remains alone; but if it dies, it bears much fruit."

Fruitfulness, therefore, begins by dying. Becoming great occurs by becoming smaller. Neither is naturally desirable. To become Savior, the Firstborn from among the dead and the First Fruits, had first to fall into the ground and die.

This dying thing was not an afterthought. It also had nothing to do with God's vindictiveness or His way of manipulating the outcome. Dying has always been a part of Eternal Life. Natural life, as well, not only exists but grows because of death. Death is woven into the fabric of life, whether it's the death of krill, some grass, or a cow.

Life exists because another gave up theirs. While death is understood primarily through the framework of the fall, there is a death which precedes it and is not tied to human failure, but to eternity.

An even better term for this type of death might be surrender because dying occurs when you stop fighting and give up your will, your preferences, and your life for another. And don't tell me that giving up or giving in doesn't hurt at times and feels like death.

Surrender has been the hallmark of the Trinitarian relationship. The Father, Son, and Spirit live in a cooperative, surrendered relationship that continually defers to the other. Relationships thrive in no other way.

Creation could do nothing but reflect this. Now, I know that a school of krill has no clue that a sperm whale has its mouth open five feet in front of them or that the blade of grass knows that it will soon become cud, but their surrender is just as real. Their life was taken in the service of another.

So let me state this as clearly as I can: a larger reason for Jesus' death had nothing to do with sin. He made that clear by saying that no spiritual life exists apart from "eating His flesh and drinking His blood". So, His physical death on the cross points beyond the Passover, where a lamb was eaten in haste, to a greater reality.

That reality is the Lamb who was been slain before creation and who is still the Lamb. But this Lamb is no longer laid across an altar. He is seated upon the throne. His nature has always been sacrificial, offering Himself up for others.

Jesus was always slated to die, regardless of sin, so that you and I could live and grow as we partake of Him. He surrendered His life to be your krill.

The writer of Hebrews also linked his death to the joy of becoming the first among many brothers (again, "brother" is not a gender term but an all-embracing relationship). He was the seed that fell into the ground to produce more sons like Himself. His death led to "being fruitful and multiplying, filling the earth and subduing it."

His death allows you to flower, and your many little deaths will also be the fertilizer that allows others to grow. Paul said that the death that was at work in him produced fruit and life in others.

But sin was and is a reality and needed to be addressed. So, Jesus' death did double duty. For Jesus, this surrender was more difficult because while He willingly gave His life, it was also taken from Him wrongfully.

Jesus was asked to dive, with His mouth wide open, into a cesspool which had fermented and was bubbling up noxious fumes. He was then asked to ingest its poison. This was His surrender. This was the death He accepted.

You, however, have a hard time giving in to a simple request from your spouse, getting a wee bit out of your comfort zone, or waiting for God to show up. So, you must be willing, in the incongruities of life, to fall into the ground and stay there while eternal and incomprehensible processes are at work. Looking back, you will know and understand the process and begin to see the outcome.

While the fall didn't create your desire to be and to achieve, it intensified your longings because, after the fall, you were unplugged from the Source. And what a terrible place to be—full of dreams and ambitions with neither the ability to achieve them nor the certainty that they will be fulfilled.

The human condition can be traced back to unplugged people, flailing about, trying this outlet and that, only to find that every one of them is faulty. Regardless of your best efforts, life succeeds or fails depending on whether you are plugged in and remain plugged into the Source of life, even when that outlet doesn't seem to be working.

When plugged into the Source, Adam and Eve had, under God, the potential to fill their space with themselves and to organize and manage their world. Unplugged, they and their progeny were left to their own devices, and we have tried ever since to fulfill that destiny, but with disastrous results.

We will look at the garden shortly, where Adam and Eve were to discover their value and purpose, and how you can both discover yours and learn how to fulfill your destiny. But for now, let's continue to wonder at the words that God first spoke to mankind. "Be fruitful, multiply, and fill the earth." These words, by the way, were restated by Jesus when He said, "Go into all the world and fill it, by making more people who are just like you, who are just like Me." (TCA)

Questions

1. How does seeing "be fruitful" as a call to express your unique essence change your view of your gifts and dreams? * Reflect on a talent or passion you have—how might God want to use it to reflect his image?

2. The chapter contrasts "being" (living as a new creation) with "doing" (Old Covenant performance pressure). Where do you notice a "to-do list" mentality driving your life? * What practical step could you take to prioritize "being" in Christ over "doing"?

3. Surrender, or "dying," is described as essential for fruitfulness, as seen in Jesus and the Trinity. Can you identify a small act of surrender (e.g., letting go of control or pride) that might lead to growth in your life? * How does this idea challenge or inspire you?

4. Being "unplugged" from God intensifies unfulfilled longings and frustrations. Have you experienced disconnection from God that led to striving or discouragement? * What habits or practices could help you stay "plugged into" the Source of life?

5. Before reading this chapter, what were the reason(s), you believed, that Jesus hung on the cross? * "Jesus died to be your krill." How did that strike you? * Does this expand your understanding of the purpose of the cross? Explain.

Adam-Become Great and Fill

I want to look at "multiply and fill" dispassionately because, I don't know whether you have noticed, I can get hyperbolic at times. "Be fruitful, multiply, and fill" has hyperbole written all over it. In God's scheme of things, however, hyperbole is an understatement.

The Hebrew word for multiply also means to become great. It is the same word that God spoke to Abraham when He told him that God was going to make his name great. So, God's word to Adam and Eve could just as easily be translated, "Be fruitful and become great, so great that you fill your space."

I want to walk around these words like a good reporter and ask some simple questions, like "Of all the things God could have said, why are these the first words out of His mouth?" What do these words say concerning God's thoughts and feelings toward you?

Also, what do these words reveal about the nature of God? And since "Be fruitful and multiply" was spoken to a whole host of creatures, we must also address the competing interests that these words have created and try to discern God's intent.

First, however, I want to remind you that God was not primarily speaking about the physicality of fruitfulness. That was built into the sexuality of humanity. Even if He was talking about sex, God always speaks in layers, with the real meaning buried under the surface.

What are the parables, for example, other than layered speaking? No, God spoke into the core of humanity, in general, and into you, specifically, the drive to grow and become great. Whatever humanity is essentially, and whoever you are, specifically, God spoke that into existence and wants it to increase exponentially.

Isn't greatness what fruitfulness means? One kernel of corn produces between 500 to 1,000 kernels, which, when planted again, can produce up to one million kernels. You don't have to be a mathematician to realize that these are crazy numbers.

So, what would you multiplied exponentially look like? If that is too much to take in, how about 30, 60, or 100-fold? What would that look like? When you were born, God intended for you to fill the space you inhabit with your giftings and personality, expand that space, and refill it again and again.

This good news was first spoken to Adam, revisited in Abraham, established in Christ, and now spoken to you. And I can't think of any better restatement of "Be fruitful, become great, and fill the earth" than "You are my beloved Son in whom I delight." Both are God's kiss that frees you to be you and to fill your space. Both declarations bring clarity to the other and expand their meaning.

Should it be any wonder then that the gospel preached in the first centuries took the poor and marginalized by storm? When they heard the good news of Jesus, they discerned that this good news was about themselves as well: "I, too, am God's beloved son in whom He is well pleased." "I, too will be fruitful, become great, and fill the earth." "My influence and significance will be immeasurable, regardless of the place I find myself in. Therefore, I will give myself fully to what is before me."

That this message has been reduced by a small segment of Christendom to be about healing, wealth, and political ascendancy (which are the smallest and least significant parts of being blessed) does not negate the good news. God wants you to shine on the stage with Him, spotlights blazing, applause resounding, and you, being fully you.

What God DIDN'T initially say to Adam was "I am God, worship me and make ME great." He didn't give him the ten best rules to live by. That came later when Adam and Eve lost their intuitive sense of who they were and who God was, what their relationship with Him meant, and therefore needed boundaries along with some sense knocked into them.

No, God said, "for freedom, you have been set free." He knew that with His blessing and with them being plugged into the Source, they would have had a proper sense of both Him and their selves. They would have flourished, and God would have been gloried, along with His will being done.

So, what must you conclude about yourself when you stand in Adam and Eve's place, hearing these words spoken to you, "(put your name here), be fruitful, become great, and fill your space?" You would have to surmise minimally that He likes the "you" He made and wants everyone to know it. Also, you would think that whatever you are today is not what you will become.

It was as if, at Adam's creation, the outline of the man and woman was sketched with the background roughed in. God then put down His pencil, took out his palette and brushes, and began mixing colors. Adam and Eve's lives were to remain on the easel with hues and textures and depth being added until the definition of God's image became unmistakable.

The desire to be on stage, appreciated, recognized, respected, and loved is part of the eternity that God has put in your heart. The desire to grow and become greater is also eternity's tug. This is the "you" that God hardwired, and you can't keep these feelings down.

Your pursuit to be noticed and appreciated is undeniable. One billion video views a day on TikTok is all the evidence you need. You push these desires down to your own detriment. These desires, however, will trip you up if you pursue them on your own or for your own aggrandizement.

Additionally, God must be comfortable in His own skin to release creation to create on its own. If He weren't secure in His person and position, the instructions would have been completely different. It would have been, "Be careful to observe all that I have commanded you." He would have kept His thumb on Adam and Eve.

Now, don't hear what I am not saying. As we grow and go through our Christian paces, there is a time to remain under His thumb, so to speak. Christian discipline is putting yourself under His thumb, and without doing it, you will be less because you don't come out of the chute feeling loved in every way.

You certainly don't know what walking in the Spirit is either, when you first submit to Christ. Because of that, the fruit that others taste can taste a whole lot like you—salty, bitter, acerbic, full of yourself, and not like Christ.

But little children grow up. Hopefully, they learn to walk and then run. Hopefully, they don't live in their parents' basement when they are thirty. Hopefully, they are self-sustained and running their own lives and dad's business. Little children are to become sons of the Jesus order.

This is what sonship is—freely humbling yourself from an exalted position to obey God and serve others. You obey because your sense of self is bathed in love. Any other obedience is "have-to", Old Covenant thinking.

How does your theology match up with "for freedom, you have been set free?" How does this align with your sense of self? Your perception of God has a greater effect on how you perceive yourself and how you act than you think.

Baxter Kruger, who is one of the leading Trinitarian theologians, tells a story about teaching his son to ride a bike. After running behind his son and holding the seat to keep him balanced, he let go, and his son began to ride.

When his son got back to him after circling the cul-de-sac, so excited and proud, Baxter told him, "Now this is what I want you to do. I want you to get back on your bike and ride around the neighborhood. Tell everyone how great your dad is for teaching you how to ride. Go ahead, loudly sing my praises! Go on now. And, by the way, when you get back, I have a few errands for you to run."

Obviously, this is a made-up story with the point of the story being that God ran behind you so you would be free and able to ride. The fruit of your freedom is that God is glorified. Yes, you will sing His praises, but the song that others hear first, and most loudly, is a set-free you. That is what others desire for themselves.

Is this your perception of God? Was it for freedom that you have been set free, or do you think that being God's servant is the primary reason that you were created? What message are you hearing at church?

That special moment of having your dad run behind you and then release you into a freedom and an adventure will cement the bond you have with Him and will cause you to want to please Him. So, do you believe that His will for you is freeing and expansive, or is it constrictive?

Your Dad's purpose in teaching you how to ride your bike is not to make Himself look better. It's not about Him, even though God does everything for His glory. It is His glory to have all of His children riding their bikes. Isn't that what you want for your children? Your freedom gives Him the greatest pleasure.

If your primary mentality is that God made you to obey and serve Him, what a small God you have and what pressure you put on yourself. He doesn't need your help, because He is able to hold everything in orbit around himself without demanding a thing because there is nothing in the universe more attractive.

He freed you, so that you would be free, and in that freedom, become like Him, a willing servant. Jesus, knowing that He was in every aspect God, willingly became a slave. It is only from this sense of freedom and sonship that anyone could become a servant, like Jesus is. According to Paul, in writing to the Philippians, THIS is the "same mind" that you are to have.

Too often, you are told to be like Jesus, the bondservant, while skipping over the first part of Paul's discourse because heaven help us if anyone thinks that he or she is "God-like". Paul wrote, "Have this mind among (literally, in) yourselves, which is yours in Christ Jesus". That is, you are to "think exactly the same way about yourself that Jesus did of Himself", who "though He was in the form of God, did not count equality with God a thing to be grasped, but emptied himself by taking the form of a servant".

Do you hear what Paul is saying? Do you understand the implications? Jesus' mindset was that He WAS, in every aspect, God because that is who He is. He didn't need to do anything to be like God. And the Holy Spirit, through Paul, said that you are to have this same mindset.

Jesus didn't have to give Himself pep talks or try to convince others. He knew who He was. Jesus knew that He was right (which is the correct definition of righteousness) and that His rightness derived from His relationship with His Father.

The question, however, is, "Do you?" You ARE a son of God because of your relationship with your Father. Therefore, you too "are in the form, God." Yes, yes. You and I are not God, just like you are not your father or mother.

But you and I have His DNA. You are OF Him. You have been chiseled out of the same cliff. John said that you have been given the authority to have His embedded image become, in you, His actual likeness. You can grow into the image of Jesus, who is the image of the Father.

That's what "made in His image" means. I can understand, though, why most cringe at the thought of "God-likeness" being applied to the likes of "unworthy" you and me. And I also get it, as to why the church is hesitant to go down this path, because it thinks that you, being God-like, somehow diminishes God's glory and therefore, borders on heresy. Most do not have Paul's inclusive, Trinitarian understanding of God and therefore tend to lean heavily on the Old Testament version of God. But it was that version that Jesus came to implode. Jesus came and said, "Surprise!"

Therefore, "He was in the form, God" and "did not count equality with God" are read to be exclusive to Jesus and skipped over to get to the serving part. But being "in Christ" means something more than you being a virus that God, in His mercy, has allowed to float around His body. No, you are vitally connected with God and essentially the same, and because of that, there is little to no difference in your essence.

"This mind", which you are to have, begins with the "being like God" part. Paul writes, "From sonship and a sonship frame of mind, act like Jesus who willingly divested Himself of every right and privilege of that high position." (TCA) The implications of this are astounding.

As I wrote in *Ephesians and All that Jazz*":

"Unless you embrace the 'you', with a small 'y' that God created, and see yourself as an equal, with a small 'e', your attempts to connect with God will fall short of what He desires. God created you for relationship, but not a relationship between dis-similars, like you and your dog.

No matter how comforting and entertaining you might find Fido, he will never get your jokes. Satisfying relationships blend hearts together who have a common heritage and a shared life. God is so over the mentality which says that you are less than a friend or a son or a lover.

Have you ever sung a duet with your dog? You can certainly howl with him, but he can never harmonize with you. To harmonize, you must be able to look into each other's eyes to blend your voices together and follow each other's lead. Only equals can do that."

You can't humble yourself from "a sinner saved by grace" position. How much lower can a worm go? And if you did, it would just be self-effort and false humility. Your humility, if it is to be like Christ's, must be rooted in a free and lofty sense of self that gives up its privileges and privileged position to willingly become someone without any privileges or rights, which is the definition of a slave.

True humility and servanthood only proceed from an identity that is rooted in an awareness that your relationship with the Father, both positionally and affectionately, is no different than Jesus'. What Jesus is in whole, you are in part. This is the unbelievably good news of the gospel, which is, "Be fruitful, become great, and fill your space."

But what happens when your fruitfulness impinges upon someone else's, or your greatness bumps up against another's, or your fullness enters a room that is already full? And what about weeds and rats? Each was also told to do their thing.

Or sheep and coyotes, what about them? Both were told to fill the earth, but the coyote's mandate mean that the sheep population is affected. Or what about sheep and grass? How is that different than coyotes and sheep? It seems that, from day one, the potential for conflict was woven into the fabric of the ecosystem because each creature and every group has its own competing interests.

What happens when your desires come into conflict with mine, or when the space you want to fill is already filled by another? You don't have to look far to see this dynamic at work. From nations seeking ascendency over other nations to you wanting a position at work or at church that is already filled, to husbands and wives and children mixing it up, your desire for greatness and mine can create conflicts within and without.

This issue exists because this righteous desire, implanted by God, is rooted in unrighteous hearts. Whereas God's intent and design were a dance, we learned how to fight. Conflict and competition replaced cooperation and collaboration.

I am sure you have sampled the conflict and competition this world offers. I'm not so sure that you have tasted God's morsels. Being ignored and dismissed, excluded, treated as a commodity, and put under another's thumb are marks of the devil's domain.

You are not an innocent victim, though, because you also use others and things to get your way. You also participate in the devil's scheme of things. You are both the victim and the perpetrator at the same time, and unless you recognize this, this cycle will not be broken.

The good news is that you don't have to put someone down to ascend to the top. That's the lie of the devil and is called a zero-sum game, where your win means another's loss. God's kingdom is anything but, because you win when others do, and others win when you do.

The top, in God's kingdom, is not a rarified space where only a few can inhabit because God's top is the bottom, and His bottom is bottomless. If the top was the goal, then coveting would be a virtue. "God has called me to be the head and not the tail, so get out of my way and submit to my will!"

A good contrast between the limiting nature of the devil's domain and the limitlessness of God's is a glass of water on a table in a room. In one scenario, you are in an enclosed space with 10 other people, no way out, and one glass of water on the table. How you would look at that glass and at the others in the room is far different than being with the same group, in the same room, with the same glass of water but sitting next to a spigot.

There are no limitations in God's kingdom, and there is space for everyone to thrive. Jesus said that He was going to prepare a place for you, and He did not just mean in the by and by. And if you go low enough, you will find how expansive that place is.

And this is how you neutralize the competitive nature that is built into the world's system. You compete to be last. You scheme to lose. You discover freedom by becoming a slave. You gain by giving. You become fat by becoming food for others. This is the upside-down logic of the kingdom.

God has called you to greatness. So, my greatness will not keep you from achieving yours, nor will the greatness of a billion other saints. God has created a system, called the kingdom, where you can shine as brightly as you want without diminishing the light of another. In fact, your light, added to another's, only increases glory.

The key is to learn how to open doors of opportunity for others and put them on the stage. We will see in a bit how this was to practically work out in the garden. But for now, "be fruitful, become great, and fill your space."

Questions

1. How does the call to "be fruitful, become great, and fill your space" shape your understanding of your God-given potential? * On a scale of 1 to 10 (1 being insignificant, 10 being highly significant), how important do you feel? * What might a 30-, 60-, or 100-fold version of you look like, and how does this potential inspire or challenge you?

2. The gospel empowered the marginalized Christians in the first centuries to embrace their significance. Can you identify a "small" area of your life where you could live out your greatness? * How might this shift your perspective on limitations?

3. Paul urges you to have the "same mind" as Jesus, seeing yourself as God-like in essence. Does this feel radical or uncomfortable? * How might embracing this mindset affect your confidence or actions?

4. Baxter Kruger's bike analogy depicts God as a Father who frees you to thrive, not to serve out of obligation. Do you view God as primarily freeing or demanding? * How does becoming a servant from a position of sonship differ from becoming a servant from a "sinner saved by grace" mentality?

5. Conflicts arise when desires for greatness compete, but God's kingdom values "competing to be last." Have you faced a conflict over recognition or space (e.g., at work, home)? * How could adopting the kingdom's upside-down logic (e.g., serving others first) reshape this situation?

Adam-Subdue and Rule

G od planted within you the sense that you are special with the need and desire to express that specialness when He spoke the words, "Be fruitful, become great, and fill". Then He gave you, with the words that followed, something to do and the need to accomplish something.

"Subdue and rule" were not just external marching orders. They were words that penetrated the very core of your being. They became your mission in life. You were born with the need to conquer and win. These words also created in you a wondering about your purpose and the desire to be acknowledged for your success. They gave a reason for you.

You were created both to be, and to do. The being part, which already has been addressed, speaks to your value, while the doing part speaks to your significance. Your satisfaction in life is tied to both. While you can't separate them because they feed off each other, it would be interesting to somehow step outside of yourself and see yourself on these two continuums.

First, do you have an inner sense that you are loved for who you are and don't need attention? Do you know that you are right in such a way that you don't have to defend yourself? Are you aware of God's focus, so you can either stay quietly in the background or be on stage without it going to your head?

Do you know your strengths and weaknesses, see their value for others, yet in that knowing, not let your personality or giftings drive you? Do you live in the restful land of "I am" or the anxious land of "I am not"?

Then, do you know the "why" of you? Do you know what you are about in such a way that you can give yourself to it without expecting anything in return? Do you have a long-term vision for yourself, so that setbacks don't set you back? Do you stay in your lane when other lanes seem easier to navigate and seemingly lead to greener pastures?

Can you take the regular beat-downs of life and turn them into an extraordinary drumline, or do they exhaust you? Is your day-to-day attached to an expansive vision, or are you going through the motions? Do you have a sense of purpose and pleasure that come from knowing that what you are doing and accomplishing pleases the Lord? A little clue—God gets as much pleasure with you doing the dishes, as He does with you raising the dead.

Without seeing your significance in the mundane, the best you can do is go through the motions, be drained, and hope that life works out. I would even say that depression and lack of motivation have their roots in either not sensing a purpose or seeing its impossibilities.

We will see in the following chapters on the garden that this grandiose vision to rule the world was put into a bite-sized, commonplace setting that looks a lot like yours. Faithful in little, faithful in much, you know. Changing the world includes dusting the furniture.

Before we look at what Genesis says about the world and your furniture, however, let's take a closer look at the words that have not only given you purpose but have also created your issues. You HAVE heard of control issues, haven't you?

Why do you think over 11 billion dollars is spent each year to organize stuff? You want to be in control and not let things run amok. God put that in your heart. Well, now we know Who and what's to blame!!

Where do you think your need to win comes from? Kids hate losing a game, and couples hate losing an argument. The need to win is hardwired into your psyche by God. Jesus, by the way, never rebuked his disciples for wanting to be first. He just told them the cost and said that it wasn't going to be achieved the way that they thought.

No, the answer is not denying how God wired you. Controlling is not the issue. Wanting to be first is not the problem. These are not the reasons for pride or selfishness. They are the echoes of a deeper part of you that cannot be dismissed as evidence of the fallen nature, even though that nature has used these words to justify selfish means and produce hurtful ends.

"Subduing and ruling" put in more colloquial, genteel terms, is "putting things in order and managing them." Isn't this the lion's share of what you do in life again and again? And aren't you the happiest when things run smoothly and not when your world is out of control?

I know that some can get used to living in a hoarder's house, but most shudder at the thought. Some can get used to unmanageable kids, but most want to lock them in a closet. And how many people suffer because they can't control their own thoughts or emotions?

This just involves you trying to hold your own life together. Then add to that, others who try to control you. I am sure that you know how that feels, unless you have been the one doing your best to control others. What a mess we have become because of "subdue and rule".

While these words were meant to establish God's kingdom here, they have been the impetus for some to carve out their own. While the focus of these words was directed toward the devil in order to squash him and his plans, this drive to control is often the reason that the psyche and dreams of children and wives are crushed, and husbands become frustrated. Words that were to establish peace on earth and in your home have resulted in unresolved conflicts and all-out war. All because you were created to put things in order and manage them.

These two words are not genteel, though. These are bare-knuckle, no-holds-barred sort of words. Fighting words. The Hebrew word for subdue is *kabash,* which means to squash bugs under your feet and grind them to a pulp.

In Scripture, this word has been used to depict the forcible subjugation of both individuals and people groups, coercing them into slavery. It was even used to describe attempted rape which is the utterly humiliating domination of the stronger over the weaker.

The Hebrew word for rule has the same flavor. It has a very hard edge to it. Both assume an obstinate environment that needs to be brought under control. Funny words for a pre-fall existence where one would think that the God-pronounced "it was very good" meant idyllic. It seems that, from day one, the world was out of control and needed someone to come onto the scene to corral it.

The fall didn't create the evil in the world. It opened the door. The chaos and emptiness, which the light dispelled, were not destroyed when God said, "Let there be." Evil scurried away and hid in the hinterlands. Adam and his progeny were given, right from the beginning, a search-and-destroy mission.

One day, though, evil did knock on Adam and Eve's door. Once they opened it, the darkness, chaos, and emptiness that they were tasked to displace entered and then controlled and consumed them. The pandemic of sin spread through the entire world.

"Now, wait a minute," you might say. "Didn't Paul, who got his revelation from Jesus, say "Sin didn't enter the world until after Adam sinned?" Well, yes, he did.

But Moses, who more than likely penned his tome on the mount in the presence of God, clearly assumed that evil was lurking in the world before Adam was created; otherwise, "subdue and rule" would have been replaced with "relax and frolic." So, how do we reconcile these two thoughts?

This is the delicious task of theologians. I am not a theologian unless you rightly say that everyone is. I am just a schlump who likes to think and, once in a while, get a few breadcrumbs to follow. This is one of them.

I need to first caution you on how you think. The Western mind finds both-and thinking difficult. It is either one or the other because we like our boxes. If it fits into your box, it's declared to be the truth, and anything outside of that box is not.

The problem is that God is not confined to your box, and as Isaiah said, "His thoughts are way higher than ours". They are also more elegant, layered, and complex in a simple sort of way. They can hold seemingly contradictory thoughts together because, at some level, they coexist.

In fact, the Scriptures purposefully express seemingly contradictory concepts. It is as if God speaks out of both sides of His mouth. He, by the way, is the only One who can, and be right, because He is able to synthesize all the oft-debated thoughts in the Scriptures without over-emphasizing one or minimizing the other.

And here is a little clue that has helped me. His words are first to be grasped by the heart, not the head. They are primarily motivational. For example, what does it do to your heart, knowing that once you are saved, you cannot be unsaved and that God has got you?

Now, what does realizing that you can lose your salvation do? One settles you, and the other unsettles. Within the Scriptures, God has placed both the carrot and the stick, and if you know anything about yourself, you need both. So, instead of hardening your theological positions by defending one or the other, you should, at least, allow for the possibility of both.

So, how do I reconcile these two thoughts—first, that evil was in the world before Adam sinned and that sin did not enter the world until after Adam fell? The distinction I make is the difference between sin and evil.

While Satan, as John said in his epistle, has sinned from the beginning, his evil presence in the world, after God brought light and order, was encapsulated. Like a submarine, filled with poison, cannot affect the ocean unless its hull is breached, so sin and death, which are the devil's poison, could not affect the world because it remained locked up.

Before Adam and Eve, who were the world's gatekeepers, opened that door, sin's energy had potential. It was active but not effective. Like yeast in a package, it couldn't permeate the cosmos until it was activated. It was poised and ready to expand, under the right conditions, but the package was sealed.

The writer of Job describes a similar scene in heaven where Satan is seen as an interloper. The presence of Satan there did not make heaven dirty or sinful because God was reigning there. It just created a situation that needed to be dealt with, and at his creation, Adam, the world's newly established ruler, had a situation of which he was unaware.

Conversely, the presence of the Holy Spirit in the world today does not make this age holy. It is still a present evil age. Peter prophesied that the Spirit is poured out upon ALL flesh, not just Christian flesh. But the closeness of the Spirit doesn't make the unregenerate righteous. As with Adam and sin, that door must be opened from the inside.

So, let me lay out my understanding of the beginning, in light of "subdue and rule". This has changed my perception of myself, my purpose, and has caused me to rethink Jesus' mission.

Having a clear understanding of the conditions on the ground at the time of Adam's creation will also help bring your life into focus and show that the warfare of Ephesians 6 was not an add-on because of the fall, but part of God's plan from the beginning.

While the fall and sin added a layer of complexity, it does not change His purpose for you because your purpose was established before the fall and that purpose was for you to establish His kingdom in your surroundings by displacing demons.

So, what did the nascent world look like? Obviously, what follows is just my imagination running away with me, but, as I read between the lines of Scripture, this makes sense, resonates, and creates faith. I love big stories anyway. So, if I am going to believe something, it might as well be big.

If the world needed to be forcibly subjugated and ruled with an iron fist (the animals, the garden, and their spouses, by the way, were not God's intended focus), then it says something about the world into which Adam was introduced. It was fraught with danger, and an evil presence lurked. The principalities and powers that exist today, existed then.

How they got there is a thing of speculation, so let me speculate. There are hints in the prophets of an age prior to the one in which we live. Paul declared that there are AGES to come, so there just might have been ages before. Ezekiel and Isaiah talk about a prior, perfect age in which righteousness dwelt. During that time, and before he sinned, Satan, the adversary, had a different name.

His name was Lucifer, or "light-bearer", because that name perfectly described him. Eyes needed to be shielded when he showed up. Ezekiel said he was "the seal of beauty and perfection." He was the standard against whom all were measured.

Sounds to me that He was, in many aspects, Jesus' twin or image with a couple of exceptions. First, he was a created being, and second, Lucifer was not allowed to share God's throne or His glory. (This makes what God purposed for you and me even more astounding because we WERE created both to share His throne and His glory.)

Lucifer had unrestrained access to paradise and to the mount of God, where he was the anointed Cherub. Created with instruments embedded and covered with precious stones, Lucifer was the covering angel who guarded the Throne and led worship. There was none greater than him under God. He ruled because he had authority over the angel armies and whoever else inhabited the world.

It seemed as well that it, like ours, was a physical, tangible world by the description of it. Ezekiel said that this paradise was traversed by a glorious Lucifer and not by a sneaky snake.

The paradise of God was his to enjoy and rule. The earth was a paradise because there was an open heaven. The presence of God was on full display. He hid nothing of Himself.

God's throne was also established on His mountain on earth. Heaven might have been one of His summer homes because He reigned here. Heaven truly enveloped the earth. As you read the last chapter of Revelation, heaven once again will saturate earth, and God's desire for open glory will be fulfilled.

Open glory, however, means no excuse. Lucifer somehow believed his own press, and when he fell, there was no redemption. Others might have told him how amazing he was (which he was) and instead of giving back to God the glory which God had given him, he kept it for himself.

A plan then crept into his heart to take the only thing that wasn't his—God's glorious throne. What he had under his authority was not enough for him. So, he gathered a cabal to overthrow the Triune and, to this day, leads the principalities and powers along with a host of demons.

As an aside, Satan must have determined that God had weaknesses, otherwise, why would he have attempted a suicide mission? He might have correctly read the heart of the Triune, who would rather wrap a towel around His waist and wash another's feet than sit enthroned. God would rather rule through weakness (love is a deferring show of weakness), than by force.

I'm not sure why God didn't crush Satan under his feet at that time, because it seems that God ceded the earth to Satan and his ilk, and this world fell and became their playground. Genesis 1:2 describes the world as empty, chaotic, and full of darkness, whereas heaven, the place where God dwells, is full of life, is harmoniously ordered, and is light-filled.

So, the question is, "Did God create the world a mess or did it become a mess?" This has been hotly debated, with the argument centering around the word "was". "It was" is interpreted in most Bibles as "that's just how God created it". "The earth WAS without form and void, and darkness was over the face of the deep."

This word, however, can be translated either as a statement of fact or as a cause-and-effect verb. The phrase, "and it came to pass", in the Scriptures is the same word. If that is the case, then this verse would read, "And the earth BECAME empty and chaotic." If it became, there would need to be a cause because this word describes an effect.

This same word, *hayah*, is used throughout the first chapter of Genesis to describe cause and effect. In fact, it is used as a cause-and-effect verb over 20 times in the first chapter. "Let there be," which describes the cause, is *hayah*. "And it was so", which describes the effect, is the same word.

I know that real theologians will argue that while it has a "cause and effect" meaning every other time in chapter 1, it does not in Genesis 1:2 for one reason or another. But in light of the "subdue and rule" mandate, this "it came to pass" interpretation deserves more consideration.

I can only surmise that Genesis 1:2 is the beginning of God's restoration project with possibly billions of years tucked between verses 1 and 2. Between these two verses would be found an age of open glory, the attempt of Satan to overthrow God, God's removal of Himself from earth, and the earth becoming a hoarder's house filled with scads of unruly children.

God had given Lucifer authority over the earth to manage and bless it. But the devil used that to his advantage when his heart became corrupt. Since God is not one to take back what He gives, it follows that when Satan fell, he retained his authority over the earth. So, "the earth became empty and chaotic, and darkness covered the deep" perfectly describes the nature of the one who ruled it.

Then the Spirit of God moved over the face of the waters, and hell gave way, while heaven broke loose. But when Satan became aware that a weak, clueless piece of dust was given what he claimed as his own, he exclaimed, "We'll see about that!", and the battle ensued. And for a moment, he won.

Only, he just saw the snapshot, not the video. Little did he know that the first man was not meant to be the last, that from the man of earth would come the Man from heaven, and that Jesus and His band of merry men and women would then permanently displace and depose him.

Why is this important? The gospel proclaims that humanity is the new Image-bearer and that these specks of dust are God's way of humbling the proud. The limited, needy, and powerless projects were created to take down the expansive, self-sufficient, and powerful spiritual entities who were completely put together and full of themselves. God's power is manifest in weakness and His wisdom, in foolishness. It has always been that way, but Satan never understood God's heart.

Adam's strength, which he was to discover in the garden, was in his identity, his need, and his dependence on the Triune. While Lucifer's relationship to God was that of a servant, Adam's was, and yours is now, as a son. And while Lucifer's sense of his perfections tripped him up, you are, more times than not, tripped up by looking at your imperfections and embracing a sinnership mentality.

Now you can believe what you want about the beginning, but I have come to believe this. Even if it is not true, believing that one of your purposes is to kick a little demon booty will put a zip in your step. And I think we all need that. Besides, isn't spiritual warfare supposed to be a significant part of Christianity?

Before you dismiss me and this as "cray-cray", let me appeal to a credible witness to add credence to my craziness. He is the renowned Christian philosopher, whose name is Augustine, to whom "The New is in the Old concealed. The Old is in the New revealed" is attributed. Augustine correctly perceived that the New and Old Testaments have a symbiotic relationship.

The Old hides behind shadows and, with subtle hues, paints pictures which only become clear by superimposing the New on it. The New then defines the Old and especially explains its most important topic, which is mankind.

Paul clearly states that Adam is the type of the One who was to come, that is, Adam points forward to Jesus, in His essence and purpose. Not only does Adam give clarity to Jesus, Jesus also paints a picture of what Adam was designed to be and destined to do. Jesus shows Adam's standing, relationship, and purpose, and in so doing, defines you and your purpose.

Jesus reveals what restored humanity looks like and what you and I were created to do. As Christ is hidden throughout the Old Testament, so Adam and you are fully revealed in Him. God's original purpose for humanity is then seen in the life of Jesus.

As you read the Gospels, you find that Jesus came as the Second Man and did what Adam was first tasked to do, but failed. In short, Jesus' call was both to be fruitful, multiply, and fill the cosmos, and to establish the kingdom by displacing the darkness that the demons ruled. The gospels show that He established His rule by loving people and by knocking demons off their perches.

He also gave his disciples the authority to do the same. Adam, therefore, is no longer the fountainhead of humanity. Jesus, in His death, burial, and resurrection confirmed that He is. And as He walked the earth and now as His believing ones do, the darkness which shrouds hearts and regions is to give way to a light which brings peace and wholeness.

As you read the Scriptures, you realize that this battle, which began who knows when, was rejoined in the creation of mankind and finally decided in the Incarnation and on the cross. Jesus, Paul wrote, defeated the principalities and powers on the cross. "Subdue and rule" was His mission, and, as He lived and as He died, Jesus neutered the devil. And He will soon crush Satan under your feet.

You and I are living in a big narrative, and God hopes that you come to see that "as He is, so are you in this world". God's mission depends on it. It is your mission to dispel the chaos, emptiness, and darkness that affect your part of the world.

Your authority has been restored, and when you come to see yourself written into this story, the gates of hell will give way. Without this story, it's on you to explain both the why and how of Satan and evil, Jesus' mission, the why of you, and the words, "subdue and rule". This explanation does it for me.

But I will let you dismiss it though, if you will humor me and let me keep my "Star Wars" fantasy because, for me, these thoughts have not created endless questions. They have helped me find answers. Neither have they been rabbit tracks that have caused me to lose my focus on God and his plan for my life. Rather, they have brought my life into sharper focus.

Faith has grown in my heart, that is, a daily believing that who I am, and what I am about, is part of a bigger picture that began with Adam and was restored in Christ. This has affected how I have looked at everything I do, from doing the dishes to loving my wife and interacting with those around me.

God has anointed you and me to proclaim this good news, to heal the broken, and to set those who are trapped in their own narrowing thoughts, free, all the while displacing the kingdom of darkness in our own little world by both being the good news and by doing it.

The veil, covering these spiritual realities, must first be removed, and a simple turning to the Lord will do that. And once removed, you will begin "subduing and ruling" because you will know who you are and what you are about. Otherwise, without this sense of sonship, your garden, which we will discuss next, becomes very small and burdensome.

So, you—honored by God. You—included in the Trinitarian relationship as an equal (with a small e). You—loved and immensely liked. You—commissioned to subdue and rule your space. You—placed perfectly in your garden to learn how to put things in order and manage.

Once you begin to believe this good news about yourself, you will find that you won't be controlled by your control issues. Rather, you will discover that, by giving yourself to serve your garden and others, you will truly be in control.

Questions

1. How does viewing "subdue and rule" as a God-given drive to bring order help you understand your need to control or succeed? * Reflect on a daily task (e.g., organizing, parenting). How might reframing it as part of this divine mission add purpose to it?

2. The chapter highlights that your sense of value ("being") and significance ("doing") are interconnected, yet many lean toward one over the other. Do you find yourself seeking affirmation for who you are or striving for purpose through accomplishments? * What practical step could you take to nurture both, fostering greater fulfillment?

3.God finds pleasure in both your mundane tasks (like dishes) and grand achievements. How does this perspective shift your view of routine responsibilities? * What small task could you approach with a sense of divine purpose this week?

4. The chapter suggests a pre-fall world required subduing, hinting at a cosmic battle against chaos or evil. Does this perspective resonate with you, and how might seeing your personal struggles as part of a larger mission to displace darkness inspire resilience? * What specific challenge in your life could you reframe as a call to bring order?

5. Jesus fulfilled Adam's call to "subdue and rule" through love and confronting evil. How does this model redefine your understanding of your own purpose? * Can you identify a practical way—such as serving someone or addressing a wrong—to "subdue" chaos in your sphere of influence this week?

6. The chapter emphasizes that embracing your identity as God's beloved child frees you from control issues and empowers you to serve. Do you live in the "restful land of 'I am'" or the "anxious land of 'I am not'"? * How might trusting in your God-given identity help you let go of a specific area where you struggle for control, allowing you to serve others more freely?

Adam-Reasons for the Garden

And the LORD God planted a garden in Eden, in the east, and there he put the man whom He had formed. Genesis 2:8

Then the LORD God took the man and put him in the Garden of Eden to tend and keep it. Genesis 2:15

After Genesis paints an extravagant and expansive picture of mankind with the words, "be fruitful, become great, fill, subdue and rule", it then puts that picture into a frame. Whereas chapter one of Genesis reveals an over-the-top image of mankind, chapter two puts them in a garden or in a limited and limiting space. If Adam was to fill his space, he needed a space to fill, and, in this chapter, we will begin to discover its purpose.

Adam and Eve, with all of humanity, were created both to be and to do. Neither happens in a vacuum. Both require a place, not just any space, but the perfect place to accomplish both. So, God planted an ecosystem perfectly fitted for Adam to stretch his wings and perfectly sized for him to begin his stewardship.

A space is also required for you to grow. You need to touch four walls to get your bearings. I'm sure that you have been through times when you have felt that you were free-falling. I know that I have. And while necessary at times, it is not comfortable or the norm.

God is the only one who can function in a limitless expanse without walls, even though He also finds fulfillment in small spaces. Just look at the body of Jesus in which all the fullness of the Godhead dwells. Yet, by contrast, the entire universe or the multiverse cannot contain Him.

So, God has prepared a place for you to dwell, grow, and manage. And it's perfect. Jesus said as much as He readied His disciples for His departure. "And if I go and prepare a place for you, I will come again and will take you to myself, that where I am, you may be also."

Most verses like this are read as a future promise. While it does point to a future hope, Jesus' words have a more immediate intent. For his disciples, at that moment in time, His promise WAS in the future because Jesus hadn't yet gone to the cross or returned physically.

But He did return to them and has, to you. When Jesus ascended, He took you with Him to His place, and when He poured out His Spirit, He established His space in and among you. He is where you are right now, and where He is, you are. You now share space with God.

Paul agreed when he quoted the poet. "In Him, we live and move and have our being." Having your eyes open to this helps you live in places that, at times, don't seem that heavenly.

This is the essence of the "you in Christ" and "Christ in you" message (which is one of the most important, yet one of the most under-taught doctrines of the church). Christ is your home and your garden, as you are His. You live in two places at the same time, and as it relates to you, so does He (or maybe in His economy, they are one and the same),

Both places have been prepared for you. The challenge of the Christian life is to synthesize both by accepting your physical space as a God-imposed limitation while embracing the expansiveness of life in Christ and then allowing His life to permeate yours.

Both places require senses that need to be developed so that you can recognize His Presence and respond to the stimuli. As you develop both your natural and spiritual senses, you will realize that your garden, with all its weeds, is perfect because He is the real garden in which you live, and He is with you in the weedy patches of your life.

In these next few chapters, we will grapple with some questions that have a direct bearing on how you discover your identity and purpose. Ultimately, whether you succeed or fail in this thing called life requires that you identify your garden and know what to do there.

Some of the questions are obvious, like "What is a garden?" and "What is YOUR garden?" Also, "what are the implications of tending and keeping your garden, and what does that look like?" Another question to examine is "What is God's interest in your garden?" Also, "How does tending and keeping relate to ruling the world?", or, in other words, "What does changing diapers have to do with your destiny?"

We also will need to examine the temptation that occurred in the garden because temptations always occur close to home. But before we do that, I want to ask a less obvious question but one equally as important. Why does Scriptures repeat the fact that God put Adam in a garden? Wasn't once enough?

Redundancy in the Scriptures is not a space filler. Sometimes it highlights and emphasizes something important, like the Cherubim's "Holy! Holy! Holy!" or Jesus' "Verily, verily." And since we don't get things right the first time, God often repeats Himself like He did when He called Samuel. Getting one's attention and learning are both dependent upon repetition.

But sometimes, repetition points to differences that need to be examined because the differences clarify the overall meaning. For example, a careful reading of the thrice-recorded Sower's parable reveals small differences that are essential in determining what the Lord is emphasizing and saying. Like a multi-faceted diamond, each facet reflects a different aspect of the whole.

Since we find the same person, the same God, and the same garden in both Genesis verses, the different words and phrases in these two verses give hints as to God's larger purpose for both you and your garden. So, let me first point out the differences and then show how they fit into a "being" and "doing" framework.

Verse 8 does not explicitly state God's purpose for putting Adam in the garden, while verse 15 does. Verse 8 adds a descriptor, "whom He had formed," while verse 15 does not. Verse 15 adds that God "took" Adam from somewhere and put him in the garden. Verse 8 just has God putting Adam there. Additionally, while each verse states that God "put" Adam in the garden, the Hebrew words for "put" are different.

Let's examine these differences. Since verse 15 states that Adam's purpose was to tend and keep the garden, we can assume that this verse speaks to the "doing" part of Adam's life or that part which gave him significance. I will look at this last.

Verse 8 is a continuation of verse 7, where it states that God formed Adam. "The LORD God FORMED the man of dust from the ground. . . and there, in the garden, he put the man whom he had FORMED."

The repetition of "formed" suggests that the garden had something to do with Adam's development or the "being" part of his life. The Hebrew word for formed is the same word that is used for a potter taking clay and creating pottery. On the surface, it might seem that, like pottery, Adam was perfectly formed and put in the garden fully developed.

But a closer look says that Adam was a lump of clay on a potter's wheel or a perfectly formed seed. The pot had not yet been put into the kiln, and the plant had not yet blossomed. Adam was not a mature plant because his mandate was to be fruitful, become great, and fill. So, whatever he was when he was planted was a shadow of what he was to become.

The garden was to Adam what the soil is to a seed. The garden was the perfect medium for him to grow. It contained all the nutrients and moisture and all the challenges that a seed requires to germinate, root, and blossom. And because some seeds do better in one type of soil than another, God prepared the perfect soil for Adam, as He has for your development.

Paul said that God has predetermined the specifics of your "where" and "when", so where you are right now is the best place for you to discover both God and God's version of yourself. If I am right that Adam was created perfect but not complete, then he began his life in developmental darkness. It follows that Adam required a classroom or garden in which he could take shape and grow. For Adam, it was the Garden of Eden. For you? Look around.

This Hebrew word for formed is also used in Psalm 139, where David wrote that God formed his inner parts, knitting them together in his mother's womb. As amazingly wonderful as this sounds, David didn't stop there. He went on to declare that this process began in eternity. God imagined him and possibly interacted with him somewhere in eternity past.

David's sense of self was informed by "Your eyes saw my unformed substance; in your book were written every one of them, the days that were formed for me, when as yet there were none of them." This is hard to wrap your mind around, but, at a minimum, it says that you are not an afterthought. The fully formed plant that God visualized was stuffed into a fully formed seed and then planted in Eden, where all of Adam could be released.

For David, it didn't matter where his "Eden" was, whether with the sheep or in the palace, because he found God there and that was enough. By keeping the sheep, David discovered the Shepherd and became a better shepherd and a better sheep. And, as a king, he worshipped the King and became a better king. So, what might you discover about God and yourself, right where you are?

Your Eden might not look like a paradise, and for some, might be a hellhole from which you need to be extracted. But for most, the place where you are, with all its thorns and thistles, is perfect. So, accepting and even embracing your God-imposed limitations is the first step toward unlocking your destiny.

Relating to God (which ranges from questioning and having it out with Him to thanking and worshipping) is the best way to embrace your lot in life. And as David wrote, your lot in life is greater and better than you can imagine. "The boundary lines have fallen for me in pleasant places; surely I have a delightful inheritance." (NIV) Your eyes just might not have been opened yet.

It might be good for you to test yourself on this because wishing you were somewhere else with a different job, a different life, or a different spouse is easy to do and an easy way out. But Paul wrote that "each one should remain in the condition in which he was called", and he did not mean begrudgingly.

You are to abide there as you are to live in your house. Hopefully, your house is not just a place to plunk your weary butt, bark orders, and scroll the channels but a place where you give expression to who you are. Whether remodeling a kitchen, creating a workout room, planting flowers, or painting walls, your home is given to you to fill with yourself and put your imprint on it.

Your gardens are the specific places in which you find yourself with their challenges and rewards. It might be your marriage and family, your workplace or ministry, or your friends or neighbors. Your garden is closer than you think. Regardless of how you got there, God has put you there. And as you allow your roots to go deeper, and as you tend and protect that space, you can grow into the person God imagined.

Verse 15 continues this thought of growing and developing as a person because, before it lays out his responsibilities, it states that God "took Adam". Adam was somewhere else before he was put in the garden, and that somewhere is instructive.

You were also somewhere else before you showed up on the scene. God told Jeremiah, "Before I formed you in the womb, I knew you." The word for "know" is not an objective knowing but an intense, interactive, and intimate knowledge. It is the same word used for Adam and Eve, knowing that they were naked and "knowing" each other, if you know what I mean.

So, where was Adam before he was put in the garden? This twice-used word, "formed", is a clue. As I mentioned before, this word is also used to describe gestation ("I formed you in the womb"), where a baby has a safe place to develop. It makes sense that before being placed in the garden with its responsibilities, Adam was safely in the presence of God.

Before Adam went to work, he was in the safest place possible—the bosom of God. Could it be, prior to the garden, like a baby in all of her waking moments, Adam was with God 24/7? I think so.

Special things happen in a mother's embrace. David wrote that he learned to hope as he nursed. There, eyes meet, and the tactile presence of the mom fills the baby's consciousness. While it can't be put into words, the baby knows that all is right in the world. So, Adam developed his sense of self and learned experientially the love of God in His presence.

But then, God took Adam and put him in the garden. The word used for "put" in verse 15 is different than the word used in verse 8. The word in verse 8 means just that—to put or place or set, or maybe to plant. But here in verse 15, the word used for "put" has a different sense.

It often means "to leave alone." It is the same verb used when God got pissed off at the children of Israel and told Moses to leave Him alone. So, God took Adam from his presence and left him alone in the garden.

There comes a point when mom is no longer present 100% of the time. In fact, a 24/7 presence will, at some point, be detrimental to the child's development. A baby must learn that when mom is not present, he or she is still safe. Separation anxiety must give way to object permanence, where the baby realizes that the physical absence of mom is okay. She discovers that mom's voice is enough, and mom becomes internalized.

So, a garden was planted where God could come and go. Didn't Jesus do the same thing after the resurrection? After being with his disciples during most of their sleeping and waking moments, He removed Himself from their presence and popped in on them at the most unexpected times.

His relationship with them changed for the better. They developed new senses, a new mindset, and anticipated His appearing while they went on about their lives. Then Jesus sent His Spirit so that He could be internalized and that His voice could be heard from within. The garden, then, was the perfect place for Adam to develop these new senses.

Verse 8 is about becoming the person God imagined. "Becoming" must take precedence over working your garden, even though you must work your garden. Otherwise, your garden will become your taskmaster. Unless you first understand that the places where God has placed you are places to grow, you will exhaust your energy trying to fix your garden.

Trying to fix your garden is a futile task, but as you grow where you are planted, that place will change as you do. How you and I need to be overwhelmed by the grace of God! If not, you will be overwhelmed by the work in front of you.

So, God took Adam from His continual presence and left him alone in the garden. This was the next stage in Adam's development. Being left alone without God's sentient presence grows your faith muscle and heightens your sense of need. Being left alone teaches you to walk by faith and not by sight.

The Christian experience begins with assurances and reassurances that God is real. Whether it comes as an immediate answered prayer or an overwhelming sense that God is present, and everything is ok, the veil is removed. God shows up and, somehow, you sense God's attention.

But then, your experience changes. You are left alone in the garden. The proverbial sun stays out, the rain stops, and you don't know which side is up. Since God is nowhere to be found, regardless of your efforts, these times can be misinterpreted.

You are left alone in your garden to be tested on the things that God has shown you. For Adam and Eve, and for you, the things you are tested on boil down to a few things—God's goodness, your goodness (isn't this what being righteous means?), and you being the focus of His goodness. Without testing, knowledge means little or worse. Paul said knowledge, in and of itself, puffs up, and a puffed-up you invites a pinprick.

Testing comes, as James and Peter and Paul wrote, to complete or mature you so that you, having done all, can stand in full awareness of your relationship with Him. This is God's purpose. As we will see in all of Abraham's tests, the test that awaits is about identity.

Being left alone has a long history in the Scriptures, which culminated with Jesus. He was left alone to be tested. He was driven into the wilderness after being bathed in His Father's presence. It was there that the devil tested him on His identity and relationship by saying, "IF you are the Son of God". The insinuation was that Jesus was not and that he needed to do something to prove it.

Then the devil used the crucible of the cross to unleash his most visceral attack when Jesus felt totally alone. When Jesus' Father removed His protection (not His Presence) from His Son, as He did with Job, the devil called every demon from their post to descend upon Jesus. They were so thick that the sun darkened.

(THE DARKENED SUN WAS NEVER ABOUT GOD TURNING HIS BACK ON HIS SON. PAUL WROTE THAT "GOD WAS IN CHRIST RECONCILING THE WORLD TO HIMSELF". SO, THE FATHER NEVER REJECTED HIS SON, NOR HAS HE EVER REJECTED YOU. You and I are the ones who had rejected Him. It's never been "sinners in the hands of an angry God". It has always been "God in the hands of angry sinners".

On my website, there is an extra chapter on what happened to Jesus on the cross and in the grave, which you will find instructive. It looks at the three sacrifices required on the "Day of Atonement", which foretells Jesus's suffering on the cross and His experience in hell.

These sacrifices show that Jesus' death and burial were not about God punishing Jesus or humanity. It was not "tit for tat". His sufferings were about forgiving sins and obliterating the sin nature, which were at odds with God, and which made the sort of relationship that God desires with us impossible. The web address can be found in the afterword.)

What is experienced in psych wards pales in comparison to what Jesus went through on the cross. Jesus' physical sufferings were nothing compared to the existential attack on his personhood. The darkness that shrouded the sun sought to darken His soul. Demonic voices are real, and, as the sun darkened, they were shouting questions and accusations, engendering doubts and fears.

The devil wanted Jesus to buckle and answer his original "If you are the Son of God" question with a "No, it doesn't look like it", and then have Him curse God and die. But the Light of the world still shined as He declared Himself to be the Son to the very end. "Father, into Your hands, I, Your Son, commit My spirit." (TCA)

Feeling alone, Jesus had to lean on what He knew of His Father and His own personhood. This was also a large purpose for Adam's testing in the garden, as it is for yours. Your garden is the place where you can learn, before the evil day comes, to resist the devil, connect with your Father, draw strength from that connection, and come to know who you are.

Adam was made in God's image, so the devil's "being like God" temptation should have been a non-starter. If Adam had on the breastplate of righteousness, that dart would have dropped to the ground because Adam and Eve didn't have to do a thing to be like God. Whatever knowledge that Adam felt he lacked, he already had but just didn't know it. Sonship or God-likeness hadn't yet dawned on him, and the devil knew it.

The temptation came to prove to Adam that he was, in every aspect, a son like his Father, if only he had passed the test. If he had rejected the devil's advances, this sense of sonship would have become clearer. But he didn't embrace his sonship, and so he fell from God's glory. Like Christ's temptation, Adam's test was about his identity and relationship.

The devil's "you can be like God" was code for "you are not His beloved son". But Adam was a son, so this test came to prove and to confirm to Adam his sonship. He failed, but you don't have to because Jesus came declaring your identity in Him and then, by His death, burial, and resurrection, gave you the right to become, in every way, a son.

The lesson of the garden is that God has created the perfect place for you to become who you already are, who is the person God imagined. And your garden looks a lot like where you are. It might not seem that way to you due to the dirt and weeds. But as you embrace it as God's garden and as the place where He has planted you, you can work to eradicate the weeds and transform it as you are transformed.

The garden, however, is not only about you and your development. It is not your garden alone. It belongs to the Lord, with you being its steward. God had interests beyond Adam in the garden. His sight was on the whole world, but for Adam, at this point, the garden WAS the whole world.

Adam was put in Eden to serve God's interests and protect them. "Serve and protect" were the two tasks given to Adam. This is the "doing" part of the garden, and I will have a chapter given to examine these two words.

If Adam was created with a global purpose in mind, then he needed to embrace the garden as his world because "serving and protecting" and "subduing and ruling" had to begin somewhere. The garden is where you learn softness by serving others and hardness by subduing your selfish tendencies and resisting the devil.

The serpent's presence in the world gives context to the harshness of the command to "subdue and rule" because you can't just say, "There, there," to the devil and expect anything to happen. You're not to play nice with him.

To understand the garden's purpose, you need to see God's ultimate intention for this world. Adam was called to fill the world and to put it in order and manage it, and this began in the garden. If that went without a hitch, then "the kingdom of the world has become the kingdom of our Lord and of his Christ, and He shall reign forever and ever" would have become a reality through the First Man. But it didn't.

God's purpose for you and for your garden is to establish the kingdom of God in your space. When you pray "Your kingdom come", you are acknowledging that your garden is God's kingdom, that you have been put there to subdue your own evil tendencies and the spiritual darkness around you, and then to tend and keep it.

So, it is important to get your hands dirty. Whether you are dusting the furniture, planting flowers, finding ways to save your company money, giving up your preferences for your spouse, going the extra mile at church, praying with your server at the restaurant, and sharing the good news, you are doing kingdom work because where you are, in your little gardens, is the kingdom.

As you give yourself to your garden, your purpose in life will become clearer. But if you continue to fight your garden, you will never discover God's purpose for your life. God has called you to surrender not only to Him but to your garden. This means that you stop fighting your spouse and stop grumbling about your lot in life. Surrender has "giving thanks" written all over it.

I assume that the Garden of Eden was a little easier for Adam and Eve to manage before the fall because the thorns and thistles hadn't yet dug in their heels. But, regardless of the seeming insignificance of your garden or its obstacles, your garden is where you will discover who you are and find your significance and reward. And as you learn to tend and keep it, the kingdom of this world, that is, the space that you have been given to inhabit, will become the garden of the Lord.

Questions

1. The author talked about your surroundings as the place where God has put you to grow (the "being" part) and to work (the "doing" part). He related that to discovering your worth and significance. Have you connected the specific places (jobs, relationships) you are to your God-ordained garden? * Have you discovered or are you discovering your worth and significance there, or are you looking for that elsewhere? Explain.

2. The chapter emphasizes that your current circumstances—your job, relationships, or challenges—are the "garden" that God has placed you in to grow and fulfill your purpose. Where in your life do you feel resistance to accepting your "garden" as God's perfect place for you? * What practical step (e.g., gratitude, prayer, or service) could you take to embrace it and discover your worth or significance there?

3. Can you recall a time you felt "left alone" like Adam—how did it test your trust in God's goodness and who you are?

4. The author said that the Father never removed His Presence from Jesus on the cross, only His protection as He did Job. The darkened sun was not God turning His back on His Son, but demonic hosts descending on the cross to attack Jesus. Is this a new thought? * How have you processed it?

5. The chapter frames Adam's temptation as a test of his sonship, which Jesus overcame by knowing His identity. How does knowing you are a "son or daughter of God's love" equip you to face doubts or temptations in your own "garden"? * Can you identify a specific challenge where affirming your identity in Christ could help you resist negative influences or lies about your worth?

Adam-The Garden

B efore we look specifically at your garden, let's further discuss what a garden is. The concept of a garden needs to be elevated in your thinking because, on the surface, dirt is not that appealing and therefore can be easily marginalized and overlooked. What you find yourself involved in can seem like a grind and inconsequential. So, what is a garden?

First, it is an investment. It has a year-over-year 30, 60, or 100-fold potential. In an agrarian society, it was their bank account and retirement fund rolled into one. If the fields did not produce because of drought or blight or insects, gold would have little worth because it can't be eaten. A garden is your daily bread being produced for tomorrow.

Jesus said that the person who discovered treasure hidden in a field purchased the WHOLE field. The treasure cannot be separated from the dirt. The good news is that Jesus didn't just come for the treasure. He chose to purchase the field. Your untamed messiness is part of the package Jesus wanted.

In fact, who's to say what is worth more, the treasure or the dirt? Yes, the treasure has an immediate value, but its worth is fixed. Inflation might increase its value a bit, but the real potential for long-term wealth is in the dirt. The real treasure that Jesus came for might just have been the dirt.

In the context of image and likeness, Adam was made in God's image, which, by itself, is an inestimable treasure. But, for God, it was not enough because He desired for that image to grow into His likeness. Through a process hidden in the heart of God, Adam was to become the person God imagined, which was a son, not under rules and regulations, but a son who filled his space with a sense of self that was bathed in love and infused with authority, not like the scribes who filled their space with empty blather.

Gold that is tested or assayed by fire is worth more than gold that initially comes out of the ground because, gold, tried by fire, becomes more golden. Sons become more sonny, as they keep believing His Father-ship and their own sonship when circumstances and their feelings say, "no". So, your worth, while inherent and immutable, will really be determined on that day.

And when you compare the treasure that is hidden in the dirt with the field that produces season after season, there is none. Just ask a farmer whether he would rather have a million dollars or one hundred acres of farmland. The ever-increasing glory that your garden produces will outshine the initial glory God has put in you.

So, what is a garden? It's just some dirt, as I said, which is easy to discount and overlook because there is not much to look at. But visit a place like Butchart Gardens in Victoria, British Columbia, and you will have your breath taken away. What began as a dug-out limestone quarry was filled with truckloads of dirt. It would have cost more to transport the dirt to the quarry than to purchase the dirt that the trucks carried.

A garden, then, is someone's vision come to life. It is intentional and controlled growth. Whether you are enjoying a tomato from a neighbor's garden or surveying a field of sunflowers, neither the tomato nor the sunflowers decided on their own to be there. Someone planned, prepared the ground, purchased the seed and fertilizer, planted, and then tended the garden before harvest.

A garden is a labor of love because it is not only work but also someone's passion. Most do not plant a vegetable, flower, or butterfly garden without, minimally, a flickering desire for an outcome. Some want to beautify. Others want to eat.

But make no mistake, a garden is work. You must serve and protect it. You have to listen to your garden and cooperate with it for it to produce. Without effort, your garden will soon be overgrown with weeds, eaten by insects or critters, or withered. You can have the best intentions, but without knowing what your garden needs and giving yourself to serve it, it will not produce for you.

A garden is also a process. In our culture of immediacies, process is not in vogue. But without embracing process, the dirt you begin with will be the dirt you end with, or possibly worse. The purpose of this book is to lay out the process so you can have hope, which, in Biblical terms, is knowing with absolute certainty that your garden will flourish. And what a difference this sort of hope makes in how you work your field.

Knowing the process allows you to interpret life because life often speaks in an unknown tongue. "What the heck is going on?" and "I don't get it" often lead to "I give up." But God has given you a Rosetta stone in the life of

Abraham, the father of faith, who, against impossibilities, produced the most fruitful garden this side of Jesus.

Embracing this garden concept gives meaning to the mundane and makes work, both less work and hopeful work. This sight-shift, this paradigm shift, has really helped me. It is easy to wonder, "what am I doing in life that amounts to anything?" because most things seem insignificant and not connected to a bigger picture. But the garden is the bigger picture.

For example, one of my jobs is to set up and take down chairs on a weekly basis. On the surface, this doesn't sound too sexy, but this is the garden that I have been called to serve at this time in my life. This mentality has made a huge difference in how I have approached these tasks.

The garden is a metaphor for your life that invites you to acknowledge its importance by embracing the mundane while you plant seeds, pull weeds, and work hopefully for better times. It calls you to stop fighting where you are or wanting to be elsewhere, and to acknowledge that where you are is your current God-ordained space.

To take it to another level, you are to let the task, whether it seems impossible or manageable, exciting or boring, significant or mundane, motivate you to invite Him to be a co-laborer, adding His touch and doing what you can't. This has always been God's great delight, that is, to work with, in, and through His creation.

What's hidden in the garden is mysteries, lying dormant, waiting to be discovered. If you have a long view of your garden, you will discover delights and a reward that will never be realized by those who have no vision for their garden or who abandon it too soon.

As I mentioned in the last chapter, the garden is another word for what Jesus proclaimed to be the kingdom of God. Heads nod and eyes glaze over when one hears, "the kingdom of God," because it seems so other-worldly, so distant, and so inapplicable to life. But if you replace "the kingdom" with "your garden", both the kingdom of God and your life come alive. Jesus' message was that the kingdom is near, but it can be so close, you can easily overlook it.

By exchanging these two, your life comes into focus, as well as what you are to do in the kingdom. For example, are you looking for fine pearls in your situations and what you are doing, in those around you, in yourself, or even in your relationship with the Lord? It's possible to look for pearls everywhere, but where you are. You can even bury yourself in the Bible and miss the treasure around you.

Let's now take some time to identify your garden because God has placed you, as He did Adam and Eve, in specific and special places with the hope that you not only grow personally but will grow it as well.

Questions

1. The chapter describes your life as a garden containing both inherent treasure (your God-given value) and dirt (your potential for growth through challenges). How do you view the "untamed messiness" of your life—such as struggles or imperfections—as part of what Jesus chose to purchase? * What specific aspect of your current "garden" (e.g., a difficult relationship or task) could you reframe as a valuable opportunity for growth in God's likeness?

2. The chapter challenges the temptation to wish you were in a different "garden" (e.g., a better job, location, or situation). Where in your life are you resisting your current circumstances, longing to be elsewhere? * What would it look like to surrender to your God-given space through gratitude or active engagement, and how might this shift help you uncover hidden treasures there?

3. How does the concept of a garden as a long-term investment with exponential potential change your perspective on the value of small, seemingly insignificant efforts in your life? * What specific tasks in your daily life (e.g., work, family responsibilities, or community involvement) do you currently view as mundane, and how might you reframe them as part of tending your garden?

4. The garden flourishes when you invite God as a co-laborer in your efforts. Choose a specific area of your life—such as a challenging project, relationship, or personal goal—where you feel stuck or overwhelmed. * How could you practically invite God's presence or guidance into this task (e.g., through prayer, seeking wisdom, or trusting His timing)? * What difference might this partnership make in your perspective or outcome?

5. The chapter emphasizes that a garden is a process, requiring patience and hope to transform dirt into something fruitful. Reflect on a season in your life where progress felt slow or unclear. How can the biblical concept of hope—certainty in God's promise for your garden—encourage you to persevere in a current challenge? * What small, intentional action could you take to cooperate with God's process in that area today?

Adam-Your Garden

S o, what is your garden? Or more importantly, where is your garden? What-ever and wherever it is, it is exceedingly more than you have thought, more important, more consequential, more fulfilling, and more rewarding. Yes, it can also be more frustrating and more work than you might want, but I think you already know that. Your present garden is the future experience of all that God is, all that He has for you, and all that God has called you into.

So, what IS your garden? It is the same as Adam's because, within his Eden, Adam had four spheres in which he lived and was to manage. I will only mention them here, but in the chapter on the fall, they will be expanded upon, and, on my website, a fuller explanation is given. Your garden is comprised of four spheres of relationship, which are yourself, God, those close to you, and your daily grind.

Firstly, you are the most important garden to nurture and care for. Both the psalmist and the prophets, along with Jesus, James, John, and Paul, liken your soul to dirt that produces vegetation. Whether alluded to as a tree planted by rivers, or likened to a watered garden, or to a vineyard, or soil on which seed is sown, or whether you are declared as God's husbandry, your soul is dirt which you are to nurture.

But you might ask, "If I am the planting of the Lord, wouldn't that make Him my gardener and the One who cares for me?" While He actively cares for you, it often doesn't feel that way because, like Eden, it seems that He leaves you alone to deal with the underbrush. As we laid out in a previous chapter, God planted His garden and then gave Adam the responsibility to care for it. God handed control of the outcome of His garden to Adam and is asking you, as well, to be responsible for your own soul.

The mandate to Adam was to nurture and protect the garden of his soul. For you to flourish, three primary soul needs must be met. When these are met, you are free to become and do. Those needs are to sense deeply that you are loved and liked for who you are, know that you have real significance, and feel safe. While you are called to meet these needs in others, they must first be met in you, and that is your responsibility.

In fact, only when you sense your own value and significance and feel safe can you begin to minister life to others. The peace Jesus spoke to relax the agitated waves came from a peace within and from the atmosphere in which He lived. Heaven impacted earth through Jesus, because He released Heaven's wholeness which resided within Him.

Jude wrote that you are loved in the Father, called by the Spirit, and kept safe by Jesus. Jude recognized that these three primary soul needs are met in your relationship with God. This is the gospel that you must first hear and believe because loved means valued, called means significant, and kept means safe. This is the faith that was once delivered to the saints and the faith that you are called upon to defend.

I don't need to be a prophet, though, to surmise that this is not how you see yourself because you unknowingly seek these from externals. If you would put yourself on a scale of one to ten, with loved/not loved, significant/not significant, and safe/unsafe being the continuum, how would you rate yourself?

Would it depend on the day? How would your actions and reactions confirm that assessment? When you take a moment to look within, what do you see? When life happens, what comes out of you? When you really think of your future, what emotions arise?

So, what's up? Why, if God's love is so palpably true, is this not your experience? Jude acknowledges this by saying that the struggle of struggles is believing God's love for yourself. The faith that was delivered into your hands, once for all time, and the faith you are to earnestly contend for, is not some arbitrary doctrinal position.

The set of doctrines that you are to contend for is the first verse of Jude, which states, "You who are swaddled in the love of God the Father, called to unimaginable greatness, and protected by Jesus Christ." (TCA) This is the faith that was, once and for all time, declared in the death, burial, and resurrection of the Lord Jesus and then poured out at Pentecost. This love defines you, but is this YOUR definition?

Your enemy, that is, the one that can sabotage your walk, is not the world or false teachers, though you need to be aware. Your contention is not with someone else's belief system but with your own. Jude was concerned that your faith does not align with God's. It is from (God's) faith, or what He believes about you, to (your) faith, or what you believe about yourself, God, and life. So, when your focus of faith is not centered on His love for you, you lose.

Believing that you are loved, significant, and safe is the struggle of struggles for several reasons. First, this is not your default position. The pit from which you were dug is deep. The reason you defend yourself, get anxious or depressed, the reason you shut down or rise up is that you don't believe that you are loved, called, or safe. You might have an intellectual grasp of it, but just let life jostle you a bit and see what happens.

It is also the struggle of struggles because you are under threat. Adam was told to protect his garden. A garden only needs protection if danger is lurking. You have an enemy whose entire strategy is to keep you experientially separated from the One who has never separated Himself from you.

When you are aware of your connection to God, you are invincible. However, if you are unaware, you are defeated before you start. Ephesians 6 is less about engaging principalities and powers in the heavens or casting out demons on earth. It is more about keeping your heart protected from the devil's schemes that keep you off balance and uncertain.

Paul said nothing could separate him from the love of God which is in Christ Jesus. He knew that to be true because each and every thing he mentioned in Romans 8 was thrown at him. His awareness of self was not rooted in externals but in his connection to God and his identity. And his connection to the Father and his identity as a son was no different than Christ's or yours.

It is also the struggle of struggles because, as we discussed in a previous chapter, sonship must be tested before it becomes operative in your life. Jesus, after being tested about His sonship, came out of the wilderness in the power of the Spirit. Adam failed his test and came out of that test in his own limited strength.

It is also a struggle because, while the battle is the Lord's, you need to fight. Jude said that God handed over to you an overcoming, all-sufficient faith which is rooted in His love. "Delivered, once and for all time" implies that, like Adam in the garden, "I have given it to you, so now it's yours. I am here to help, but you must lead the charge."

Paul describes your armor primarily as defensive. The attacks, whether they come from without or within, are against your identity or sense of self. The question that you need to answer is, "Are you going to believe who God says that you are or the devil's lies and your sinnership mentality?" This is the test.

You too will come out of your testing in the Spirit's power as you keep believing your sonship against all odds and against all enemies, both foreign and domestic. You will come to know and believe that "in Christ" means that you are as much of a son as Jesus is.

This struggle makes living in the awareness of God's love both the most difficult and the most important thing you can do. It is your mission if you choose to accept it. As Abraham was called to walk out his faith journey alone, you also must face down the phantoms of your past and the giants of your present, "mano a mano" or "womano a womano". Hopefully, you have encouragers in your life, but while others are important, they are not a substitute for yourself.

So, Jude admonishes you to "keep YOURSELF in the love of God." You who are loved, created for a unique purpose, and are safe in His arms are to do everything in your ability to live with this mind and heart-set, all the while expecting God's great mercy. You are to serve and protect the garden of your own soul.

Again, don't expect others to do that, even if you are blessed to have a good friend in your spouse or in life who sees in you what you don't. Take all the encouragement that's given and believe the best that others tell you. But if that is the only way you can go forward, crutches are poor substitutes for two good legs, even though everyone needs a crutch from time to time.

As I wrote in *Ephesians and All that Jazz:*

"This will only work if you let the truth you hear from others become the truth you tell yourself. You are the most influential person in your life. You are the best preacher you will ever hear and the best audience you could ever have. . . The junk you have recorded about yourself from the earliest years can be overwritten, but only you can do it."

Your own soul is the most important garden that God has given you to tend and keep, and as you give yourself to nurture it and protect it, you will be in a better position to positively affect your other gardens. And since Jesus said that the kingdom is near, the rest of your gardens are also.

Your spouse, if you are married, is chief. Your children are a close second, and then those in your family. For those who are single, you know the few whom God has put in your life to care for. They might (and probably do) annoy you from time to time because relationships can be messy. However, if you think or feel that you are alone, be intentional about finding a group and have your antenna up to find kindred spirits.

Now, I am not stupid. Sometimes the extended gardens of your life don't want to be cared for and, over time, will make it abundantly clear that they don't want you to mess with their dirt. You can only care for a garden that wants to be cared for, but don't walk away from your garden either. If it walks away from you, though, you are free.

Then there are those whom God has given you. Jesus repeated many times in His high priestly prayer, "Those whom You have given Me." This little phrase might have come from the book of Isaiah, where it's written, "I and the children whom You have given me." The Father didn't give everyone to Jesus, but the ones He did, Jesus embraced.

I know the ones whom God has given me to care for, and I am intentional about staying connected with them. I am amenable to others, but to the ones God has given, I give myself. They are my gardens which I am charged to serve by nurturing and protecting through prayer and intentional interactions. It might be a good exercise for you to identify those given-ones in your life and do the same.

Another sphere or garden that you are called to serve and protect is your work, whether it is setting up chairs or being the chairman. The daily tasks associated with your job, you know, the ones which frustrate the heck out of you and which you have to do again and again, are the stuff gardens are made of. Whether dusting furniture or delegating assignments, these all fall under the "serving and protecting" paradigm that God has given you. Adam was called to put his world in order and maintain it, and this has house chores and responding to emails written all over them.

I have a good friend who had a light bulb turn on when I told her about this garden concept. She is also retired and helping out with janitorial stuff at church. Retired folk can flounder because a large part of who they were, retired with them when they did. But as I shared this, she saw her two cats in an entirely new light. They were a part of her garden that she was called to serve and keep safe.

You might discount this and say, "Cats? Most cats don't even care if they are cared for, so that isn't much and can't be all that spiritual." But you say this to your own hurt. It was God who put a love for cats in her and for hers, in particular. While she is involved in others' lives and ministries, her garden also includes cats.

Finally, and probably first, the Lord is your garden. While you can't make God any better or more productive in one sense, you certainly can magnify

Him in your life and give Him the freedom to make Himself known through you. The Scriptures tell you to magnify the Lord because He then becomes clearer and more operative in your life.

Paul writes that you and I are to "sing and make melody to the Lord in your heart." That is a strange way to fertilize your garden. I don't know about you, but not even my wife wants me to invade her space with made-up little ditties. But the Lord invites you to do just that because that is exactly what He wants in your relationship with Him, that is, each invading each other's spaces with song.

Has this chapter changed your perception of what God is calling you to, what He is asking you to do, and where you will find that call fulfilled? The four spheres of dirt that you are to serve and protect are you, your relationship with others and the Lord, and your day-to-day responsibilities. Your high calling is not only buried under a pile of dirt, it IS the dirt. Your garden is there for you to get your hands dirty, and as you work and play in your garden, you will grow into an awareness of who you are and what you are about.

Questions

1. The chapter identifies your personal garden as four relational spheres: yourself, God, those close to you, and your daily work. Which of these spheres feels most vibrant or neglected in your life right now? * What specific action (e.g., prayer, self-care, or intentional connection) could you take this week to nurture the neglected sphere and align it with God's purpose for you?

2. What "junk" (negative beliefs or past hurts) might you need to overwrite by speaking God's truth to yourself, and what practical step (e.g., journaling, affirming Scripture) could you take to begin this process?

3. The chapter emphasizes that believing you are loved, significant, and safe is a struggle due to external threats and internal doubts. Where do you find those threats coming from—within or without? * How does this perspective challenge you to confront your own barriers to embracing your God-given identity?

4. The author, in discussing caring for your own soul, quoted this: "This will only work if you let the truth you hear from others become the truth you tell yourself. You are the most influential person in your life. You are the best preacher you will ever hear and the best audience you could ever have. The junk you have recorded about yourself from the earliest years can be overwritten, but only you can do it." Do you agree or disagree? Explain. * What junk might you need to rewrite? * If true, what can you specifically do to help "rewrite" over the junk?

5. The author suggests that even mundane tasks, like caring for pets or doing chores, are part of your God-given garden. Choose one daily task you find frustrating or insignificant (e.g., work duties, household tasks). * How might viewing it as a sacred act of "serving and protecting" your garden shift your attitude? * What difference could this perspective make in your sense of hope or purpose?

Adam-Serve and Protect

I hope, by this time, that you have gotten a different perspective on both Adam's and your own worth, significance, and purpose. You were created with an expansiveness which includes being transformed and transforming your world. Your world, however, can look rather smallish.

The reach of some, like Paul's, is far-flung. Others have a seemingly small space. But regardless, your reward is based on what you have done in your garden, regardless of its size. Anyway, God is responsible for the breadth of your ministry. You are responsible for its depth.

Adam, along with his progeny, was tasked with putting the world in order and ruling it. With the task came the God-implanted need to control. An honest look at your own heart testifies to this.

You try with varying degrees of success to control life, control your surroundings, control your spouse, others, and your own impulses. You are happiest when life is ordered and unhappiest when it is out of control. The fall made this impulse worse because your default mode of ruling is to exert external pressure on things and on those around you. This need then became a drive which, for some, has become an art form.

We have discovered all sorts of delicious ways to control others and outcomes. From brute force and arguing to passive-aggressive, emotional crap, you are hard-wired to control. Jesus saw this paradigm clearly when He said, "You know that the rulers of the Gentiles lord it over them, and their great ones exercise authority over them." Even us small ones, though, want to lord it over others.

I can safely say that you would rather control than be controlled and that conflicts occur when the control-ee does not cooperate with the control-er. And then put two controllers in the same space and watch what happens. You often don't have to look any further than your marriage, your family, or work to see this dynamic at work.

But whether it's the strength of your will or personality, whether it's your logic or emotions, your physical strength, or its opposite, playing wounded, the one with the strongest grip wins. Winning, however, comes with a huge cost. Feelings are hurt. Relationships are destroyed. Hardening of hearts occurs. And ultimately, your control issues control you. But this method of controlling is not how it was from the beginning.

When God put Adam in the garden, the intent was control. He was put there to put things in order and manage them. Just plopping Adam in the garden, however, with the words, "subdue and rule", without some practicalities on how that should be done, would have left Adam to his own devices. On the important issues, leaving things to your own devices is not how God operates.

While He can be cryptic at times, God always points you in the right direction. I have alluded a couple of times to a "following the breadcrumbs" metaphor, and I believe that following breadcrumbs is the primary way that God uses for you to discover who He is, who you are, and what you are called to. He scatters a thought or desire your way, or He presents an opportunity, with the hope that you will follow.

But here in the garden, He is direct. Genesis says that God put Adam in the garden to tend and keep it. "Adam, remember the first thing I told you—that I created you to subdue the world and rule it." "Yeah, I do." "Well, here you are. This garden, for now, is your world. This is where you are to fulfill your mandate of controlling the cosmos. And this is how you are to accomplish your task—you are to serve and protect it."

This is so counterintuitive it must be God, that is, to subdue by being a slave and to rule by protecting your turf. *Abad*, the Hebrew word for serve, means to serve as a slave, and *shamar* means to protect or defend. So, try to process this: "Lord it over someone by being their slave" or "Break down their walls by protecting them". It messes with your brain. But this is exactly how God rules. This is exactly what love looks like.

I am sure that you have been messed up by "conquer and rule" because that experience is never pleasant when it is done to you. Yes, a few get to enjoy a victory dance when they have gotten their way, but, sadly, their dance floor is often the heads of others. Doesn't the marriage dance look and feel this way at times?

But the way Jesus came to "subdue and rule" was by *abad*-ing and *shamar*-ing. Jesus, the fullest expression of both true Divinity and true humanity said that He did not come to be waited upon but to serve with every ounce of His being because this is His being. Lording as a slave was not a new or a "have to" experience for Jesus, neither was it His way to teach those unruly people how to be happy.

Throughout eternity, the Father, Son, and Spirit have taken off their outer garments and have washed each other's feet. This attitude that has always been in Christ Jesus is the attitude of the Trinity. This has kept their relationship humming. Serving and protecting have been their delight. Creation just gave them another way to express and reveal their nature.

The devil messed it up and, in doing so, tried to redefine ruling. But, if you want to know who God is and align yourself with Him, this is God. When you see the One on the throne, you will see a Lamb sacrificing Himself for you.

Not only does the Triune sing "Be our guest. Be our guest. Put our service to the test" to everyone, He also holds all things in His hands, that is, He keeps all things safe in their orbit. He both serves AND protects.

In His High Priestly prayer, Jesus told His Father that He had protected the ones whom the Father had given to Him and then asked His Father to take over. So, as it relates to His garden, it was not only Jesus' heart to serve and protect, it was also His mission.

Jesus knew that His mandate was to do what Adam was created for, that is, to retake the earth for His Father by revisiting paradise-lost and reclaiming it by *abad*-ing and *shamar*-ing. He also gave Himself to teach his progeny or disciples to do the same. So, when push came to shove, He chose not to call on His angel armies to squash the bugs in His garden but to lay down His life for it to come to life.

Violence is His last resort, and at the end of the age, He will come with His angels. But that moment will give way to the fullest expression of God. Lions will lie down with the lambs. The lions, however, will still be lions, and the lambs will still be lambs. Yet somehow, they will look out for each other's best interests and serve each other.

Let me repeat, what Jesus accomplished, Adam was first tasked to do. It is so important, as I wrote in a previous chapter, to overlay Jesus on Adam and overlay Adam on Jesus to read them correctly. Paul said that Adam was a type of Christ—a failed one, for sure, but a type.

That means that who Adam was, and what he was about, points to who Jesus is and what He is about. And reflexively, Jesus points back to Adam, more clearly defining Adam's identity and his mission. Jesus' story is read in Adam's, and Adam's story comes to life in Jesus'.

Both Adam and Jesus are sons of God. (Adam, the created one, and Jesus, the Creator.) They were both the Father's delight and both had the same mission—to subdue and rule by serving and protecting. The gospel writers confirm this by regaling us with stories of Jesus serving humanity and displacing demons.

But guess who Adam and Jesus point to? Who are they a type of? The amazing and astounding answer is you. This is the gospel. So, you are to overlay Jesus and Adam on yourself. Otherwise, you will have no context for yourself.

You too are His beloved. You too have been put in your garden with the same mission. A large part of the "who am I?" and the "what am I about?" questions are answered by the meta-stories of Adam and Jesus, the first and Second Man.

You have been placed in your garden to make it thrive because a garden needs someone to care for it if it is to blossom and grow. Gardens produce when plants are put in rows, fed, watered, and protected. Kids blossom when they are loved, given boundaries and age-appropriate challenges, and made to feel safe. Individuals, marriages, organizations, and communities grow the same way.

You, tending your garden, is the way God communicates His heart to the world. He has created many yous so that no one would have to face the world alone and that each would come to sense their worth, feel safe, and grow into the God-version of themself. As each tends their garden, His kingdom comes.

When you serve your garden, your garden will begin to feel and believe that it is special. (Some will still disbelieve and resist because of past trauma. The roots of some weeds go deep). Like a sunflower which lifts its head when the sun comes out, gardens have the most potential to come to life when you shine on it.

As you prioritize your garden like Jesus did, you also will begin to discern what is behind the weedy issues that present themselves. Not all things are the devil, but as you read in the Gospels, at times, they are. If you are the gardener who cares for your garden, and not a hireling, you will know and be able to deal with them.

A garden will also do its thing when it is protected. Chicken wire keeps out those nasty munching bunnies, along with other animals who would trample it. Only when you feel safe will you let your guard down. I am sure a large reason that some allowed Jesus to touch their uncleanness or endure glaring looks while washing His feet was that, in Jesus' presence, they felt safe.

To serve and protect has profound implications because it speaks to the three primary longings and needs in the human heart, which are to sense value, to know their own significance, and to feel safe. Right from the beginning, God wrote this into the ethos of humanity by kneeling before Adam and releasing him to rule. Kneeling before another (remember, this is what *barak* means) is a show of the greatest respect.

Then, the Lord told Adam to do the same thing in his garden. Adam was to grow his garden by kneeling down to serve it and then, having done all, to stand up to protect it. God revealed how gardens grow and when humanity failed, He came in person to reestablish the principles laid out in the first garden.

On a practical level, you will never have a successful garden unless you listen to it first. It will tell you how to care for it and make it feel safe. This is what serving as a slave looks like. The garden is in command. While your desire is to see it fruitful, it tells you how. For example, you don't plant potatoes in a rice paddy or rice in Idaho.

The writer of Proverbs knew this when he instructed parents to train a child in the way he should go and not the way that parents would want their child to go. Like a garden, your desire is for a flourishing young adult, but your child's temperament, along with their likes and dislikes, will point you in the right direction. Pushing a child with an artistic bent into a square, rigid opening will end in frustration for both.

You first need to know the personality, the desires, and the way a child learns in order to help him on his journey to adulthood. Your vision for them must align with theirs. Yes, you train them up in the ways of the Lord, but that is just the bones. The flesh is theirs.

There is no one-size-fits-all when it comes to your garden. My first pastor told me that I needed to earn a PhD on my wife. To value her and make her feel safe requires me to know her in the real Biblical sense, that is, knowing not only what makes her tick but those things that make her tock. Shouting might bring the walls of Jericho down, but it will only strengthen your spouse's.

Also, doing your job, whether it is making your bed or running a company, is as much an art form as it is a list of things to do. To accomplish any task first requires you to understand it and to know what it needs before you can bring your giftings, personality, and effort to bear upon it.

Serving your garden, wherever and whatever it is, as a slave, and making it feel safe is the definition of love. When God, who is love, finally arrived to establish the kingdom, He defined love with the verbs, *abad* and *shamar*.

For Jesus, serving as a slave and giving Himself for others aligned with His nature. So, while there were moments of intentionality (either the many times of pulling aside to connect with His Father or the few times when He resisted His natural desires and the devil), Jesus' life was an outflow of who He was. It was His joy to wash His disciples' feet.

You, however, will need to give yourself to the hard work of converting your self-centered and self-protecting mindset by intentionally centering your life around those God has given you and serving them until it becomes your second (or rather, your first) nature. In the kingdom, nature follows nurture, even though when you were born from above, God gave you His nature.

The whole process of serving as a slave and making yourself vulnerable, so that others feel safe, might seem that you are being asked to be selfless. Doormat-ish, as it were. But this is far from the truth because the Servant-in-chief neither was, nor is, a doormat. His Lordship, in no way, conflicts with His servanthood. His servanthood confirms His Lordship.

He *abads* and *shamars* for His glory. When all the trees of the field clap their hands, He gets the credit. When the desert blossoms, it shows off His handiwork. When the potatoes are harvested, He gets to eat.

This is why I wrote a chapter on self-interest. The Christian life is not selfless, even though a superficial reading of the Scriptures might seem to indicate that. It is an intentional, self-given life that has an expectation of a glorious outcome. Serving your garden is the absolute best thing you can do to position yourself for success. It is the best strategy for you to walk into your destiny.

Whether it is an actual garden or the relationships which God has given you, their increase becomes yours. I don't know of a greater joy than seeing your children flourish in life and acknowledging your influence, unless it is seeing your own broken life being made whole and acknowledging Him.

Sometimes, however, your garden is not cooperative. Yet even in that God is working to achieve His end, which is seeing you blossom and being fruitful. I have a good friend who married a Christian lady who had both a critical spirit and no self-awareness, which is not a good combination.

He married late in life, and a large reason for that was his very small view of himself. (Yes, size does matter.) He prayed and prayed for a wife until that fateful day when he fell head over heels for her.

I had the privilege of being his best man, and I thought as he said, "I do," "Beware what you wish because you might get it". Over the decades, there have been seasons of détente, but, for the most part, her gift for discerning lacks and negatives, and his self-perceived lacks and negatives have been a match made in heaven.

On the surface, it would seem that she was the worst choice for a lifelong partner. But quite the opposite has occurred because he has discovered grace in the wilderness. He has heard God call him "beloved", and he has embraced his garden with all of its thorns and thistles.

The wilderness HAS flowered, but not the wilderness that he has hoped for, because she hasn't changed. But the wasteland of his soul sure has, with the fruit of the Spirit being evident.

Is he still believing that she will change? Not so much, yet one can only hope. The only way she might change is when she feels safe enough to answer the Jacobian "What is your name?" question by confessing, "I am a ___ (fill in the blank)."

He is doing his best to make her feel loved and safe, so he has learned NOT to call her out or to intimate her lack because that is the work of the Spirit. He does his best not to step on her toes and loves her the best way he can. Love for him is not a joy but a commitment.

He has, however, found great joy in his children, who are amazing. He has also found great joy in his relationship with God while he puts one foot in front of the other.

He has seen how much he has changed, of which I am eager to remind him often. While his efforts have not resulted in a happy marriage, his garden has flourished, and for that, he will be rewarded.

This is the reason for the garden and your purpose in the garden. God has put you (and sometimes leaves you alone) in your garden so that you discover the three greatest treasures in life—the God whom you could have never imagined, the "you" imagined before time, and your purpose, which is caring for and protecting others. And this all happens as you *abad* and *shamar*.

And as you give yourself to serve and protect your garden, however unruly it is, you will find, as paraphrased from Paul's writing, "that your love will overwhelm your garden and, with your eyes wide open, you will sense the quality of your work and will put your own stamp of approval on it.

And on that day when you present yourself and your garden to the Lord, He will also be blown away at the produce He samples, along with its variety and volume. And while He pats your back, you will raise your glass to Him because you know that, without Him, all your efforts would have amounted to nothing." (TCA) Philippians 1:9-11

Questions

1. The chapter contrasts the human impulse to control through force or manipulation with God's call to "subdue and rule" by serving (abad) and protecting (shamar). Reflect on a situation in your life (e.g., marriage, work, or family) where you've tried to control outcomes or others. * How might adopting the approach of serving and protecting, as Jesus modeled, change your interactions or perspective, and what specific step could you take to implement this shift?

2. The author describes God's guidance as scattering "bread-crumbs"—thoughts, desires, or opportunities—to help you discover your identity and purpose. Can you identify a recent breadcrumb in your life (e.g., a new interest, an open door, or a prompting) that you've followed or ignored?

3. The chapter emphasizes that gardens—whether self, relationships, or work—thrive when served and protected, meeting needs for value, significance, and safety. Which of your gardens feels most challenging or neglected right now, and what barriers (e.g., frustration, fear) prevent you from tending it? * What practical action (e.g., listening, encouraging, setting boundaries) could you take this week to nurture its growth and align with God's purpose?

4. The story of the man who found joy in his children and God despite a difficult marriage illustrates that serving an uncooperative garden can still yield personal growth. Have you experienced a challenging garden (e.g., a strained relationship or unfulfilling job) where serving and protecting led to unexpected fruit in your life?

5. The text mentions that conflicts often arise from competing desires to control. Reflect on a situation where these control dynamics have caused tension in your life—how might the approach of "abad and shamar" (serve and protect) have altered the outcome?

Adam-The Fall

F or all have sinned and fall short of the glory of God... being freely justified.
Romans 3:23,24.

This verse describes, in a nutshell, the human condition and your conundrum. On one hand, you sense, or at least you hope, that you were made for more, and for glory. On the other hand, you strive unknowingly to capture that expansive sense of self that God purposed for you at creation because you know intuitively that you are lacking. Your attempts to fill the voids, however, miss the mark.

It is important to note that Paul said that the place from which you fell is GOD'S glory. Take time to think about this because it is too wonderful to believe, and I don't think that we will ever fully comprehend it.

Every created thing has its own glory or essence, or that thing which defines it, or makes it who and what it is. A table, for example, has its own glory and, by being in your dining room, tells everyone what it is and why it exists. A duck has its own glory as well. It does duck things that express its glory or essence.

But note, Paul didn't say that you fell from your own glory, that is, that you became a lesser version of yourself, even though you did. You became a lesser version of God. (Now if your version of God is primarily God Self-sufficient, Separate, and Sovereign and not the Relational God, who is the Servant of all, then being a version of God will chap your butt. But your butt probably needs to be chapped.)

The measure of humanity, the measure of you, is God and His glory or essence. You were created to live and share in, to be clothed with, and to emanate His glory. It is the same glory that He would share with no other because you are not other. You are bone of His bone and flesh of His flesh.

This is the place from which you fell and, if Paul is to be believed, the place to which you now have already been freely restored in Christ. As laid out in the previous chapters, Adam was designed for a God-measured fullness, which is a more correct definition of righteousness than being "right with God." Full of a right sense of self and life, fully fruitful, full of resources and ability. Full of yourself in the best of ways and full of God.

The reason I spent as much time as I did, looking at Adam, pre-fall, is that your default mentality is post-fall. Post-fall is important and the reason we are now going to talk about what happened in the fall. But post-fall humanity has been redeemed because Jesus pushed the reset button.

If your sense of self is rooted in a post-fall understanding of yourself, you will never become the person God imagined. The prodigal son, as he returned home, knew that he had blown it and rightly came with a post-fall understanding of himself because he self-identified as one who missed the mark. That sinnership mentality changed a little in his father's arms because now he understood himself to be a sinner saved by grace.

But his father kept calling him, "Son." I can only imagine their exchange as the prodigal, looking down, told his father, "Your sinner-saved-by-grace is here and is forever grateful", all the while his father kept lifting his chin, saying, "Son." How long do you think it took for the prodigal to finally submit to his father's naming and give up his own?

The real question, though, is "How long is it taking you?" It is entirely understandable that you would feel less because your experience, coupled with what you know of yourself, is pretty convincing. Sin is real and has done a number on you.

In the fall, the unassuming righteous sense that Adam possessed vanished in a moment and revealed a glaring glory-void that you and I have ever since sought to fill. His glory-clothing also evaporated, being replaced with some home-spun fig leaves. You also dress yourself up in order to present a presentable you to the world (that is, until you are annoyed). Then those fig leaves fall off to show how ugly you can be.

Adam's righteousness, which was of God, became a righteousness of his own making. Self-righteousness was Adam's reaction to his fallen sense because when God made him, Adam was infused with the need to be right. Since Adam was made in God's image, that righteous sense was implanted, and when it left him, he had to find a way to satisfy it, as you do.

The atmosphere in which Adam and Eve lived, prior to the fall, was the Spirit. Since they lived in the Spirit's milieu, it was hard for them to stand outside of it and put it into words, nor did they need to. They were fish swimming, here and there, in crystal clear water, just being fish, unaware of the reason that they could happily go about their business.

When Adam and Eve, however, became fish out of water, they still existed, but in a foreign ether. It was the ether of self-effort and condemnation. You can thrash about, gasping for air, even after becoming a Christian, and still find this normative because you don't know anything different. This, by the way, is the Romans 7 experience where Paul became aware of his desire to do good, coupled with his inability to accomplish it.

The effect of the fall, as described in Genesis 3, is instructive here. Genesis 3 describes four sub-spheres in which you live, that is, the four areas of relationship that define you and which you try to hold together. These spheres describe righteousness and unrighteousness, and life and death, in pictural terms. It also shows practically what sin-consciousness looks like. Self-preservation, self-promotion and self-righteousness took center stage.

And lastly, it reveals what Adam experienced pre-fall, as a righteous and sinless Adam, because his life was turned upside down when he disobeyed. So, if you just flip it over, you will see what life and righteousness looked like for Adam before the fall. The fallen Adam reveals, by contrast, the glory from which you fell and the place to which God in Christ Jesus has restored you in each of these four relationships.

It is important to understand what happened both in and to Adam, so that you can also understand your starting point because, as this verse implies, you were in Adam when he sinned and also fell from that high estate when he did. What happened to and in him happened to and in you because he was the fountainhead of all humanity.

(I am sorry that this is the way it is. It doesn't seem fair. Being born on the wrong side of the tracks is not your fault. And I think that God takes this into account. He will be a lot kinder and more merciful on that day than you think because you were born into darkness and have been deceived. The opportunity, however, is now at hand, for you to discover a rightness amid all of the wrongness.)

The change in atmosphere brought along with it a constitutional change in Adam. This constitutional change was revealed immediately after he sinned and showed itself in how he perceived himself, how he perceived God and others, and how he reacted to life.

You and I live with a "missing-the-mark" or a "something-lacking" consciousness and, for the most part, don't know it. For Adam and Eve, however, that moment was a shock to their system. For them, the switch that had always been on was, for the first time and from that time forward, clicked off.

Genesis takes note of the four spheres that changed immediately when Adam and Eve sinned, and this is written in a most sublime way. So, when God told Adam, "In the day that you eat of it, you will surely die," this is what He was talking about.

It was not, however, a physical death at that time. Being buried, in fact, was the least of his deaths. "In dying, you will die" might give a better sense to this verse. Physical death was the final evidence of these initial deaths. Death by a thousand cuts, as it were. Not only was he cut off from the Source of Life, these four areas also immediately shriveled, just like the fig tree did when it was cursed.

First, his relationship with himself changed. For the first time, he knew something against himself. Before this, Adam knew himself through the acceptance of the Lord, the admiration of his spouse, and by the respect and response of creation.

His conscience was clear. But now, Adam became unsure of himself and was aware of his vulnerability and lack. He knew that something was wrong, which is why he attempted to cover and protect himself.

Then his perception of God changed. What formed in his imagination was an image of a vindictive, judgmental God, one from whom he had to distance. "Where are you?" can be heard in many ways, from playful and inviting to demanding, or as a "gotcha". By Adam's reaction, He did not hear, "Come out and play," as he did the other times that God approached.

(Please note that God's heart toward Adam did not change one bit. Yes, He had an issue to address and gave Himself from that moment both to change Adam's mind and heart and to rectify the situation, but God was still who he was. God is love, so sin just brought out the best in God. Paul understood this when he wrote that grace is released in its greatest measure where sin seems to be out of control.)

Third, his relationship with his closest friend ruptured. Eve became a "suitable hindrance" from that point and was one to blame. And finally, his world, for the first time, resisted him. Instead of flowers, his garden produced thorns. These were the four streams in which he swam, and each of them was poisoned.

These are also the four streams that God redeemed when He redeemed you. Whereas each sphere was to confirm who Adam was and to encourage him to press on into the high call of God, they now condemned him. And if you take a moment to examine your life, you will find this to be so, as well.

He was put on the defensive. His internal digital recorder looped, "I am not", rather than "I am", and Adam, from that time on, acted from that paradigm. Adam tried to make himself look good any way he could. He, over time, created even fancier clothing to keep his sin-conscious self from being fully exposed to himself or others.

Shame and self-consciousness redrew his image of God. God was no longer considered a friend, a lover, or a caring father. As an aside, I think that God, in His kindness and mercy, established the Old Covenant's rules and regulations with its veils and rituals, so that the unworthy you could have a way to feel worthy enough to come to Him.

He, however, has never needed any sacrifice or ritual to forgive. We are the ones who need that assurance. The psalmist said, "Burnt offering and sin offering you have NOT required" and "You, Lord, are so good, so ready to forgive, so full of unfailing love." (NLT)

You and I are the ones who need rules to keep and break, and a way to settle accounts, in order to be convinced that He does forgive. You and I live with a "tit for tat" mentality, not Him.

He came down to our level and spoke to us in a way that we could understand. So, the law preceded grace. Not many in the Old Testament understood the extravagant grace of God, and sadly, not many, living under the New Covenant, do either.

David was the huge exception. He knew God in an intimate, immediate, and most familiar way. He ate the bread reserved only for the priests. He removed the Ark of the Covenant from behind the veil and brought it home with him which, by the way, was punishable by death.

When he sang and wrote about worshipping in the shadow of His mighty wings, he meant exactly that—the wings of the Cherubim, which sat on the Ark of the Covenant which should have been behind the veil in the Holy of Holies. But David took the Ark of His Presence from behind the veil home with him. (Look it up.) He danced in a Presence that killed others.

It's no wonder that James declared that this tabernacle, that is, David's most intimate place of worship, which required no veils or rituals, and the one which invited a closeness without a smidgen between, is the one which God has reestablished. "After this, I will return, and I will rebuild the tent of David that has fallen; I will rebuild its ruins, and I will restore it, that the remnant of mankind may seek the Lord, and all the Gentiles who are called by my name', says the Lord, who makes these things known from of old."

But the moment Adam sinned, he was plunged into darkness and had to navigate life with only his limited physical senses, his logic, and emotions. He began walking by sight and interpreted what he saw through his natural senses and limited logic. Since he knew himself as un-right, Adam couldn't imagine a God who was good, so his perception of God became twisted.

Adam kept away from God and created his own rightness to justify himself. He also created a god in his own image and created his own religion, as well, so he could placate an implacable God. This is evidence of a sinnership mentality.

If you could step outside of yourself and look at your own actions and reactions dispassionately, you would see the residue of the fall at work. Feeling dissed. Making sure to get the last word. Trying hard to get ahead. Stepping on others. Allowing yourself to be stepped on by others.

Making excuses. Blaming others. Beating yourself up. Beating others up. Stewing on things. Shutting people out or up. Justifying yourself. Feeling overwhelmed or underappreciated. Thinking others are stupid.

Anxiety. Fear. Arrogance. Selfishness. Depression. Guilt. Annoyance. The list is endless, and I am sure that if you stepped outside of yourself, you could add to this list. All of these reactions point to the way you handle perceived threats to your own personhood, and all of these reactions are rooted in the fall.

Whether it is your self-image, how you think God feels about you, how you act and react in your interpersonal relationships, or whether you think the world is for or against you, the starting point for you to escape this corruption is to acknowledge that you have fallen short of God's glory. For most Christians, this is an easy thing to do. You know, that "sinner saved by grace" thing.

The next step is harder. You need to believe the gospel, that is, that God has already freely restored you to wholeness and has redeemed each of these poisoned spheres of relationship, even though your world might still look wrecked.

As you, in your imperfections, behold Perfection, who is the image of you, and as you declare your garden to be perfect, you are transformed into that image. Transformation does not happen as you look at your faults or as you beat yourself up or excuse yourself.

Again, don't hear what I am not saying. There is a time to confess your faults to one another. While that will keep you grounded, it will never let you fly, and you were created to fly. Beating yourself up and marginalizing yourself is the devil's job anyway, not yours.

This is what your faith was designed for. It was designed to respond to the overwhelming grace that God has revealed. If the grace you perceive is fuzzy, however, so will be your perception of self. If your grace only gets you into heaven, well, to heaven you will go, but heaven will never come into your world in full measure.

I have a chapter on how Paul turned these four spheres on their head on my website and how you can participate in God's reclamation process. Those four streams which were poisoned have now been filtered through the redemption that is in Christ Jesus, but you have a part to play in cleaning up your own rivers.

So, here you are—knowing that you were made for more, but also knowing, deep down, that you don't measure up. Depending on your personality type, you might try harder, project a macho or Wonder Woman image, or hide in the shadows and wallow in your lot in life. Your response to life is as unique as you are and is reflective of how you are wired and how you respond to life.

But, regardless of who you think you are, you have missed the mark. Unless you know that the reset button has been pushed, unless you come to realize that He has already stepped into your darkness, you will continue be "too much you," that is, full of yourself, and not full of God. You will not become the God-version that He intended for you.

So, let's leave Adam, pre-fall and post-fall, knowing that you inherited from Adam, pre-fall, a glory you can't begin to put into words, and, post-fall, all of his self-righteous tendencies, and examine the meta-story of Peter. He was called Simon Peter in the Gospels for a reason. He showed flashes of brilliance, but for the most part, he was Simon.

Simon Peter's story is the story of every Christian who wants God and His will, who gives him or herself to please God, yet lives in developmental darkness and might even celebrate their blind spots. Peter did. His is the story of all those who think that their personality and giftings, and the way they have controlled their life and have gotten their way before they were saved, are God-blessed after, just because they are now Christians.

What passes through regeneration, complete and intact, are all the ways that have protected yourself and gotten your way before you were saved. Sanctification is the Biblical term which describes the process of unwrapping those self-centered attitudes to reveal your God-center.

And it doesn't matter if your giftings are apparent to all or hidden from view. Jesus is out to get you and expose you in the most beautiful of ways. Peter's story, as seen in the gospel, is about a bubble, called Simon, that Jesus burst to reveal the Petrine rock within. His transformation began with a flash of insight that showed Simon that his version of himself was suspect at best. This is your story as well. Are you ready?

Questions

1. Paul wrote that you fell from God's glory, not just your own, implying that you were created to reflect God's essence. How does this perspective challenge or reshape your understanding of your own worth and purpose? * How might believing you've been fully restored in Christ change the way you approach your daily struggles or sense of worth? * And in what ways can you believe the you have already been perfected, even while you are still unfinished?

2. The text mentions that you may try to fill the "glory-void" left by the fall through self-effort or self-righteousness. Can you identify a specific way in your life where you've tried to compensate for a sense of lack, and how might embracing God's restoration change that approach?

3. What's harder for you: admitting you've fallen short or accepting that God sees your beauty as His son or daughter? Why? * How could focusing on God's grace, rather than your faults, reshape your understanding of your purpose or identity?

4. What do you think of the portrayal of David's intimate relationship with God, free from the veils and rituals of the Old Covenant? * How does this example of extravagant grace inspire you to rethink God's heart toward you and your own approach to connecting with Him?

5. The author painted a picture of the prodigal son's struggle to accept his father's naming of him, "son", because he self-identified as a "sinner saved by grace." Does that struggle resonate with you? * Reflect on how a persistent "sinnership mentality" might hinder your ability to embrace your restored identity in Christ.

Peter-Reading His Mail

J esus looked at him and said, "You are Simon, the son of John. You shall be
 called Cephas" (which means Peter). John 1:42

From their very first encounter, Jesus had Peter's number. He knew and liked
Simon, but, as we will see play out, wouldn't commit to him until after the
resurrection. Simon Peter showed flashes of brilliance, but, most of the time,
he was just "too much Simon".

The gospels are full of Simon Peter's stories. He is mentioned over 160 times
in the gospels, while the other disciples, combined, only equal 130. When the
disciples are listed, his name is always first. He was the undisputed leader and
not just because Jesus appointed him. This was because that is who he was. He
was going to fill the leader's space, even if that space was already filled.

For most, it might be difficult to identify with Peter because of this. Only a
few have his personality and leadership qualities. But on a deeper level, every
Christian who sets his or her heart to respond to God's call is Simon Peter
because Jesus must unravel you just like He did Peter.

One reason Peter's story is so prominent in the gospels is that you can read
your life in his and interpret the sometimes puzzling and painful moments of
your life. As with Adam, Peter's life is a meta-story, but it depicts a different
part of the Christian experience.

Peter's story is about the moment the light turned on and how Simon
became Peter. It is how Jesus reoriented Peter to make a rock from shifting sand
and bread from sifted wheat. And it is the same way that He begins to remake
you.

Adam's story, pre-fall, reveals God's over-the-top picture of you and,
post-fall, why you are bifurcated, conflicted, and struggle. But Adam's story
does not tell you whether he changed or how. That is Peter's story to tell, and
Abraham's.

Peter's story begins where Adam's left off—outside of the garden with all of his God-implanted desires, needs, and giftings but without the God-connection that would fully satisfy them. And while Adam knew that he had blown it and was lost, Peter did not. Peter was fairly confident about who he was and how he did life.

Simon knew that he was right. The way that he handled situations worked for him. People naturally gravitated toward him. He was competent, and he knew it.

And now, a charismatic Rabbi chose Simon to be one of His closest disciples. For Simon, righteous was an apt description, but it was a rightness that was rooted in his own personality, judgments, and abilities. He is the perfect picture of Christian self-righteousness.

Now, everything might not be working for you. It wasn't for me, but I still felt that I was right, and if life would just change, everyone would know. I didn't have the confidence or personality to make life bend to my will, but I did what I could to put myself in the best light. And, depending on how you are wired, you do the same thing to protect and project yourself.

You want to be on top and not at the bottom, and so you do what you can. You want to be heard and not ignored, so you go to social media. You want your kids, spouse, or whoever to do it your way, and if only they did, life would be so much better for both you and them.

Then add a religious component to this, and you have real justification for your opinions and actions. You now know that God is on your side, so you are going to make "God's will", a.k.a. your will, be done your way. This is Simon Peter's story.

Simon was on top. His voice was always heard, and he had a way to get others to follow him. And now, he could really say, "God told me", because God really did. Simon Peter was so sure that he was right, he even had the chutzpah to correct God.

So, there had to be, for Simon, a moment when reality hit him because it is easy to live with the illusion that you have your life together and that your opinions and attitudes are right, even though your spouse or kids or boss or employees or life resist and say otherwise. Being clueless and self-assured is a shaky place to be.

You need to be exposed as the fraud that you are and discover that how you have done life has only dug a deeper hole for yourself. God will let you continue to be "too much (fill in your name)" for only so long. You, like Simon, will, at some point, come face to face with the image you have created for yourself.

Simon Peter's story does not chronicle the process of transformation after he became aware, however. The gospels bring Peter to the point of change, and the book of Acts chronicles the exploits of a transformed Peter. But you don't see how he changed, though you know he did. And I hope that you know that, as with you, Peter's change didn't happen overnight.

You might assume that the outpouring of the Spirit magically transformed him, but if you know anything about the outpouring or being filled with the Spirit, you know that it doesn't. The Spirit did light him up, though.

I'm sure that you are aware of "anointed" people who are messed up, have messed up, and have messed up others. Their giftings are obvious, and how God uses them can make you jealous. But the outpouring and their giftings have nothing to do with transformation.

In fact, the anointing can set you up for failure if you misinterpret it. You can assume that you are right because spiritual things happen. It didn't help King Saul, nor did it help David when he was on the rooftop.

Simon also operated in the gifts of the Spirit before Pentecost and led the other disciples. But Saul and David and Simon, regardless of the anointing, missed the mark and screwed up. The anointing is not the answer for your messed-upness.

Peter's story is about beginnings. He was an initiator. He was the first out of the boat. He was the first to declare Jesus' divinity. He was the first disciple whom Jesus met after His resurrection. Peter initiated both the Jewish and gentile churches.

He is also the first disciple to be broken by the Lord, and in that, the first disciple to realize that he was not the person he thought he was. So, Peter's story is instructive because it depicts the initial steps toward transformation.

Whether you know it or not, the change that the Bible talks about does not occur by reading, memorizing, or even obeying. Nor does going to meetings or witnessing make you more Christ-like. Even though these are important and essential components, externals do not change you.

Transformation, like all things, is of Him and through Him and to Him, as you will see in Peter's life. It is encountering Jesus and walking with him, even when things don't seem to be working out, because these times open you up in ways that the outpouring of the Spirit doesn't.

Peter's "Christian" life, that is, his becoming Christ-like, began with an encounter, and Peter's initial encounter with Jesus was one for the ages. As he approached Jesus, Peter became aware of this Person's penetrating gaze.

John wrote that "Jesus looked at him". This Greek word for "look" describes a sustained, locked-in gaze. It speaks of a look that goes beyond the superficial. Jesus was reading Simon's mail.

I'm not sure how uncomfortable Simon was with this. I know that I would have been. But knowing his personality type, he might have been thinking, "This is weird. What's up with this guy?"

Peter didn't know that he was walking through a full-body scanner. Jesus was not only assessing the person in front of him, but He was listening to the Spirit. "You are Simon, son of John, but you will be called Peter."

"Whoa! Who is this guy who knows my name and my dad's name?" "Hey, Andrew, did you tell Him?" "No, He hasn't a clue." "Hmmm. This guy knows my name, and he is giving me another name? I'm intrigued."

Who isn't impressed with parlor tricks? Or was it? Jesus' gaze held a whole lot more than an "I know your name" trick that some have up their sleeve. Jesus really knew who Simon was and who he was to become. That gaze captured the entire scope of Simon Peter's life from sinnership to sonship.

So, what did Jesus see? First, Jesus saw an individual with a unique personality and giftings. He saw someone whom He created and lit up when Simon came into the world. Jesus saw the person that He held before his birth because Jesus also knew him before time began. I am aware that we are entering holy ground here, but this is exactly what God showed both Jeremiah and Paul.

Then Jesus knew his name. There is a reason God acknowledges names in the Bible. If He wasn't enamored with individuals, He would have said "that disciple with a birthmark on his left arm" or "disciple #1".

No, it was Simon Peter, as it was Simon the Zealot and James and Matthew and John and Mary, and especially Mary, because Jesus revealed Himself to her in her deep need, as He lovingly called her name at the tomb. Jesus knows and speaks your name because He knows you in the fondest and most intimate of ways and wants you to know Him as the One who knows you intimately.

While God identifies people groups and incorporates people into groups, He sees individuals. Now, I hope that I don't need to defend this "grouping" statement to you. Groups are important to God and having the privilege of being part of any group or family or culture is of God.

The psalmist says that God puts the solitary in families. God also arranged the children of Israel according to sub-groups, and heaven is not going to be any different because there will be nations, tribes, and various dialects. You were made for groups, and you come to know a big part of yourself among those with whom you associate, and that is a privilege. But with all of that, God knows YOU.

I don't think that there was another person in the Bible like David, except Jesus, who lived in this awareness. He connected the dots as a teenager while he was tending his dad's sheep. "Hmm, as I know each sheep by name and temperament, God, You know me."

Then, when He looked up into the night sky one evening and was struck by its vastness, David didn't think, as some philosophers do, how insignificant he was. No, he turned that paradigm on its head. "How insignificant the universe must be because all of your attention is focused on humanity, and especially on me. You can't get me out of your mind. So, what sort of creation am I?"

And then years later, as David had time to mature and think this matter through, he didn't add qualifiers to this understanding. He didn't tamp down his youthful exuberance. No, David amped it up. "How can I get away from You? Stalking doesn't even come close. When I try to quantify how much you think about me, I give up. But Lord, please don't stop!" Psalm 139 (TCA)

God sees YOU, so it might be good for you to stop, maybe for the first time, and just stop. Stop what you are doing and take up and take in Psalm 8 and Psalm 139. As you consider all the things that make you feel insignificant, ask God, "Who am I, Lord, and with all that is going on in the world, why am I the center of Your attention?"

And then listen. Just wait for your heart to quiet and for your eyes to adjust to the light. Wait until you realize that you ARE more than you think you are.

Simon, however, did not have the time, nor did he take time, to stop. That was for a future moment, arranged by the Spirit. He was a man on the move, running his business. And now, as he encountered Jesus, he was a man with a real mission, in fact, the mission of missions because he was called to follow the Messiah.

Jesus, gazing at Simon, saw through him, all the way back to Adam. He saw Simon, the son of Adam. "Now wait a minute, John wrote that Jesus saw 'Simon the son of John.'" Yes, yes, we will get to that, but follow me on this. Before Simon was the son of John, he was the son of Adam.

Before you were the son or daughter of _____, you too are a son or daughter of Adam. I know that I have spent several chapters trying to flesh this out, but let me take a few paragraphs to summarize. Paul wrote that all have been born with Adam's yearnings and desires, along with his nature.

At creation, God spoke into Adam, or maybe a better way to put it is that He hardwired humanity with desires and needs, which would become a part of our operating system. A significant part of Adam's pursuit and fulfillment in life centered around being able to satisfy them.

By kneeling before Adam, Adam was filled with the need to be the center of one's attention, to be honored, valued, and loved. That this was corrupted in the fall does not negate what happened there or God's original intent.

The fall just confirmed this because the need for attention that God intended to fill became a compulsion that has both defined and doomed humanity. Self-centeredness, wanting to be noticed and loved, and having your way stem from God putting His image in you and you doing your darnedest to fulfill it.

Then, when God told Adam and Eve to be fruitful, to become great and fill, He set in motion a people who were born to express their own unique selves to such an extent that their influence would be undeniable. Who hasn't had the fantasy of being recognized on stage for some unique gift, real or imagined?

Where do you think that nudging comes from? Most of your issues stem from not having this need met. Most of your wrong choices come from trying to fill that void. You were created to put your signature on life. Most, however, settle for less because life seldom responds to their efforts.

And do I also need to revisit, "subdue and rule?" Control issues can't be controlled. They are as much a part of you as your fingers which you use to tightly hold onto things. You were made to put your life in order, and to the degree you do it well, you prosper. Whereas God rules by holding all things with an open hand, you do by squeezing and applying pressure, both to your own hurt and others.

So, I hope you can agree that Peter was, in every respect, Adam's son, and I hope you can also agree that you are as well. You have been hard-wired to give expression to your own unique self, to be noticed, and loved for both it and you. You were also created to sense your own worth and significance, and to be satisfied with what you accomplish. So, all of your unfulfilled frustrations began with Adam.

So, here you are, clueless and conflicted, just like Adam and just like Simon. And like Adam and Simon, you are unaware of your condition until the light turns on.

Jesus then said, "Simon, son of John." "Simon you are not only like Adam in general, you are specifically like John, your old man." For some of you, it might be "like your old woman". Each of you have a unique way of trying to make life bend to your will which is not only inherited from your folks but is also learned both directly and indirectly.

It should go without saying that the presence or lack of a dad or mom has profound effects on children. Moms are just as important, if not more, but for Peter, it was his dad he took after. The presence or absence of physical parents become resident phantoms which can affect you for your entire lifetime.

How Simon protected and projected himself, his personality, and how he tried to make life work for him didn't happen in a vacuum. He was predisposed to lead and exert his will on others, and he learned how to do it by watching his dad fish and fight for ascendancy, and by being infused with his dad's DNA.

You can read the gospels and know what Simon's dad was like. He was a man's man and sure of himself. He made split-second decisions, even if he didn't have all the facts. He was able to handle life. People made space for him. And, as typical of "type A's", Simon and his dad believed their own press.

And then on top of that, Jesus acknowledged Simon Peter's personality and giftings by making him the top dog. It is obvious by Simon's actions, which included rebuking Jesus, being the one, and being right, fit Peter's assessment of himself.

Jesus has an elegant way to set people up for failure by using their strengths against them. For example, I don't believe that Jesus wanted Judas to fail, but knowing that Judas had an issue with money, one has to question the wisdom of putting Judas in charge of the purse without any oversight.

Jesus knows that the way out of your entrenched behavior is facing your own demons and coming honestly to Him. Judas kept his issue a secret, however, and it destroyed him. If I were Jesus, I would have put Judas in charge of keeping the attendance records and Simon, cleaning the latrines, so they both could learn humility. But Jesus' ways are higher than mine and more efficient.

After scoping Simon out, Jesus said, "But you will be named Peter." In Greek, this word, Peter, means "little rock." I can't help but return to this book's introduction, where Isaiah said, "Look to the rock from which you were hewn."

Peter was going to be look-like and taste-like Jesus. Even his shadow was going to be Jesus to others. And Jesus once again would become incarnate in Peter at the end of his life because Peter also willingly embraced a cross. Peter's life ended with an exclamation point.

But before this could be done, Simon had to be undone and look deeply into the "pit from whence he was dug". Simon had to realize that he was not Peter and that he was covered with an Adamic residue and clothed in his dad's shirt. Simon needed first to look at the pit from which he was pick-axed before he could be Peter. He had to be exposed and weep bitterly.

This is Peter's story, and the next chapter will tell of the moment when everything changed for him and when he began to change. This is also your story from a Simon's sort of sinnership to a Peter's sort of sonship.

Questions

1. The text describes Jesus' gaze as one that saw Simon Peter's entire life, from his flaws to his potential. Have you ever felt truly "seen" by God or someone else in a way that exposed both your strengths and weaknesses? * How did this experience impact your understanding of your identity or your relationship with God?

2. You, like Simon, may try to protect or project yourself to feel valued or significant even though you might not have Peter's personality. What is one way you have done this in your relationships or daily life, that is, make yourself look good, and how might embracing your God-given identity as a "son" shift your perspective?

3. The author suggests that transformation begins not with external actions but with an encounter with Jesus that "undoes" you. Can you recall a moment when you felt God challenging your self-perception or way of living? * What did that moment reveal about who you thought you were versus who God is calling you to be?

4. Simon's story shows how his self-righteousness and need to be "right" stemmed from his Adamic nature and personal tendencies. In what ways do you notice yourself striving to protect or project an image of being "right" or significant, whether in relationships, work, or faith? * How might embracing your identity as God's beloved child change how you approach these situations?

5. The text highlights that God knows you intimately, as He knew Simon, even before you were born. How does this truth—that God sees and loves the real you, including your unfulfilled desires and struggles—impact your willingness to trust Him with your transformation process? * What is one step you could take to lean into this trust?

Peter-Self Awareness

S imon, Simon, behold, Satan demanded to have you that he might sift you like wheat. Luke 22:31

And the Lord turned and looked at Peter. And Peter remembered the saying of the Lord, how he had said to him, 'Before the rooster crows today, you will deny me three times.' And he went out and wept bitterly. Luke 22:61,62

For three years, Peter was taught by the best of them. He was rebuked by the best of them. He was affirmed by the best of them. He hung out with the best of them. He was encouraged by the best of them. Peter was loved in ways he couldn't put into words.

Even with all of that, Peter remained Simon to the very end. "It doesn't matter what anyone else does, I know me. I'm not going to let You down. I know that my 'ya know' doesn't stink. I know myself. I know! I. . . I. . . I. . . I am right in my own eyes."

The image Simon had of himself was pretty convincing. He had certainly convinced himself. He had also convinced others. But he didn't fool Jesus. His sense of rightness or his righteousness was rooted in his own self-assured self. Or, to put it another way, Simon was self-righteous.

This, by the way, is the default position of every person who comes to the Lord, and that means you. I am sure that you know of some Christians who, even after years of walking with the Lord, have glaring blind spots. You can see it, but they don't.

But, the more important question is, "Have you seen your own?" If you have had your antenna up, you would already be aware because others have already clued you in. The way that you protect and project yourself, the way you try to make life work and get your way, does not magically mend when you "repent". Your message or mission might change when you become a Christian, but you keep banging your drum the same way.

Repentance is not just about sin. In fact, sins committed are the smallest part of repentance because the sin-weeds in your garden are only cut off at ground level when you say you're sorry. The roots, however, of your Adamic nature go deep. Peter only realized this when Jesus' eyes met his at the moment of exposure.

Self-awareness is always a work of the Spirit, which you can neither anticipate nor manufacture. And it often occurs when your life falls apart despite your best efforts. But the signs are always along the way. Jesus tried to tell Peter that he was off more than once.

You might be alerted when your spouse or kids, or folks are having a hard time with you. It might be your work or ministry grinding you. But, at some point, how you do marriage or parenting or friending, work or ministry will catch up with you and bring you to your knees. It is important, so important, not to be a Judas and give up at this point, but to be a Simon who humbles himself.

I am sorry that I have been a little more pointed here in pointing out your attempts to protect yourself and your turf, and how you try to make your world bow to your will. It is easy to conflate God's will with your own, but that is exactly what everyone who bows their knee to Jesus does initially. You try to make everything bow to your will or make yourself noticed, that is, until Jesus catches you, and you become aware.

One of the lines of a Wesley hymn is, "Adam's image now efface. Stamp Thine Image in its place." This should be the prayer of every Christian, inviting Jesus to do in you what He did in Peter.

Jesus was about to do a little Simon-effacing, so He said, "Simon, Simon". Not just, "Simon". Saying his name once would have left room for interpretation. Once said could have a hard edge to it. Once said could have been dripping with disapproval. Once said could be an "I told you so".

But "Simon, Simon" is filled with gentleness and kindness. "Simon, Simon" does not condemn. It entreats and embraces. "Simon, Simon", says, "I know that you're trying to do your best, but you are heading for a fall, a fall into the abyss of your own soul and of your own making. And how I wish it weren't so."

"Simon, Simon" was Jesus' way of speaking past the actions of Simon, which spoke so loudly, and to the Simon who animated those actions. Sin is one thing. The sin nature, that is the engine which drives the car, is another.

Forgiveness is remedial and takes care of sins, and praise God for that. But only the devastating realization that what you have believed about yourself is a lie, and how you have done life, is hurtful, will begin to address the pre-fall nature that you inherited from Adam.

"The devil has demanded," Jesus then said. Just an aside. I'm not sure how this "devil thing" works (not sure anyone does), that is, knowing when he is involved or how circumstances coincide with spiritual activity. I do know, however, that there is a power animating many things in the world because this world is under Satan's control.

The devil is a puppet master. But here, Jesus gives us a little insight by telling Simon that He was giving the devil permission to use a servant girl to lob an existential grenade his way. The devil has complete freedom to enact his will in the world, but it's the same freedom that a pit bull, who is held on a short leash, has.

I don't think that the devil would have asked God's permission to do God's job of perfecting Simon. Rather, I think the devil asked permission to blow Simon's house down like he did with Judas. But Jesus had re-purposed the devil's request and let Simon know. I wonder whether Simon Peter clung to these words during his dark time, and I wonder whether they became a glimmer of hope. God always repurposes the devil's threats and attacks.

So, we come to an epochal moment in Peter's life and its apex. There is no higher point in Peter's life than this, because, at this moment, everything changed for him. Pentecost, and all that followed, could not have happened without this campfire experience. Self-awareness is one of the best gifts God can give.

Before this "Jesus looked at Peter" moment, Peter was living in the flesh, and he was about to be introduced to walking in the spirit. These two phrases, however, as I have discussed previously, have a definition but little meaning for most Christians.

Walking in the flesh is the starting point for every Christian, and it is not about sin and sinning. In fact, it is often about doing good. It is you trying to be a Christian, the best way you can.

Like Jacob, you want what God wants, but also like Jacob, who is the Old Testament's Peter, you use your personal strengths, your personality, and what has worked for you in the past to do God's will and hold your life together after you become a Christian. It is living from your soul which houses all your natural ability and gifts. It's what makes you, you.

If you were opinionated before you became a Christian, you are still opinionated after. Only now, you fancy yourself as a Christian apologist. If you got angry before, you still get angry after. Only now, it is called righteous anger. If you were a yes-person before, it is now called a fruit of the Spirit. Do you catch my drift?

God has created you to live from your spirit, where you are no longer controlled by your personality. Everything is a nail, if you have hammer giftings and are living from your soul. Living from your spirit begins when your natural strengths are broken, and Christ begins to shine through. (Watchman Nee's books are an excellent resource if you want to look further into this.)

Your spirit is that ginormous place within where you and God intersect, intertwine, and fellowship. Your spirit is to take the lead, but while your body and soul are noisy (if you are hungry or if your feelings are hurt, you know it), your spirit whispers in a way that requires you to be attuned. That is why there needs to be a breaking of your natural, outer person.

Only when you become aware of God's awareness (Jesus' knowing look) will you come to the realization that you are living out of your soul or natural abilities. This is Simon Peter's story. You will never hear the Spirit in your spirit or even be aware that you have a spirit, if your default operating system is your own strengths, your personality, and giftings.

Luke then wrote that Jesus turned and looked at Simon. With all that Jesus was enduring, His thoughts pulled Him toward Simon Peter. And this wasn't a cursory glance because the look He gave Simon was the same look he gave him in their first encounter.

This is the same word that was used when Jesus first looked deep into Simon's soul. But this time, the look which was then dismissed as weird, now penetrated and exposed Simon as a fraud.

You have to be amazed and humbled at the elegance of Scripture. When Jesus first met him, He called him, "Simon," and you would think, especially at this moment when Simon was completely exposed, Jesus would be looking at the culprit, Simon.

But no, Jesus looked at "Peter." Jesus looked at the one whom he had known from eternity. Peter, the little rock, was emerging from the shell of Simon and about to become like the Boulder Himself. Jesus looked past Simon and saw something of Himself—someone stable and strong and on whom He could establish His church.

Jesus affirms you into your destiny and identity. You do, however, have a part to play. Jude wrote that you are to keep yourself in the love of God by building up yourselves in your most special faith. Most Christians, however, keep themselves out of the love of God by embracing a "sinner saved by grace" mentality. I expand on Jude's understanding on my website, but part of building yourself up is not tearing yourself down or beating yourself up, though, like Peter, you might go through seasons of self-flagellation.

You will only have a moment or two when God exposes you, and you know it. But after that, your life is about building yourself and others up and not doing the devil's job for him by tearing yourself or others down.

You are to present yourself before Him and declare your sonship. You are to use your thoughts and direct your words to persuade your own heart as to the truth about yourself.

Glorious things are spoken of you, but are you speaking these glorious things to yourself? They must first be spoken to you, by yourself, before what God says about you will fully resonate within. Only then will your words resonate with others.

What does a glorious you look like? I am not sure, but I am sure that Jesus saw Peter in front of him and not Simon. As I wrote in the chapter on calling, your lack is God's call on your life. So here, as Simon saw his great lack, the Spirit was both calling out Peter and calling him to come out. Lazarus was being resurrected once again.

Paul later codified this upside-down logic when he shared that the secret strength of his life was his weakness and exposure. Because of that, Paul desired to be shown how empty he was, so that the fullness of Christ would fill him. But Simon Peter didn't know this at that time. He had to look back at this experience to gain that insight.

Being exposed shakes you to your very foundation. It strips away all the things that have held your life together. Free falling is an apt description because the walls that helped define your life are gone. All you can do is cry, "Ooooh, nooooo!" all the way down, hoping that when you hit bottom, you aren't destroyed. But you will be, in the most edifying of ways.

"And he wept bitterly." Peter's nadir was his apex. While you cannot force this moment, you can surely invite it. And I can only imagine what happened in Peter when Jesus looked again into his now opened and humble eyes after the resurrection.

David's Psalm 139 gives voice to someone aware of God's all-consuming gaze. "You have searched me and known me." While that gaze will, at times, reveal fault lines as it did with Peter, that is not God's primary intent. Jesus was looking at the wonder of Peter and He is looking at the wonder of you, as He looked at the wonder of Adam when He first saw him and fell to His knees. That is how I read Psalm 139.

Is that how you read it? That this Psalm is too good to be true is why it IS true. It also ends with an invitation for God to search your heart more so that God's glory can more fully shine through.

This is Peter's story. This is your story too, whether you have realized it yet or not. It is also Paul's. Paul, for most, seems to be the exception to the rule because he came out of the spiritual womb on fire. His exceptional life, when preached, is often held up as the gold standard for Christian living and used to motivate the saints.

But the end result of preaching this is dubious. To those who are workers, it will certainly work them up more. For others, though, who are not as motivated, his story can demotivate and actually condemn them for their lack of effort.

But Paul's story is none of the above, and I will have a chapter discussing the two biographies of Paul that will show that Paul is no exception to the rule. This should encourage you because you will find yourself in good company.

Before I do that, I'm going to tell you my story as it relates to self-awareness. I am an anti-Peter and an anti-Paul. I am not a "type-A", leader type. Though I have developed some of these traits over the years, I am still basically a slouch. I am a plain wrapper who likes to stay in the background and who had to be convinced of the treasure within.

I think that most, while they would be like a Peter-type who steps out of the boat, are quite comfortable sitting on the cushions. In my early years, I had little confidence in God or myself and kept in the background.

While God has used, over the years, my secular work to push me outside of my comfort zone, I had to be convinced of my giftings and beauty. That convincing, though, came from God and from a few outside encouragers (especially my wife).

How the Spirit brings change in your life and brings you into your destiny is the same whether you are larger than life or smaller than dust. I definitely landed on the smaller-than-dust side.

But regardless of where you are on the continuum, the Lord will, at the right time and at the most opportune time, or should I say, the most inopportune time, fix His gaze on you, and you will be aware of it. And that will be the moment everything changes for you.

Questions

1. Have you ever experienced a moment when you felt exposed, like Peter, and realized a truth about yourself that was hard to face? * What was that moment like, and how did it shape your understanding of yourself and your relationship with God? * Reflect on whether you saw God's gentle gaze in that experience, calling you toward your true identity.

2. The chapter suggests that others often notice our blind spots before we do. Can you recall a time when someone pointed out a flaw or behavior you hadn't seen in yourself? * How did you react—defensively, with humility, or otherwise? * What might it look like to respond differently in the future, trusting that God is using others to help you grow?

3. Jesus' address of "Simon, Simon" is described as filled with gentleness and kindness, not condemnation. How does this portrayal of Jesus influence the way you approach your own failures or moments of weakness? * Are there areas in your life where you struggle to receive God's grace, and how might you invite His gentle gaze into those places?

4. The author writes that God affirms you into your destiny, but you have a part to play by persuading your own heart of your true identity. * What are some ways you tend to "tear yourself down" or agree with negative thoughts about yourself? * How could you begin to speak "glorious things" to yourself, aligning your thoughts with what God says about you?

5. The chapter emphasizes that transformation often comes through brokenness, when our natural strengths and efforts fail. Can you identify a time when life fell apart despite your best efforts, and you sensed God working in the midst of it? * What did you learn about yourself and God through that experience, and how has it impacted the way you live out your faith today?

Peter-My Story

There have been two moments in my life when the image that I had created for myself was effaced. Once was devastating, and the other was more matter of fact. Both, however, were catalysts for change.

One exposed the fiction I believed about myself. The other revealed how I operated and the way I protected and projected myself. The veils were removed, and I was exposed. Both brought a self-awareness that began to change me.

Before I get to the stories, let me tell you what led up to those moments. To say that I was messed up and didn't know it, growing up, would be an understatement. I did a pretty good job of hiding from others and myself.

I don't have many memories of my childhood, and fewer of my dad. But the ones I have of my father are all negative—being chased with a belt or being yelled at, and I wasn't a rebel. I was a compliant kid.

My older brother was his favorite and was cut out of the same cloth as my dad, so he also took delight in highlighting my lacks. My mom loved me in a German sort of way, that is, with little expression. So, there I was.

I never dated because I was too scared to ask. The only time, however, that I mustered enough courage to ask, the girl demurred with "oh, we're just friends." If that wasn't the kiss of death, I don't know what is.

I comforted myself with the knowledge that if I went to Europe, girls would flock to me. Pretty pathetic, right? I thought, however, that I was ok, even though I knew deep down that something was wrong.

All of that began to change in college when I began dating, that is, until, in the second semester of my freshman year. I got hit with acne, but not the normal run-of-the-mill pimples. I was beet red with infections all over my face, my chest, and back.

That drove me further into a shell, until sometime in my junior year a girl took notice of me. And after a two year, on-again and off-again relationship, she finally determined that it was off. She knew what she wanted to pursue in life, and I was not part of her plan.

I was devastated until she called to tell me that she was pregnant. This was 1973, the year Roe v Wade became law. We did the right thing, though, and got married. I was ecstatic. She, to say the least, was not.

For me, it was a dream come true because the only dream I remember having was to have the perfect marriage. And now it was being fulfilled before my very eyes because I knew that I would be the perfect husband.

You see, I was a servant-type. I got people to like me by being nice, saying, "yes" and serving. And my wife, I was sure, would fall under my spell.

Not sure how dreams form in one's heart, but everyone has a unique dream for their life. It could be a wish, a desire, or even a fantasy. For some, it comes with certainty, though for most, it seems fanciful. I believe that these are not childish whimsies, but a part of the eternity which God plants in one's heart, calling you. At least, it was for me.

I think that a large reason for this dream was that I didn't see it in my parents' marriage. It was not perfect. While there was little bickering, there was little interaction. They just lived together, doing their own thing. My sister and brother, like myself, did our own thing as well. I knew that I wanted something more, and I was now in a position to make that happen.

In the few times of conflict, mom would always have the last word. My dad would try to stand up for himself, but inevitably he would sulk away in defeat. That interaction was the basis for my first moment of self-awareness.

To that point, if you told me that I was anything like my father, I would have rejected it out of hand. He was loud and impulsive. I was quiet and reserved. But I had a Darth Vader/Luke Skywalker dream-scene experience where, after Luke kills Darth and pulls off Darth's helmet, he sees himself.

I would come home from class and ask Nancy to take a walk with me. She would say, "no". I would insist, but she refused to go. I would then sulk just like my dad. Did I say, "Just like my dad!!?"

My world imploded. Not only was my dream of a perfect marriage evaporating, but I realized that I was not who I thought I was. And, on top of that, I was like the person whom I didn't like or respect. It was at that moment that I said, "God, if you are real, help!"

Now I was fairly theologically minded, having gone to Lutheran grade school, high school, and college. I had a relationship with the Lord, but it was mostly head knowledge. But here for the first time, I connected honestly with God from my point of need.

This was my Peter moment. I was exposed and desperate. I realized, as Peter did, that I was a fraud. The Lord asked for Jacob's name, and he replied, "I am a cheat." I replied, "I am my father."

Peter might have been ok with being compared to his dad because he was proud of him. But whether proud or not, whether embraced or rejected, whether formed from a good, bad, or non-existent relationship, the image you have of yourself must have a pin put into it because your image of yourself is not God's. And this takes a moment of self-awareness.

That began my journey, and our journey, from brokenness to wholeness, from sinnership to sonship. We were still a mess, but Nancy and I committed ourselves to the Lord the best we could.

Both Nan and I knew that we were lacking and without the resources to fill the hole in each other. For me, I had a big and empty "love and worth" hole that I needed Nancy to fill. Nancy had a big and deep "significance" hole that she knew I couldn't fill. It was not good.

Going to church and being involved, while important, didn't help much because externals, no matter how godly, can never meet those needs. During my early years of walking with the Lord, I would even crawl into bed in a fetal position when I felt overwhelmed. Both Nancy and I were living from a sinnership mentality and not in the sinning sense, but in the "I am not" sense.

For over eight years, we held on by our fingernails. Nancy was clinically depressed, and I was clueless. I would come home from work and find her staring at a wall, and I didn't know what to do. We recently had friends tell us that they never thought we would make it. During those years, however, we had kids, went to church, developed friends, and did our best to serve.

But we were at an impasse. We couldn't go forward because Nancy and I were trapped in our own limiting and limited sense of self, which affected our marriage, our kids, and life. But then God stepped in.

He interjected Himself into our marriage by speaking a word just like He did with Abraham. When God wants to do something monumental in your life, He will first give you a word or promise that you will sense.

It is that word, once spoken, which you must hold on to because, as I have laid out in the life of Jesus and as I will lay out in the life of Abraham, the way God brings you into your destiny is to first speak a word which hopefully is believed and received. Then that word is assayed or tried before He brings it about; that is, fire is put to what He has said.

Jesus was driven into the wilderness for this very purpose. After the rush of God's presence, the Spirit rushed him into a place where all He could do was wait and hope. It will seem to you that what you sensed from the Lord is not real, and often, the exact opposite happens. That is what happened with us and in our marriage. The promise that God gave of beauty and wholeness blew up. But that is a story for another time.

But knowing this principle (a sense from God leads through the wilderness into the experience of His promise) can help set your expectations and allow you to press on when your world falls apart. Again, the principle is this: when God wants to do something epochal, He first speaks a word (by His initiative and grace), then He tries the word (your believing and hoping), and then He makes it come about.

Jesus hinted at this, in the Sower's parable, when He connected the sun that baked the ground with the seed being planted. "When trials come BECAUSE of the word, or on account of the word, or for the word's sake." TCA The reason for trials, at times, is God bringing about His good purposes in you.

God's speaking to you invites trouble because He wants His word to become flesh, where you no longer try to live the Christ-like life, but you become it, and therefore you live it. For that to happen, the word must have some fire put it. Since you are the word's crucible, you will experience the heat as well.

I don't believe in "name it; claim it", that is, if it is in the Bible somewhere, you put your finger on the verse, can claim it, and somehow it will happen. That is presumption. But I do believe, if God has witnessed something to your heart, you better hold on to it, or it won't happen because it is by grace, through faith. Your faith must hold on to what the Spirit witnessed to your heart, regardless of the circumstances.

Let me repeat, it is by grace through faith. It is not just grace or God's efforts, though He is the One who initiates and works in you. Nor is it just faith or you trying to make it happen. It is a collaborative effort where you sense something of God for your life, and then hold on to it, while He makes it come to pass through you.

The second moment of self-awareness came some fifteen years after we were married. Our marriage was stable and getting better. But I was still myself and not making much of my life. I was content not to push myself in order to make our life better, and that was a sticking point. Nancy was committed but not happy.

But ever the servant-type, I thought I was ok because I served Nancy. my family, and church, along with my employers, the best I could, and I believed in that "if you want to be great" thing. Serving suited my personality. It was my strength, and I thought it worked for me. And it did to a point.

But it didn't suit our finances. I had marginal jobs that allowed me to have a sense of accomplishment, but it barely got us by. Employers liked me because I owned my positions and made them look good. But I still hid.

I think that I can safely say that how you perceive yourself and how you make life work for you is skewed, and, since you are immersed in it, you can't see it objectively. Objectivity is not a strong suit for either you or me.

So, there must be moments when you are exposed from the inside, but with an outside-looking-in perspective. Having your spouse point these out normally doesn't work, though it should.

These moments are not scripted. They just happen. But somehow, you need to recognize them and be open to them. For me, this moment was not earth-shattering like the first moment of self-awareness. It was unremarkably remarkable, though, because I saw how I tried to manipulate life to make it work for me, and from that time, I began to change.

It happened when I was going for my master's in counseling. The program required each student to attend counseling for a semester. I was assigned to one of the professors who was brilliant. My first session looked just like my second, third, and fourth.

I would sit down. The professor would ask me a simple question and then would either close his eyes and put his head down or he would turn his eyes up inside of his head, so all that I would see were the whites of his eyes.

I don't know how you would have reacted, but, after he asked his question, I found myself stammering and stuttering because I had no feedback. He had no expression. He didn't affirm, correct, or comment. He seemed disinterested.

After three or four sessions, I realized that he was being a blank screen on purpose and that I was seeing myself projected on that screen. I couldn't get my bearings, and it hit me that I got my juice from others. I didn't live from the inside. I saw how I did life and ultimately how I perceived myself, and it wasn't good.

If someone showed interest in me, I would be engaged and engaging. However, if someone did not show interest or respond positively, I would shut down. This reflected what I believed about myself. I let others define me and give me, in the moment, permission to express myself. Others controlled me, and I didn't know it.

My servant-type personality controlled me, and I saw that it was nothing more than my way to get people to be interested in and like me. It was my safe space and soulish.

My serving, while admirable, was not of the Spirit. It was just my personality, my perceived strengths, and giftings that controlled me. I used serving to protect and project my best side, but this wasn't serving us well.

I didn't purposefully do anything to change, but from that point, I did. Once the light turned on, I became aware of more than my lack because light lights the way out of sinnership and reveals sonship. The perfections of beauty began to shine through.

Now, I can't give you an amazing success story, filled with riches and recognition. I told you from the beginning that my life has not been that interesting. I still have small, and, to the outside eye, insignificant gardens to tend and keep.

But I can tell you that I know who I am and the importance of what God has given me to say and do. I have come to know my sonship, as has Nancy, and this has affected how we navigate life. I can lead and confront, or stay in the background and serve, depending on the moment.

I use my giftings, but if they are not received, I neither push, nor do I lose my stride. As John the Baptist said, "I am a voice." I am not an echo, but a unique voice with a unique message.

Some will receive. Some won't. Yet it doesn't matter because this is what God has put in me. The word, which became flesh in Jesus, has become flesh in me.

I am at the center of God's attention, so while I give myself to build relationships, relationships don't validate me. God also has created me to be fruitful, to become great, and to fill my space with me. And I have seen Him do this in the areas that are important to me.

My part is to make sure that I am focused on making Him and others great and on opening up space for others to fill. This defines my greatness and will define yours. And, by the way, after over fifty years of marriage, Nan and I are best friend and getting to be better friends as we face life and serve together.

For me, *From Sinnership to Sonship: The Story of Becoming* is my story. I have written this book from a place of experience. The Lord's eyes have caught mine like Peter's, and those moments of self-awareness have been turning points.

This has created in me a sense of self that has been bathed in God's acceptance and love.

When you glimpse Jesus, you see yourself. So, I have begun to see myself in the light of the glory of God in the face of Jesus Christ, that is, in His smile. And as I describe the path to sonship laid out in Abraham's life, I also write this from a place of experience.

I have read my life in Abraham's, who also was insignificant when he was called, and discovered that when he left this life, his influence grew exponentially. I have walked in his steps that have been marked, at times, by unbelief. I have hoped against hope, and I sacrificed my Isaac willingly upon the mount of Moriah. And because of that, I have heard Him say, "Now with blessing, I will bless."

But before we look at Abraham's life, I need one more chapter to drive home the point that God proclaims the bad news of you before you can receive the good news. The Peter principle affects all because all are right in their own eyes until they are proven wrong. All use their personality and wiring to make life work for them, and becoming a Christian will not change that. So, let's look at Paul, whom most feel is the exception to this rule.

Questions

1. Reflect on a time when you realized that the way you were presenting or protecting yourself—through your personality, strengths, or self-image—was flawed or rooted in your own efforts rather than God's truth. * What was that moment like, and how did it change your view of yourself? * Did you turn toward God for help, or did you pull away, and what impact did that choice have on your journey?

2. How has the author's story of self-awareness and exposure resonated with your own experiences, particularly in light of Peter's moment of realization after denying Jesus? * Knowing that God's grace allows you to respond to past or present moments of exposure, what might you say to God today about any areas where you've relied on your own efforts or self-image instead of His truth?

Peter-Paul is No Exception

W hen I say "Paul", what comes to mind? He is certainly a Christian who should be emulated. The word that I associate with Paul is full. He had a full life. He was full of the Holy Spirit. He was full of confidence. He was full of compassion. He was full of the mind of Christ and purpose. He was full-filled.

But he also began his Christian journey full of himself. "What! How could you say that? Right after conversion, he boldly proclaimed Christ." Yes, he was doing what God has commanded all Christians to do with a vigor few have.

But if the Peter principle is more than a principle (and it is), then Paul is no exception. What catches one, catches all. So, Paul might be more like you than you think, and I am not talking about his personality or the entrapment by specific sins that catch everyone.

He was not a super-Christian because no one comes out of the spiritual womb as a mature adult. He had to go through the same process everyone does. While Paul had a special call accompanied by special giftings, he was as clueless as you. He was as messed up as you. His personality and the way he got his way also controlled him, as they do you.

He also needed the work of the Spirit in his life. He needed the light turned on to see himself, otherwise, Paul would have continued to do God's work in his own way with disastrous results. He might have been able to build a kingdom, but it wouldn't have been God's.

Now, these assertions, you might say, are interesting, but back them up with Scripture because it's easy to fit things into your own narrative just to make a point. Ok then, I will.

My understanding of Paul opened up while I was puzzling over Paul's two seemingly conflicting biographies. As I read these accounts, I began to see the process that I had also observed in my own life. Reading your own heart, at times, is as good a commentary on the Bible as most and, in some ways, better.

The first biography is found in the Book of Acts which Luke wrote after he interviewed Paul. The second was Paul's own autobiographical account written to the Galatians. This one's veracity, to my amazement, was sworn with an oath as the truth.

I find this strange because I can't find Paul using an oath when it came to proclaiming the gospel. He just declared it. But he got worked up over this piece of personal history. It was as if the Spirit knew, while he didn't, that Luke was going to write his own piece of history that seemed to conflict with Paul's.

First, let me give you the order of events, as laid out in these two accounts, and then I will read between the lines. Luke's narrative describes Paul's first journey to Damascus and his return to Jerusalem after his conversion.

Saul left the Jewish leadership in Jerusalem with papers which gave him authority to do what was needed in order to stop the spread of Jesus' followers. Paul told Luke that he was "breathing out threats and murder". As he approached Damascus, Jesus was revealed to him from heaven. Paul was both blinded and enlightened at the same time.

Then, after three days of physical blindness where he could do nothing but let this experience sink in, his sight was restored, and immediately he began to preach Jesus. Luke wrote that he kept getting stronger in Damascus, confounding the Jews by having an answer for every counterpoint they could throw at him. In a matter of weeks, he was the best Christian apologist around.

After a short period of time, months perhaps, the disciples knew that this was going sideways, so they helped Saul escape. Saul then headed back to Jerusalem.

While there, and again it seems for a relatively short time, Saul did what Saul did best. He argued. Luke wrote that he argued against the Greek Jews. Not sure why they were his special target, but it seems that Saul wanted to press his point and convince them that he was right and that they were wrong. He did have the truth on his side this time, however.

Saul proclaimed what he had seen and experienced because he wanted all to know the truth. The church, however, soon realized that this wasn't working out because they heard of a plot to kill him. So, they took him to the Mediterranean Sea and shipped him off to Tarsus.

This is where Luke's account stops. He ends this phase of Saul's life with an interesting comment. Immediately after Saul leaves Jerusalem, Luke writes, "Therefore, INDEED, the church had peace and grew." (A literal translation from the Greek). "Indeed" is not included in most translations because it seems inconsequential, but "indeed" says something. But we will leave it there for now.

Paul writes of a second visit to Damascus because he writes in Galatians that he returned AGAIN to Damascus, and after being there for three years, he went to Jerusalem for fifteen days to interview Peter and visit briefly with James.

It is important to note that these are two different visits, pointing to two different times where two different persons are on display. In the first, Saul was front and center. The second time around shows a person who was content to be in the background, to be a part, and a learner.

The best we can piece together of Paul's history is that between these two visits, there was a space of time. After being in Tarsus for a bit, he went to Arabia because Paul wrote that God wanted to do something IN him. He wrote "when God. . .was pleased to reveal his Son IN me . . . I went into Arabia." (NIV)

I am not sure how God alerted Paul that He wanted to do something new IN him. But Paul knew that whatever it was, he had to get alone. So, he chose not to go to Jerusalem to consult with the apostles about this urging.

Just for the record, Paul didn't go to Jerusalem the first time to "consult" with them either. He knew what he knew and didn't need anyone to tell him about Jesus, even those who lived with Him. For Saul, ever the leader type, it was "follow me" or get out of the way. He wasn't into, at that time, sitting at anyone's feet.

So, to Arabia, he went. It is a matter of speculation as to exactly where, or why, or for how long he remained in Arabia, so let me give you my best guess. Paul is to grace what Moses was to the law. God gave Moses the gospel of the law, and He revealed to Paul the gospel of grace.

So, what better place to unravel justification by works and to redeem all that was old than on Sinai, the place where all stood condemned? Moses was on the mount for forty days and nights, receiving the best God could do at that time, which was the Old Covenant. When he left that space, his face shone.

However, when Paul left, possibly forty days later and after receiving the revelation of the New Covenant, he shone on the inside. The light of the glory of God began to shine IN him.

On the first trip to Damascus, Jesus was revealed TO him. This Jesus, after you meet him, is the One whom you want to proclaim and defend with all of your might and with the strength of your persona.

In the wilderness of Arabia, though, Jesus was revealed IN Paul. No longer an objective reality, Paul began to realize "Christ in me", which he exegeted to the Galatians because "Christ in me" is a major theme of Galatians. This second time, Jesus became Paul's animating life force because Jesus was transliterated.

The contrast in Paul's behavior between these two encounters shows that a constitutional change occurred in Paul. Let's unpack this by looking at Paul, first pre-Damascus, then post-Damascus, and finally post-Arabia.

Pre-Damascus, Paul had a keen sense of rightness. It drove him. You don't "breathe out threats and murder" unless you have been breathing in an all-consuming hatred for wrongness. His verse for that season of life might have been "I have hated with perfect hatred." (KJV)

He was hardwired to be all in and fully on for whatever he thought to be the truth. He lived for a higher purpose and could justify his actions according to the Scriptures. So, he used the force of his personality to do God's will his way to accomplish a greater good.

Saul was passionate, forceful, self-assured, and convincing, and aggressive with a "take no prisoners" personality. To his credit, he honed his personality to a sharp edge and then did what came naturally to him. Paul, as he wrote in Galatians, exceeded all his contemporaries in his zeal for the Lord.

He acted. He led. He inhaled mission and breathed out plans which he then enacted, and everyone applauded. The Pharisees, who were politicians, loved him because they had their enforcer.

He saw a bug and was determined to squash it. Everything he saw was a nail because he was a hammer. He lived for the fight and since this was a righteous cause, Paul could give himself wholly to it. Paul's personality and how he approached life was on full display.

But then, oops, he realized that he was wrong. Paul was, in his mind, God's hammer who was to beat down the rabble. But when he encountered Jesus for the first time, he realized that he was bringing the hammer down on God.

So, what did he do? He took his hammer out to beat down a new rabble. This time, however, his targets were the unconverted Jews. While his message and audience changed, he didn't. He was still passionate, forceful, self-assured, and aggressive with a "take no prisoners" personality.

Luke wrote that he began to boldly proclaim Christ in the synagogue, and, as he engaged the Jews, he threw them into a state of confusion. He knew that he was right and was going to prove it.

Paul fed off his personality and knew that he was a complete package. He had a strong intellect, strong passion, and a stronger will. If there was a destination,

Paul knew only one way to get there and that was straight ahead because he had the ability to go through any obstacle.

So, Paul used every ounce of his strength to convince the Jews that he was right, and I am sure his motivation was also right. He wanted them to know the truth. But the more he pushed, the more they pushed back, which just caused Paul to exert even more of his personality to push back harder.

What happens when two immovable forces collide? Well, it depends on the numbers, and the Jews had that on their side at this time. So, the church did the right thing and, for both his sake and theirs, got rid of him.

Then he went to Jerusalem and did the same thing. As noted, he had no time for the apostles who had already gone through the wringer and were seasoned. He knew his mission, and nothing was going to take precious time from him accomplishing that.

Coming from what Paul thought to be a victory in Damascus, he found another group to be against. He argued and let his personality and the way he got his way shine through, with the same questionable results. Luke writes that when he was sent away again by the church, "The church, THEREFORE, INDEED, had peace and grew."

Luke felt that "therefore" was not strong enough to make his point, so he wrote, "therefore, indeed". Indeed means "take note of this" because "indeed" emphasizes the reason for, and the result of, Paul being shipped off. This is not a throwaway statement. Luke was connecting Paul's departure with growth.

The cause was Paul's leaving. The result was peace and growth. How about that for the key to evangelism? Ask the toxic leader to leave, and God brings growth.

As I wrote in *Ephesians and all that Jazz*:

'That's really what happened to me (Paul speaking) in Damascus. I knew that I was right, and everyone was going to know it, whether they liked it or not. The saints, however, finally had enough of the trouble I caused and "helped" me escape with my life. However, they were really helping themselves because they wanted to escape from me. They said, "Too much Saul" after I left.

Then when my brothers in Jerusalem saw the effect that I had on everyone there, they had enough as well and escorted me to the boat. I heard later that, after I left, there was a huge sigh of relief, and the church came alive again and began to grow once more.

That was hard for me, but I am so glad they had the courage to confront me because I would have continued to be a pompous ass. (When I told you about talented people hurting the church, I was talking about myself.)

This has been one of the most important lessons of my life. I could have gotten angry with them and went somewhere else to prove them wrong. But that would have just created another crisis in a different group.

Thankfully, I directed my anger toward Jesus and had it out with Him. But the madder I got, the quieter He became until I was quite spent. Then I realized that Jesus was the One sending me to a time out, and this shattered my world."

Paul, pre-Damascus and post-Damascus, was "too much Saul", just like Simon was "too much Simon", and just like you are "too much you" before and after conversion. What passes through conversion, unscathed, are all the methods that are used to get your way, to press your point, and the way you protect and project yourself. (By the way, one of the great values of marriage is exposing your fault lines or your "too much you". Its other great value, as you hang in there, is its ability to heal.)

The direction changes. The message changes. But you are still you. Yes, you are redeemed and forgiven, but the "you" that booby-trapped your life before still blows up after. While "converted," you still do the best you can with your unconverted personality and natural abilities, like Paul. Peter's principle rules!

After Arabia, though, Paul changed. He was still passionate and ever the leader-type, but his passions and personality, his giftings and natural ability did not control him. When he returned AGAIN to Damascus, it was almost like returning to the scene of the crime for a redo.

This time Paul was there for three years. Doing what? We don't know, except he was not stirring the pot. Paul was part of the community of believers, going to prayer meetings, sharing as he had opportunity, developing friendships, and, I think, learning his new trade, tent-making.

Then he went again to Jerusalem, but not to tell them what for. He didn't go proclaiming anything. Paul went to sit at Peter's feet for a couple of weeks and then to visit James. That's it.

Could he have preached the gospel to the crowds? You bet, but that is not what the Spirit laid on his heart at that time. His natural strengths, abilities, and his great desire to share Jesus were harnessed. It is said that meekness is power under control, and Saul, the bold, became Paul, the meek.

There comes a moment in time when you realize that how you are trying to live your Christian life is not working. You try and try and nothing, and sometimes less than nothing, which is something.

Your spouse is still resistant. You still feel that others don't get you and life should bow to you. You still fall into the same patterns of life even after prayer and fasting, and repentance and confession.

These are very critical times because you can lose your bearings. You don't know which side is up. Your assumptions about Christianity are found faulty, and you can fall several ways.

Some give up at this point and say that Christianity doesn't work. Some deconstruct, whatever that means. Others continue to go to church but go through the motions. Others stay in church and continue to beat others up with their "gifts". Some become adversarial while others go silent. All because this moment is misinterpreted.

As I said of marriage, being in relationship at the church has the potential both to expose and make whole if you hang in there with a modicum of self-awareness. You CAN fall into the grace of God like Peter and Paul did when they were exposed. You can discover the essence of Galatian's message, which is, "not I, but Christ who lives in me." That requires, however, remaining in the wilderness alone for a time, and possibly weeping bitterly.

This moment comes to all because God has a greater plan for you. For you, to become fruitful, to become great, and fill your space, you must first recognize that the engine that powers your vehicle is your own efforts. This is the reason Paul wrote about "you in Christ" and "Christ in you", with the hope that you too would repent of your own efforts and learn to walk in the power of the Spirit.

When it pleases the Lord to reveal His Son IN you, you will no longer be controlled by your passions, your personality, your natural strengths, or giftings. You will walk in the Spirit and into the awareness of your sonship. You will begin to know what being led by the Spirit is when your natural strengths are broken.

After Arabia, Paul could be in someone's face or sit in the back row. He could comfort or chastise. He could command or entreat. He could demand his rights or not. He could go forward or not move at all. His instrument was finely tuned but played by Another.

God wants to meet you in Arabia, where He can reorient your life and where you no longer need to defend Him or yourself. You will no longer beat others up or yourself. Nor will you hide from life any longer because the life that you now live in the flesh you live by the Son of God's faith, who knew He was loved and who has always loved you and has given all of Himself to, and for, you. His faith and life, not yours, will animate you.

A Christian is more than living as a forgiven sinner. God's version of Christianity is living an exchanged life. You give Him your life and He gives you His. Your inabilities for His ability. Your cluelessness for His wisdom. Your smallness for His expanse.

Watchman Nee, writing in *The Normal Christian Life*, (which I highly recommend), makes the point that the normal Christian life is not the average one. The norm or standard for living the Christian life is Christ living in you because the only person who has ever lived it is Him. And the only ones who can live it are the ones who, like Peter and Paul, have their eyes opened to their own failings and inability and then live a surrendered and exchanged life.

Questions

1. What were the key differences between Paul's behavior during his first visit to Damascus and Jerusalem after his conversion and his behavior after his time in Arabia? * According to Luke's account in Acts, what actions did Paul (Saul) take in Damascus and Jerusalem immediately after his conversion? * How did Paul's behavior change after his time in Arabia, as described in his Galatians account? *What does the chapter suggest was the cause of this change, particularly in terms of Christ being revealed "to" him versus "in" him?

2 .How did the church's response to Paul's actions in Damascus and Jerusalem reflect the impact of his reliance on his natural personality? * What specific actions did the church take in Damascus and Jerusalem to address Paul's behavior, according to Luke's account? * Why does the chapter highlight Luke's statement, "The church, therefore, indeed, had peace and grew," after Paul was sent away? * What does this suggest about the consequences of Paul's initial approach to ministry?

3. What role did Paul's time in Arabia play in his transformation, according to the chapter's interpretation of his Galatians account? * Why did Paul choose to go to Arabia instead of consulting with the apostles in Jerusalem? *What does the chapter propose happened to Paul during this time, particularly in relation to the revelation of the New Covenant? * How did this experience differ from his initial encounter with Jesus on the road to Damascus?

4. How do Paul's and Peter's experiences of self-awareness illustrate the universal need for Christians to confront their self-reliance as described in the chapters on Peter and Paul? * In the Peter chapters, how did Peter's denial of Jesus lead to a moment of exposure and self-awareness? * In the Paul chapter, how did Paul's reliance on his personality in Damascus and Jerusalem lead to his need for a wilderness experience in Arabia? * What does the comparison of these moments suggest about the role of failure or exposure in moving from a "sinnership" to a "sonship" mentality as discussed in the second Peter chapter?

5. In what ways do the wilderness experiences of Peter and Paul, as described in their respective chapters, demonstrate God's process of transforming Christians through humility and dependence on Him? * How do these experiences, along with the author's story in the second Peter chapter, highlight the importance of embracing difficult seasons as opportunities for God to reveal "Christ in you"?

Abraham-The Meta-story

I began this book by saying that this book is about meta-stories. A meta-story is an overarching narrative in which you find your own story written, and which answers the "Who am I?", the "What am I about?", the "Why do I struggle the way I do?", and the "How am I righted?" questions.

I identified these stories as Adam's, Peter's, and Abraham's. Each has been recognized in the Scriptures as a father of sorts, and as the saying goes, "like father or mother, like son or daughter." Adam and Eve are the reason both for your hopes and dreams and your struggles and disappointments because the imprint of "the glory from which they fell" has impregnated every cell of your being.

Adam's story is about God's estimation and purpose for all of mankind and how to achieve greatness. It is about the high call of God in Christ Jesus. His story is about your sonship, which was lost in the first man and found in the Second. Adam's story is about you, your intrinsic value, and your significance in the world.

It also explains the reason for your struggles and failures. The Fall left you on a road toward fulfilling your hopes and dreams, along with your desires for worth and significance. But it also left you without a roadmap or mode of transportation. In fact, it left you in an even worse place. The path was washed out, so even if you knew the destination, there was no way of getting there.

Peter's is a perfect picture of this conundrum. His life, as narrated in the gospels, is the foundation for all who comprise the church, that is, those who have left their old life behind to follow Jesus and yet are unaware that their old life hasn't left them. His is the story both of glaring blind spots which kept him from seeing his own self-righteousness and the way Jesus exposed him as "too much Simon".

Peter's story is not so much about specific sins, but about the nature that produces them. Sins are easily forgiven. Nature, however, is a different animal.

Peter's story is about doing Christianity the best way you can in the strength of your personality and giftings, and then discovering that the best you have doesn't come close.

It is about the image which you have created or adopted or accepted for yourself. Your sense of self will dictate how you do life, and Peter's image was bigger than life but was wrong. Yours may or may not be bigger than life, but it too is wrong.

So, Jesus allowed Peter, in the most exquisite way, to glimpse himself, and that began his journey into being the rock Jesus knew him to be. As with Peter and Paul, you too will be exposed. Their stories were written so you can interpret these moments correctly. Otherwise, you might give up too soon. Peter and Paul's stories help with that.

Abraham's story, however, is the meta-story of meta-stories because it describes the journey from sinnership to sonship. While Adam's story paints a glorious before and a terrible after-picture, and while Peter's continues the after-picture until Jesus shined a light on him, neither describes the way out.

Abraham's story, however, does. He, even more than Adam and Peter, is your father because Abraham is called the father of those who believe. His faith took him from Ur to Moriah, from unrighteousness to righteousness, from glory to glory, from faith to faith, and from sinnership to sonship. From his initial believing to faith's flowering, Abraham's story is written so you can walk in his steps and discover the Abrahamic blessing, which is meant for you.

Abraham's story is the story of becoming. Paul specifically wrote, in Romans 4, "that he might BECOME" because life is neither supposed to remain static nor be unfruitful. Becoming means that a change has occurred and transformation is happening.

Abraham began his journey in Ur, not knowing who he was. He ended his life with the inner certainty that he was like his Father—fruitful, multiplying and filling his space. On the mount, this was evidenced because Abraham was willing to give up all physical evidence to his fatherhood because the only evidence that he needed was the word that God spoke to him.

The word "might" in this verse should also put you on notice because this word implies uncertainty. The implication is that Abraham might NOT have become. He had to be put through his paces and go through a process in order to become. The scary thought is that you might not become the God-version of yourself, that is, unless you go through the same process.

What God purposed for you and what He imagined you to become is not a given. As I wrote earlier, image might not become likeness unless you participate in the process. It has always been "by grace, through faith." Persistent baby steps are required, and you need to get up again when you fall on your butt. You need to stay on the path that Abraham blazed.

So, if you don't know the process, you are DOA before you begin. But God has given you the story of Abraham so you can join him on your faith journey and find exceeding greatness.

Abraham's story is also about the intersection of faith and righteousness. While "accounted to him as righteousness" is often viewed as Abraham being declared righteous, a closer examination suggests that God, at that point and for the first time, highlighted and underscored Abraham's act of believing. His believing, or his faith, was accounted as right. God seemed to be saying, "YES!!! Now your faith is aligned with mine."

Others, before him, were said to be righteous, but Abraham's faith was different because it elicited, not only a response from God, but one which the Spirit insisted that it be noted because this connection of faith and righteousness is brought up again and again in Scriptures.

The assumption is that Abraham's faith, at one point, wasn't quite right, and then it was. But a casual examination of the faith Abraham exhibited, before the Genesis 15, shames most. He left all. He did exploits. He built altars and worshipped.

The surprising thing is that the rightness of his faith was NOT primarily about being right with God. Again, look at his life before this moment under the stars. He was right with God. All of these faith-works proved that alignment. This moment, however, was about becoming right with himself or becoming the person God imagined.

This "accounted as righteousness" comment, inserted by the Spirit, occurred at least a decade after he began to follow God. God visited him in Ur many years before God's righteousness was declared, so righteousness has to be more than just "being right with God". As you will see, Abraham's rightness was more about his relationship with himself than with God, though both are linked. And so, it is with you.

Paul and James deliberately connected "and it was accounted to him as righteousness" to different moments in Abraham's life, other than when it was quoted. Instead of using it as it is recorded in the Scriptures, they inserted it at two different times in his life. Rather than pointing to the Genesis 15 event,

Paul referred to the faith that Abraham exhibited in Genesis 17, and James referred to Genesis 22. They knew that becoming righteous was a journey and much more than being right with God.

Abraham's story is about discovering your identity and, from that place, living your life. This is the heart cry of every person. Who doesn't want to know the reason for you? Who doesn't want to sense their importance? Who doesn't want to know their worth? Righteousness speaks to these because righteousness is about sonship and identity.

As this story applies to you, you too are called to a greatness beyond your wildest dreams, to righteousness, and to sonship because Abraham is your father. His story is yours. Paul even wrote that "his being accounted right" was also written for you. Without question, Abraham's story is a meta-story and one which, if you are to become who God imagined, describes the path you must and will follow.

It took Abraham about 40 years and specific moments when God reiterated to Abraham who Abraham was before he arrived at Moriah, where James said that what God purposed to do in him was fulfilled. It might have taken Abraham four decades because he didn't have the advantage of having a manual to read. He was the manual, being written on the fly.

But you have a manual, if you can read yourself into his story, though it still might take decades as well. I think that one purpose for his story is that you have a clear vision and don't give up. Abraham's story is a meta-story which can be overlaid on yours, and one by which you can interpret the often, confusing times of your life. His story is to bolster your faith and cause you to hope against hope so that you too might become.

You can then both rest and press on because, in Abraham, you will find yourself in good company. He followed the Lord imperfectly to begin with, just like you. He was also as clueless as you are. But by the time the Lord finished with him, Abraham's name was lit up with as many stars as you can count, and billions upon billions more.

As you read your story in his, be attentive to the voice of God. You may hear for the first time, or possibly hear the echo of what God has been speaking to you, "You are my beloved" and "So shall YOUR seed be".

Questions

1. How is this phrase, "accounted to him as righteousness" applied by Paul in Romans 4 and by James? * How is it different than how it is originally placed in Genesis? * How does that expand the meaning of righteousness for you?

2. Abraham's story serves as a manual for believers to interpret their own confusing times. Are you willing to accept the possibility that Abraham's life into greatness is God's intent for you, and that how God grew Abraham is how He will grow you? * How could seeing your life's challenges through the lens of Abraham's journey provide clarity or encouragement during difficult seasons?

3. Peter's story reveals the challenge of confronting one's flawed self-image. How has this idea of being "exposed" by God impacted your understanding of your own identity? * Have you ever experienced a moment where your self-perception was challenged, like Peter's? How did it shape your faith or actions? * How can recognizing your "blind spots" lead to spiritual growth, as it did for Peter?

4. The chapter emphasizes that righteousness is tied to identity and son-ship, not just being "right with God." How does this perspective shift your understanding of your worth and significance? * How do you currently view your worth in light of Abraham's story of becoming? * How might embracing this identity influence the way you navigate life's challenges or pursue your purpose?

5. According to the chapter, what does Adam's story reveal about your intrinsic value and struggles?

Abraham-Abraham's Gospel

K now then that it is those of faith who are the sons of Abraham. And the Scripture, foreseeing that God would justify the Gentiles by faith, preached the gospel beforehand to Abraham, saying, "In you shall all the nations be blessed." Galatians 3:7-8

This last section of the book is written to the sons of Abraham. Paul makes it clear that more than those of his bloodline, those who walk the path of faith are the sons of Abraham, both male and female. So, you mustn't skip over Abraham's gospel because his gospel foreshadows and explains the one that Jesus proclaimed.

Everything hinges on Abraham because he introduced a whole new way to connect with God and become whole. The covenant of promise made with Abraham preceded and negated the covenant of "maybe if you try hard enough, but probably not", and points to the New Covenant which is infused with God's "I will do it". It was about making the unrighteous, righteous; the broken, whole. It was about restoring God's image in the world. It was about revealing the sons of God.

Abraham initiated the renewal of God's restorative work in the world. He was the door through which God came into the world. And what greater blessing is there than having God show up through you? Also, through Abraham, faith and faith's journey were explained.

So, if you want to know what faith looks like, look to Abraham. If you want to know how faith is sparked in your heart and how to hold onto it, look to Abraham. If you want to know what a justified and exceedingly fruitful you looks like, look to Abraham. If you want to know what you must go through to become that person, look to Abraham.

You needn't go through life clueless, and maybe you can avoid some pitfalls. As the book of Hebrews says, "These things were written for your learning that through YOUR patience and the encouragement and confidence which the Scriptures give, you might live in the absolute assurance of an expected and glorious end." (TCA)

"By grace, through faith" was Abraham's theme song. It was, for Abraham, God's initiative and his response. It was God's call and Abraham's, "Here am I." When Abraham's faith followed God's grace, things worked out. When his faith took the lead, a teachable moment followed.

And it all began with the gospel being proclaimed to Abraham. In Ur, he heard it for the first time and responded the best way he could. Over his life, Abraham was brought back to the good news of Abraham because God proclaimed it to him again and again. Then, on Moriah, this good news was depicted in graphic form because there, on the mount, God responded to Abraham's faith with a giant "Amen!".

Now, if I were to end this chapter here, you might scratch your head because the gospel of "sins forgiven and going to heaven" doesn't seem to fit into Abraham's good news. Neither does "sins forgiven" translate into the long-term, Abrahamic relationship that released the far-reaching blessing of God into the world. In fact, sin is not addressed in Abraham's story, at least in the evangelical sense. God seemed to overlook Abraham's faux pas, and, at one point, even blessed it.

The good news proclaimed to Abraham, however, got him up in the morning and got him going. Does the news of sins forgiven and going to heaven do that for you?

And how does "Christ died, was buried, and rose again" affect your everyday life if it is only talking about Jesus? What does it mean for you? The gospel, proclaimed to Abraham, was about God working through Abraham and about his significance in the world. The good news proclaimed to Abraham was about his sonship, which I defined earlier in this book as a glorious you in relationship with the Father and with a position of authority in the cosmos.

The gospel preached to Abraham is the same gospel that is proclaimed to you and about you. While the cursory meaning of the word, gospel, is good news, that meaning just gets you looking in the right direction. The gospel is the unbelievably breathtaking and an "entering a wormhole of an amazing and wonderfully new universe" sort of news which astounds and disorients. Anything less than this is just ok news.

I'm sorry but "sins forgiven and going to heaven" doesn't cut it. These are great blessings and side-benefits, but they are givens and ones which you were "born-again" into. Forgiveness is remedial and gets you to square one, with heaven, a bonus.

Again, don't hear what I am not saying. Everything God does and offers is exceedingly good news with forgiveness and heaven being the bookends of this gospel of glory. But just being a recipient and not a world-changer makes one bored and boring. This was not the gospel proclaimed to Abraham, and it is not the one being proclaimed to you. Forgiveness and heaven, though included in the package, are not the package. As I wrote in *Ephesians and All that Jazz:*

"For Him, forgiveness is such a small thing. It might seem big to you, but forgiveness, for Him, is just the beginning. It is the crack in the dam. It is a door ajar. It is a thimble you have dipped into the ocean. Yes, you hold the ocean, but not really.

Lift up your eyes. Forgiveness is the beginning ripples, alerting you to the vastness of His heart surging toward you. Your thimble cannot contain what's coming your way. The tsunami of grace is rushing in to overthrow every structure you have built to hold your life together.

Grace will undo you so you can be done right. And its waves keep coming in, doing what nit-picking and threats, timeouts, and punishment can't. They change you. While you play in its surf, His grace changes you."

The gospel preached to Abraham was proclaimed by the God of Glory Himself. Stephen gave the Pharisees a history lesson in the book of Acts, when he began his sermon with "the God of Glory appeared to our Father Abraham." I don't think that God had to say a word because good news filled that space. Glory appeared to him, and what better news could there be?

The good news, being expressed at that moment, was a glory that beckoned Abraham from sinnership to sonship, from his own meager glory to one he couldn't put into words. This news was about blessing, increase, and glory.

While Abraham's shortcomings were exposed, he didn't need to be told about them. There was no need because glory stood before him, calling him to leave his darkened understanding of God and himself and to go into a land yet undiscovered.

Stephen said that it was not the God of judgment who appeared to Abraham, pointing out his faults, even though he had faults. "You helped your dad make idols. That makes you an idol-enabler, and I can't have anything to do with you unless you repent and ask me into your heart."

No, this is the same God who walked with Adam in the garden. It was the God of glory, inviting him into a relationship that would focus the spotlight on Abraham and glorify him. He is the same God beckoning you. Abraham realized at that moment that the glory from which he had fallen was now within reach if he left where he was and journeyed to a place he did not know.

"In you, all will be blessed" is what Abraham heard. The blessed God promised to make Abraham a blessed Abraham, just like He promised to make Adam, a blessed Adam, just like He promised to make Paul a blessed Paul, and just like He has promised to make you a blessed you. A recipient of blessing, for sure, but more than that, a conduit of God's increased blessing into the world. They were, and you are, called to be a world-changer.

Now reread these words slowly. "In you, all will be blessed." These words were the good news preached beforehand to Abraham. Now replace this "you" directed toward Abraham with YOU because this is the same gospel being proclaimed to you. Do you hear it?

"In me? No, that can't be. That news, preached to Abraham, was referring to Jesus because it's in Jesus that all nations will be blessed." You are right about that, but the problem with this sort of superficial thinking is that this same Jesus who resided in Abraham's loins now lives in you.

If anything, Jesus resides in you in greater measure than He did in Abraham. So, what else can the gospel mean and be, but "In me, in you, and collectively in us, all nations will be blessed" because Jesus lives in you? This is the gospel you are called to believe.

The blessing that fills Christ fills you, waiting to be released into your world. Paul wrote, "For in him the whole fullness of deity dwells bodily, and you have been filled in him." Don't read over this verse. Read it again slowly. You filled. You filled, with Him. You filled IN the One who fills all things. You and I do the Scriptures and the Spirit a disservice when these words are casually read because these words house your destiny.

It means that you don't know squat, nor do I. It means that it's time to cry out to God for revelation. Quite possibly, the reason the world has been kicking the church's butt is that we have neither heard this gospel nor taken the good news to its natural and supernatural conclusions.

Now do you see why Paul prayed that God would give you "the Spirit of wisdom and of revelation in the knowledge of him"? The Spirit is the One who practically unfolds what He knows of the One He knows intimately to longing hearts to the end that they know how to navigate life because they intimately know Jesus also.

The good news is directed toward you, and, like Abraham, you, are called to respond in faith and journey from the land of "I am not" into the land of "I am". "Yes, in ME, all nations will be blessed." As I look at my family, my peeps, my work, my ministry, which comprise my world, they all will be impacted by God through me because Christ lives in me.

Paul believed this gospel for himself. He told the Romans that when he came, he would bring the fullness of the blessing of God with him. Paul lived the Abrahamic gospel. He knew who he was and also knew what and Whom he carried.

Paul knew that God resided in him, along with every blessing that heaven contained. Where did his understanding of being God's blessing container come from? This understanding came from hearing Abraham's gospel and believing it for himself— "In you, Paul, all nations will be blessed".

This blessing, which is the good news of the glory of God, was released through Abraham and then fully revealed in Christ. It was then proclaimed by Paul with the hope that all those who would hear and believe Paul's gospel would also be blessed in Abraham's blessing.

This is the exceedingly good news that is proclaimed to you, and the good news you are to proclaim to others. Only as you begin to believe Abraham's gospel can you leave your sinnership mentality behind, follow his footsteps, and discover what it means to be a son of God.

My prayer is that you begin the last part of this book by believing the gospel. As we will soon see, it was over a decade before Abraham finally believed the good news about himself. He, however, had to figure it out on his own (with the help of God), so a decade is understandable. Hopefully, it might not take you that long because the universe is waiting for the unveiling of the sons of God.

Questions

1. The author states that Abraham's "In you, all will be blessed" is directed toward you, not only because you are his child, but because Christ lives in you. How does this sit with you? Explain. What struggle might you have to embrace this new paradigm? What would your life look like if you truly embraced "In YOU, all nations will be blessed"? And can you begin to believe this?

2. Why might the traditional evangelical focus on "sins forgiven and going to heaven" fall short of the fuller gospel message presented in the text? Does the good news that you believe motivates you to get out of bed in the morning?

3. How does the idea that the gospel is about you becoming a "world-changer" rather than just a recipient of blessings influence your perspective on your role in your community? Reflecting on Paul's confidence that he carried God's blessing, how might believing that you are a blessing container influence your interactions with family, friends, or coworkers?

4. What have you have sensed about your life in that past that was something much bigger? What does it do for you to know that these thoughts and dreams were not fanciful, but God-planted? Can you resurrect them and tell God that you believe?Knowing that there is a process you will go through to become, how might reading the rest of this book and understanding the process help steady your faith?

Abraham-Conversion

C onversion is not formulaic, and neither are there typical conversions. They come in all shapes and sizes. But a couple of components are always present, which are an honest assessment of one's own life, coupled with an honesty toward God.

Conversion is also a lifelong process because what is being converted is your understanding of God, yourself, and life. You hold onto many things that you think hold your life together. Your identity is wrapped up in these things. So, it takes time to figure this out. While there is a moment in time when the light turns on, conversion is a dimmer switch.

You give yourself to the Lord, but you are unaware that you are also giving Him a bunch of stuff of which you are unaware. You still carry hidden baggage, which at some point will be dumped out on the floor. You, like Lazarus, come out of your grave with your graveclothes still on.

The rest of your life, God helps you unwrap and usually does this through people around you who, at times, are annoying. Whether it is because of a lack of awareness, pride, fear, defensiveness, or an unwillingness to give up everything (even though you often tell the Lord that you do), conversion takes time because you don't know what "everything" is. Nor do you know what you are converting from or to. It is that developmental darkness thing.

But as you take baby steps (those are the only steps that you can take), God steps up in you and works in you what you desire but can't accomplish. And He is excited for every step you take, as He was with your father Abraham.

Conversion always begins with a connection, that is, connecting with yourself at some level, and with that awareness, connecting with God. God, by the way, has made it easy to connect because He is the one who wants it the most.

Watchman Nee, who was used by God as an evangelist both individually and corporately, had three principles which governed him as he engaged unbelievers. (This works, as well, for unbelieving believers.) He asked this question,

"What is the minimum needed for conversion?" As he examined the Scriptures, he found three things at play.

First, he discovered that Jesus is the friend of sinners and freely touches the unclean, drawing to Himself all who feel their need. Then he recognized that the Spirit's outpouring was upon ALL flesh, not just Christian flesh, as Peter first prophesied at Pentecost. The Spirit is only a hair's breadth away from everyone and pushing on their heart. All that is required then is a crack in the dam for the Spirit to rush in and begin the work of conversion.

That crack, for Watchman Nee, was an honest heart. He saw many who had no time for God give their hearts to Him. When a person would say, "I am not interested," Nee would invite them to tell that to the Lord. That honest exchange brought the Spirit's conviction and a desire to connect with God.

He even saw a former professor, who was an atheist, find faith. "How can I tell a something that doesn't exist that I don't believe it exists?" With a little encouragement, the professor told God that he didn't believe in Him or His existence. Within a couple weeks, the rest was history.

How did this happen for Abraham? We don't know exactly, but for him, it was dramatic. Having God show up on your doorstep would stop anyone in their tracks. But how did this happen for you? More than likely, you were also arrested, but in a more subtle way.

Not sure if Abraham was like Nathaniel under a fig tree, thinking about God, or rather indifferent before God showed up. Not sure if he was a Saul who became Paul, raging about this or that, or just following the crowd. Not sure whether Abraham was aware of his brokenness or not. All we know is that God appeared to him.

And we don't know what that looked like either. It seems that, for most of us, Abraham's experience has not been ours; that is, God showing up in all of His brilliance and giving specific direction. Jesus said that only a few are chosen this way, that is, with an exclamation point. Most are called with question marks. "Are you going to catch my drift?", the Spirit asks.

Jesus appeared in the flesh to over 500 after His resurrection, but for most, He appears in non-physical, tangential ways and often disguised as roadblocks. Regardless, the only way that you come to the Lord is by realizing that your life is not as glorious as you thought and that God has the fix or the glory that you desire.

Abraham realized something about God and himself in that first encounter. Perfection stood before him, and instantly, Abraham's entire life was put in a different light. No one needed to talk with him about sin because glimpsing perfection revealed his imperfections.

But this glory didn't just point out the negatives, God's glory opened Abraham's eyes to the glory lost in Eden and called him. This is the beauty and wonder of God. He flashes his excellencies like a lady of the night flashes her leg. It stirs a primordial urge that beckons. (I know that I am writing from a male perspective, but that's the only one I have. But you know what I mean.)

It creates an awareness, stirs a need, and it becomes an urgency. You know that what is being offered, you don't have, but you want and need it. And when you see His leg, you know that He is inviting you to taste and see. The glimpse creates a belief that you can have what He has, so, in the encounter, comes faith.

"Faith comes", Paul wrote. Faith comes by sensing something of God, that He has come and is willing and within reach. For Abraham, the word he heard, as he beheld glory, was "leave and go", which was code for "come". The glory that Abraham beheld was calling him from his own glories, which by comparison were garbage, to a glory not seen since before Adam's fall.

And for you and me, what better leg, what better glory, is there than the resurrected Christ? The man, Christ Jesus, in His rising, destroyed every iota of everything which have limited and marginalized your existence. The resurrection is calling you to an eternal potential because what God has done for the One, He has done for all. And the Spirit is telling you to "leave and go".

So, let's look at Abraham's conversion in the attempt to understand your own. And as you will see, his conversion was not just an event, but a process that unfolded through a series of events.

You first meet Abram in Genesis 11. Terah, his dad, had led Abram, Sarai, his wife, and one of Terah's grandsons out from Ur. They came to Haran and set up camp. Then in Haran, Terah dies. At this point, God appeared to Abram and told him to leave his family and country with a promise of greatness and fatherhood.

But without Stephen's history lesson, which Luke recorded in Acts 7, you would have an incomplete picture of Abraham because this is not when the God of glory first appeared to Abram. And, in this discovery, you find someone like yourself, one who follows imperfectly while trying to do your best.

At some point, years before, Luke wrote that "The God of glory appeared to our father Abraham when he was in Mesopotamia BEFORE HE LIVED IN HARAN and said to him, 'Go out from your land and from your kindred and go into the land that I will show you.'" Yet, we find that Abraham did not leave his family of origin as he was told. In fact, Terah, his father, took the lead.

So, the picture is this: Abram, upon encountering God, tells his dad about the experience. In that culture, sons, regardless of their age, were under the authority of their father or grandfather, whoever the patriarch was at the time. Abram either convinced Terah or Terah realized something remarkable had happened with his son and then took over. Terah said, "Let's go," and Abram didn't buck the system.

I am amazed at the way God flows with the situation without getting His nose out of joint. It was not His plan to have the whole family leave. In fact, it was His plan for Abram to leave his entire old life behind so he could come to know himself in a new way. This required Abram to distance himself both metaphorically and physically from his extended family, however close they were.

Your identity is wrapped up in your family of origin. It could be bad or good. It seems that it was good for Abraham. It was, at least, comfortable and familiar, so he didn't have the desire, the courage, or the faith to leave. But he left the best way he could, and in that leaving, God was pleased.

Your old identity, like Lazarus' graveclothes, clings to you. It is wrapped up in your culture, your work, your family, your friends, your music, your routines, your lifestyle, your political persuasions, your past, and a whole lot more "yours". These things define you. It is the air that you breathe.

So, the journey into the "land I will show you" is dicey because it is hard to stand outside of yourself to identify those things that give you your sense of self or identity. So, you don't know how ensnared you are or by what. And initially, you might not know why you need to separate yourself from these, but the call is to leave.

God's plan behind your leaving is about His glory and yours, about His identity and yours. Clothing yourself with this new identity cannot happen until the old clothes are removed. But without knowing how bad your clothes smell, you keep wearing them until, by God's grace, they fall off. Sometimes your "dad" just needs to die. That's what happened with Abraham.

So, Abraham continued his journey. God wanted Abraham to distance himself from the environment, which corroborated who he thought he was. He had to remove himself because, unbeknownst to him, that culture kept squeezing him into its mold.

To become the person God imagined, Abraham needed to know himself in a new way which was not going to happen where he was, even with the life-altering revelation of God. This was going to happen in the land that God was going to show him.

This is a large reason for the body of believers. The church is many things, but as it relates to your journey into wholeness, it is both the path you are to take and your promised destination where you discover both who you are and the reason for you. This is why joining and committing yourself to the church is so important, and why the devil attacks it and discourages you.

Paul said that he knew no one after the flesh, not even himself. He came to know himself as a new, never-before-seen creation, that is, a son, which is why the church is paramount. The church is the gathering of sons. There is a knowing of yourself that also goes beyond anything you can imagine, and this is discovered with those who are heading in the same direction.

God is calling you to know yourself as He knows you, and that is, in the context of a Father/son relationship. This is why you are called to leave and join with those who are following the same call. This is the journey from sinnership into sonship. This is conversion.

Since God knows the pull of the past, He keeps calling, and all He needs, or even wants, is a step. So, when Terah died, God appeared again and said, "Leave." Again, no upbraiding or chiding. No, "This is the last time that I'm telling you." Just "it's time to hit the road." But this time He added, "And I will make you".

When God first arrests you, there might not be much more information than "leave", but as you go, God begins to color the edges. Most of the time, the specifics of your life are filled in after you leave. The general call of BEING a son morphs into specific DOINGS which only a son, like you, can do.

"And I will make of you a great nation, and I will bless you and make your name great so that you will be a blessing. I will bless those who bless you, and him who dishonors you I will curse, and in you all the families of the earth shall be blessed." This call to Abraham is Adam's reframed, that is, to be fruitful, become great, and fill the earth.

It is God's call and His deep desire that you know that you are blessed and that you are a blessing to your world. God's call is for you to know that you are loved, significant, and safe because only then can you image and represent God to the world.

The call to be like God was first expressed in their dialogue when they agreed that "In Our image and into Our likeness" was man's ultimate purpose. But after Adam's failure, the Father found a son in Abraham who would in time become a father like Him.

While there are specifics for each person, your primary purpose is to become like the Father because that is who a son becomes. And the process for Abraham was as much an inward journey as an outward one. Before the world would come to see who he had become, Abraham first had to know, within himself, that person.

So, God spoke into Abraham, his destiny, and if you notice, God did not say much more than that to Abraham over his life. He just came back to sonship and fruitfulness and greatness. Though God would tweak Abraham's understanding as time went by, God only said a few things to him. God will also speak only a few things to you about your life over your lifetime. He then will look over His word to perform it.

In talking with other believers, I find that this is a most disconcerting and puzzling topic. For example, if I asked you, "What has God planted in you that He desires to blossom," what would you say? I know that, as many read this, eyes glaze over and stare blankly at the page, having no clue. I know because I have been there.

But if you are a child of Abraham, then not only what God did in him, but how God led him is exactly how He leads you. You will and must sense a few specifics over time, but what is most important and the thrust of this book, is that you hear and believe what He spoke to Adam, to Abraham, to His Son, and now to all his sons (meaning you), "You are my beloved, in whom I am delighted."

As you leave your current mindset and journey into the land of the beloved, you will begin to know the specifics. But along the way, as John wrote, you will need to be the one who persuades your own heart before Him. That is what Abraham did, as you will see. And why did John say that you need to persuade yourself? Because, like Abraham, you don't believe the unbelievably good news about you. So, this is a large part of conversion.

Jude wrote the same thing. "Keep YOURSELF in the love of God". This is what the journey of leaving and going into looks like, that is, convincing yourself that you ARE loved, that you ARE significant, and that you ARE safe, even though that might not be evident to others or yourself. A large part of "keeping yourself" is tied to confession.

For most, confession has a narrow and limited definition because it is typically tied to the lacks and missteps of your life. Confession has been largely about sin. This type of confession is important, however, because it describes the leaving part.

But once you have left and are on your way, confession becomes an important part of your "going into". You are to confess your sonship. You are to confess the "it is finished" part of salvation. God says, "You are My beloved, in whom I am well pleased", into the caverns of your being with the hope that its echo will find its way out of your mouth.

John wrote that you overcome, not just by what Jesus did, but by giving voice to it in both word and deed. "They have conquered him by the blood of the Lamb and by the WORD of their testimony, for they loved not their lives even unto death."

Confession, in the Greek, means to SAY the same thing. I emphasized the word, "say", because it means to speak, not just to think. Obviously, this should be in your thinking as well, but you are called to rebut thoughts that negate God's thoughts with words.

This is what Jesus did when he was confronted by the devil. He SPOKE truth. He confessed His Sonship and authority when He said, "Go away." Paul also talks about taking every one of your thoughts captive, that is, not letting them run wild. You are to subdue and rule over your thought life. and one way to do that is to speak to the "I am not" that attacks you with the "I am" of the word.

"I am loved." "I am safe." "My life and what I am doing is important." "What God has purposed for my life is already accomplished and it is glorious! I don't need to fret, just follow." These are to be your confessions.

God's words need to come out of your mouth. Paul confirmed this when he asked the question, "What shall we SAY to these things?" before he gave you the things to say. Just thinking will not cut it. You are to SAY, "If God is for me." You are to SAY, "Who can bring a charge against me?" You are to rebut the circumstances which seem to say otherwise, by SAYING to them, "What can separate me from the love of God?"

When you feel unloved, are you giving voice to your feelings, not talking at all, or are you saying both within and out loud, the same thing as God? "I am God's great delight." "I am the focus of His attention." "He can't get enough of me." "I have a glorious end." Is this your confession?

If it is, you are on your way. If not, you are still hanging around Haran waiting for your dad to die. In time, hopefully, he will, but it would be better if you would put a knife in it yourself by confessing the truth about yourself.

"Go, and I will make you," is God's call on your life. This is the journey from sinnership into sonship. This is what you are being converted from and being converted to, and it begins with one step, followed by another, and then another.

Questions

1. The chapter identifies honesty with oneself and God as key to conversion. Reflect on a moment when you honestly assessed your need and connected with God. How did this spark your faith journey, and how can embracing these components guide your ongoing walk with God?

2. Conversion is described as a lifelong process of reshaping your identity, not just behavior. How does viewing conversion as gradual encourage patience with your growth? * Do you envision the end result as a "glorious you"? * What specific aspect of your identity are you currently wrestling with?

3. The chapter likens old identities or "graveclothes" to baggage that needs removing, often through others. What personal "graveclothes" (e.g., past habits, cultural ties) do you recognize in your life? Who in your church community could you ask for help in shedding these?

4. The author said that confessing is a large part of leaving and entering. Is confession, as the author explains it, a new concept for you—that is, you speaking truth to yourself more than confessing sin? * How comfortable are you declaring truth to yourself, and how can this become more operative in your life? What specific things do you need to begin confessing?

5. The church is portrayed as both the path and destination for discovering your sonship identity. How has your engagement with the Christian community shaped your sense of self? * What step could you take to deepen your involvement and uncover more of God's vision for you?

Abraham-The Faith Stage

I began this book by saying that if the church had a better definition of righteousness, I could have titled it, "From Unrighteousness to Righteousness. The Story of Becoming." But since righteousness is one of those Christian words that, for most, have a book definition with little internal meaning, I didn't go there.

Righteousness, however, is one of the great, if not the greatest, themes of the Bible. Paul, after declaring that all were un-right due to missing the bullseye of God's glory (which is His essence and image), said that we have been freely justified or made right and restored to that image by the redemptive act of Jesus.

Being made right is typically defined as being right with God. While this is both true and exceedingly great news, it seems a little sterile. Book definitions always are.

The definition of being righteous, however, is not found in a dictionary. It is discovered in a narrative and, more specifically, in Abraham's story because he was the first to have his faith declared right and, by so doing, discovered that he was right also. His believing had something to do with his being declared right.

While there were those before him who were said to be righteous before Abraham, this was the first time someone's faith captured God's attention and elicited a response. But if you have followed his story, Abraham had already been a "Christian" for over a decade and was already "right with God." So, the book definition of righteousness must give way to the shades, the hues, and to the texture and depth of Abraham's story.

To review, before this moment, Abraham met God in a way that few have. He obeyed God and left the comfort of his home to go to a land he didn't know. Abraham built altars and worshipped. He let Lot choose the best land for himself and then took a few men to defeat the armies that had captured the same Lot. who took advantage of him.

On top of that, Abraham was the first one mentioned to give the tithe and, in doing so, the first to recognize the pre-existent Christ. Then he refused to take anything from the king of Sodom, who is the picture of the ruler of this world. I don't think that many have credentials like this. So, if Abraham wasn't righteous before Genesis 15, what was he? And if Abraham wasn't righteous at this point, who is?

Genesis 15 is where the phrase, "it was accounted to him as righteousness", is first stated, and this was, at least, a decade after he left his home country. There was something about this moment that brought an expression of God's approval. Not that God didn't approve of Abraham before, but this moment brought an "At last! Now we can get down to business" from God.

The business at hand was Abraham becoming righteous, or right, or the person God imagined, or someone who was to become just like Him. In the Genesis 15 encounter, God was not concerned about who or what Abraham thought of Him. As already stated, Abraham had proved his faith with his actions, and even this Genesis 15 exchange revealed an honesty and relationship with God that few have.

Abraham was called out under the stars to believe what God had told him many years before about Abraham himself, and now, under the stars, Abraham finally did. God was concerned about what Abraham believed about himself. This was the moment that God accounted him righteous, and, in so doing, God expanded the meaning of righteousness. It's about a lifetime, not a moment. It was about Abraham himself, and not just about God.

Righteousness has two legs, with one being faith in who God says He is, and the other one, believing who God says you are. He, your Father, and you, His son. But many Christians find themselves hopping around on one leg, wondering why the Christian thing doesn't work. Only an active believing that explores, pursues, and presses into both will allow you to walk.

Abraham's encounter began with the Lord getting out into the open, the unbelief which was hidden in Abraham's heart. Your unbelief must also be exposed before faith can be implanted. Honesty works both for those who don't know the Lord and for those who do. "I am your reward, Abraham." "No, you're not because I'm not who You said I am. I don't have the child that You promised me. I am not a father."

God has various ways to get what you are harboring out in the open, and usually it manifests as a complaint. Complaining is ok, if you are open to its counterpoint, which is God's big "but".

"But" is one of the most powerful words in any language. It can change the direction of your life. It can bring God into your situation or keep Him away because what follows your "but" is what you really believe. "God loves me, but I'm not going to make it" is vastly different and expresses a vastly different reality than "Life sucks, but God loves me."

So, Abraham heard God's "but" —which was, "So shall your seed be" and believed. The words which he heard decades earlier finally sank in, and therefore he was declared righteous. This began a faith journey into God's call to be fruitful, to multiply, and fill the earth. Abraham began to live life by faith and not by sight.

Your definition of righteousness needs to expand for you to expand your definition of God and yourself, and to grow into your calling as a son. To be declared right in the Abrahamic sense, you must come to the place where you agree with God about yourself.

"You are my beloved in whom I am well pleased" is your identity and the definition of righteousness. Your identity is not "I am righteous, but." Any other mentality is rooted in your own understanding and is pride, even if it is clothed with a humble, "sinner-saved-by-grace" sackcloth.

As Abram's dad needed to die before Abraham could go into the land promised him, so, a "sinner-saved-by-grace" paradigm might need to die as well. Or maybe it has already died or outlived its usefulness, and the church is dragging around a cadaver. That body needs to be buried because when Jesus arose, all that was attached to sin, including the sinnership mentality, was left behind, and a brand new, never-seen-before humanity arose.

A "sinner saved by grace" theology is a large reason many Christians don't know how to go on because they are entangled in these chains. Paul never wrote to saintly sinners or to sinnerly saints. He wrote to saints who, at times and for whatever reason, hadn't lived up to their calling.

You need to repent, not only of your sins, but even more, of your sinnership mentality. Unless you believe that you who have confessed Christ are already right in yourself as a son, you will never become right. When Jesus said, "According to your faith, be it unto you," He also meant this. You have a part to play in your future, and that is to learn to walk by faith.

If you don't come to the place that your father Abraham did, that is, hearing and believing for yourself the glorious gospel of your belovedness, you will, like Abraham, harbor resentment and wonder why God hasn't done whatever for you. You might beat yourself up. You might take it out on others. You might deflect with self-deprecating humor. You might give up. You might quietly go through the motions.

There are as many ways to deal with disappointment with God and with yourself, as there are people. But God's answer is to get that out in the open, so He can take you out under the stars. A friend of mine actually encountered Jesus while effing Him out under the stars. God just desires honesty.

But maybe, just maybe, you need to take YOURSELF out under the stars and say to YOURSELF, "This is MY influence. This is MY significance. In Christ, I am more than the few stars which I can count. Now bring out the James Webb telescope and keep counting. I might now be getting close."

Is that what you believe about yourself? If not, then you may be right with God, but not right in the Biblical sense. You are not right or righteous until you believe the unbelievably good news about yourself, which was the good news preached to Abraham.

As with Abraham, believing without physical evidence was the start of his journey into becoming a son like the Father. The perfect seed of righteousness, which is the seed of sonship, was planted. The process had begun. However, even though God declared Abraham right, he wasn't yet holding a child.

This is why Abraham's "becoming" story was comprised of the three stages that Abraham went through to become the father God imagined. Genesis 15 ended the first stage, which was the faith stage. Before this moment, Abraham was an unbelieving believer, that is, one who believed God's estimation of God, but not God's estimation of himself.

For Abraham, it took over a decade. Hopefully, it won't take that long for you. Most Christians haven't heard that the gospel is unbelievably good news about them, but now you have. You can sing, "I am a child of God" on Sunday and hold onto that on Monday and Tuesday and Wednesday because it is the truth.

Genesis 15 began Abraham's journey toward an inward and quietly confident knowing that he was like God. This first stage is the believing part and the fun part. To sense God's pleasure is wonderful.

To have the heavens open and hear God's approval creates a rush of excitement. To have a flash of insight into your destiny is exhilarating. Being at church and being caught up in the moment, well, there is nothing like it. That God would make you aware that you are His delight and has a huge plan for you is both humbling and thrilling.

But Monday morning comes. And what do you do with that? Life remains a grind, and the surge of Sunday gives way to the worry of the week. The time and distance between the seed and the fruit is the process that we now want to examine because this part of your journey can tamp down your enthusiasm.

What follows the faith stage is the hope stage, where that thing that God has purposed to do, doesn't happen, at least, according to your timeline. But before we do that, let's look at the New Testament and see how it says the same thing about growing into righteousness.

Questions

1. The chapter challenges traditional views of righteousness as a lifelong journey of becoming. How has this perspective shifted your understanding of righteousness? * How does seeing it as a process rather than a moment encourage you in your faith journey?

2. Righteousness involves faith in who God is and who He says you are. Which of these "two legs" do you find harder to embrace, and why? * How might balancing both impact your daily walk as a Christian, particularly in living out your calling?

3. God exposed Abraham's unbelief to implant faith, a process vital for growing in righteousness. What doubts about your significance or belovedness do you need to bring before God? * How does this reflect God's approach to growing your faith today?

4. Affirming your God-given significance, like taking yourself "out under the stars," may feel bold. What would it look like for you to declare, "This is my influence"? * Are you willing to embrace this practice to counter doubts about your worth?

5. The chapter critiques the "sinner-saved-by-grace" mentality as limiting. How does embracing your identity as God's beloved son or daughter free you from this mindset? * What practical step could you take to live from this new identity?

Abraham-The Faith Stage in the New Testament

For each stage of becoming, I will highlight a couple of parts of the New Testament to corroborate the understanding that Abraham's life is a meta-story about the journey of becoming the person God imagined and about laying out the stages that you must go through to become unimaginably fruitful.

Augustine said, "The New is in the Old concealed. The Old is in the New revealed," and there is no better example of this than the Parable of the Sower being overlaid on Abraham's story.

The Parable of the Sower is Abraham's life retold by the Sower Himself. Each point to the other and expands their meaning. Both are about a seed being planted. Both are about the challenges to becoming fruitful. Both are about the process. Both are about the potential for amazing fruitfulness.

It should be little wonder that this is the only parable which Jesus calls His own because it is singularly His story. He was the seed sown who let His roots drink deeply of eternity while the sun baked the ground. He was the seed that fell into ground and died. He also is the resurrected vine that allows each of His branches to bear much fruit. The Adamic mandate for exponential fruitfulness, and the filling of all things, found its fulfillment in Jesus.

He also called it the "Parable of the Sower" because He is the invested Sower. He is the word sown, with you being the soil. You are His garden. You are the return on His investment. You and Jesus have a symbiotic and mutually beneficial relationship.

The parable can be read in many ways and is often interpreted as descriptive and almost fatalistic, that is, describing the different types of soil that a person is. While this is instructive, it is better understood as a narrative describing the path to becoming fruitful and the various threats faced along the way. It is the roadmap toward your future you.

The Sower's parable is not fatalistic because Jesus said, "Those who have ears to hear, let them hear." So, if you are resistant to His word, you can change. If you have buried your dreams, they can be resurrected. If you are clueless, you can be clued in. The seed has the power to transform anyone who receives it, so the parable describes the three challenges that you must address and the three stages the seed must pass through to reach its full potential.

The seed, let me remind you, is the unbelievably good news about you. The good news of Jesus is the good news of you because a resurrected and glorified Jesus means a resurrected and glorified you.

For most, it is easy to receive and believe the bad news about you, but the seed that Jesus sows is the good news about you. That is why this parable is so important, because you can, as a Christian, reject what Jesus is sowing and not know it.

While there are depths to explore in this parable, my intent is only to highlight a few points to get you thinking about how to recognize and engage the good news of God's word, which is the seed. If I can get you thinking about the word in a new way and its relationship to you, I have done my job.

Make no mistake, the story of Abraham and the story of the soil are one and the same, and they are your story. Both talk about how the seed interacts with the soil. So, how you hear the word, how you hold on to the word when the sun comes out, and how you deal with distractions will define your life. It is all about the primacy of the word.

The Sower's parable and Abraham's life say that the path to fruitfulness is predictable and includes the same developmental challenges. This is good news because you have a way both to see the end from the beginning and fit your life into a larger narrative. It is hard to interpret what happens in the confusing moments of your life without this.

The other good news is that the seed has no problem producing with the right conditions, and that you are the right medium. With the right conditions, it will do the rest. The right conditions, however, are your responsibility. The purpose of both stories is to show you your potential, your challenges, and then give you tools to address them.

And as it relates to the first soil, hardened ground will not grow plants because the seed doesn't have a chance. Unless a seed can penetrate the caked surface, it is just devil's food. The soil must receive the seed. This is the initial believing stage.

If you have been tracking with me, the seed that I am NOT talking about is your belief in God, though this applies as well. If you have been reading this far, that is a given, because you have already opened your heart to Jesus.

The seed I am talking about is the same seed that Adam disbelieved, and that Abraham believed after he first disbelieved. That seed is the unbelievably good news about you, that is, you, becoming God-like and glorifying Him by multiplying exponentially and filling your space with your unique giftings and personality.

The first soil describes the condition of your heart when you become a Christian. Yes, your heart is softened and humbled because it has received the good news of God's salvation. You have been saved FROM something but aren't aware what you are being saved TO. You also bring into your new life some of the crustiness of the old life.

The hardened pathway is the assumptions and beliefs about life and yourself that you brought into your relationship with the Lord, just like you did in your marriage. You don't know what those are, until, after your honeymoon, your spouse's assumptions and beliefs collide with your own. What you bring of yourself up the aisle also walks down the aisle, even though you made promises.

What passes through regeneration are all the ways that you had protected yourself and projected your strengths before you said, "Yes," to the Lord. What passes through regeneration is your unconscious perception of yourself, which animated you before regeneration.

The pathway heart is the first obstacle because it is your default position. It has been walked on for years, with each step hardening your perception of self. Again, it doesn't matter if your image is healthy or not, it doesn't come close to God's perception of you. This was Simon Peter's heart when he encountered Jesus. And it is yours.

Each time you have felt unloved and under-appreciated, each time you have felt that your life hasn't amounted to much, another step tamps down the soil of your heart. Every time you think that you are better than someone else. . . crunch. When "Oops, I did it again" happens. . . stomp. Each success or failure confirms your faulty assessment of yourself.

So, when the "You are My beloved who excites Me" seed is sown, the crust of "Yeah, that can't be right" or "I've heard that before" rejects it. Or the crust of "I'm good, so I don't need it" dismisses it. And since "I am not worthy" fits so much better than "I am His beloved", you remain an unbelieving believer.

While the direction of your life has changed, the soil of your heart has not yet been tilled. Like a neural pathway, your patterns of thought are habitual, and they unconsciously measure any thought about yourself against your own. The good news of an amazing you will not get past the watchful dragons, which Jesus describes as the first soil.

Jesus' answer to this condition is an honest heart. Only painful honesty and vulnerability will loosen the soil enough to allow you to take in God's estimation of yourself. God had to get Abraham's assessment of himself out in the open before He could take him out under the stars.

Sometimes the pathway is so hard, only a jackhammer will work. But this is your starting point—acknowledging that you don't believe God's estimation of yourself and then looking at the stars long enough to have the word of God's amazing grace penetrate.

You must also do the continual hard work of combating every thought which is contrary to this good news. And it is hard work because the ground IS hard and because no one else can do this for you.

You must find a way to soften your own heart to put yourself in a position to believe. This, at times, requires prolonged effort. Paul called it a work of faith and a labor of love for a reason.

You have to love yourself enough to take yourself in hand and lecture yourself. You might be pretty good at lecturing others, but you are the one who needs to be told what's up, and only you can do that effectively.

Jeremiah likened the word of God and your heart to a hammer upon a rock. When a hammer first hits a rock, it might not seem like anything has happened, even after the second, third, or fourth blow. But within, little fissures form until it finally breaks apart.

His word is as effective as a hammer. Your heart is sometimes as hard as a rock. The question is, "Which will win out?" Hopefully, both, when you finally believe. When, regardless of your feelings or circumstances, you keep agreeing with the Lord that you are loved, significant, and safe, the pathway soil will become soft enough for the seed to germinate.

These stages are also seen in how the New Testament handles the phrase, "and it was accounted to him as righteousness." Four times this verse is used in the New Testament. The first time this phrase is used is in the beginning of Romans 4, where Paul begins to argue for a righteousness that is based on believing and not on doing, and then by pointing to Abraham's life.

The other three times this phrase is used in the epistles point to these same three stages found in Abraham's life and in the Parable of the Sower—the stages of faith, hope, and love. You will find this phrase used in Galatians 3, then at the end of Romans 4, and finally in James 2. While God spoke this word only once in Genesis, that is, when Abraham first believed the good news about himself, both Paul and James rightly apply this phrase to other times in his life.

In the book of Galatians, Paul contrasts trying to become right by your own efforts with believing that God has already made you right through Jesus's redemptive act. He ties this phrase to the working of miracles. Besides not being able, in your own strength, to raise the dead, the act of raising the dead is not a process. There is an immediacy to the gifts of the spirit. You don't wait for years to see the body come to life. It opens its eyes and sits up, or it doesn't.

There is also an immediacy to righteousness upon your initial believing in whom God declares you to be. That is what happened to Abraham under the stars. You believe who God says you are, and God says, "Done." Jesus, by the way, has already said, "Done" when, on the cross, He declared that it was finished. You and I and all of creation are just playing "catch up".

Abraham did not believe before God took him out under the stars, but once he did believe, God said, "Now you are." A seed either penetrates the ground or not. The seed which housed all that God had imagined for Abraham was received, and the One who sees the end from the beginning said, "righteous", even though there were years before righteous Abraham came into clear focus on the mount.

And so, it is with you. Believing that you are His beloved son and standing in all the perfections of Christ, all the while you know the mess that you are, is your starting point. God sees the seed of His word in the soil of your heart and says, "I see the harvest already". God also walks by faith.

But now, as with Abraham, you face a new challenge as you enter the hope stage. Here the sun comes out. Here you will wait and wonder why that thing you have sensed of God hasn't happened. As you began the faith stage as an unbelieving believer, you also begin this stage as an unhoping hopeful.

Questions

1. The Parable of the Sower is presented as a roadmap for spiritual growth through developmental challenges. How does this perspective reshape your view of your faith journey? * What specific challenge in your life could you approach as part of this fruitful process?

2. Hardened soil represents assumptions or past experiences that resist God's good news about you. Can you identify ways your heart may still be hardened by self-perceptions (e.g., "I'm not worthy")? * Why might it be easier to believe negative views of yourself, and how can you soften your heart to receive God's estimation?

3. In Galatians 3, Paul links righteousness to the immediacy of your faith being declared right when you believe what God declares about you. What does this suggest about the journey of faith? * How can trusting that God sees you as complete, despite your ongoing journey, strengthen your faith?

4. The concept that God counts your belief as "done" may feel new or radical. What thoughts or emotions does this idea stir in you? * How might embracing this truth help you stand firm against doubts or circumstances that challenge your identity as God's beloved?

5. Abraham's faith stage began as an "unbelieving believer" and concluded with believing God's promise about himself. Where do you struggle to believe the "unbelievably good news" about your divine identity? * What practical step (e.g., confession, prayer) could you take to align your heart with God's word about you?

Abraham-The Hope Stage

G od spoke to Abram about his identity in Genesis 15, and this time Abram believed, and he and his faith were accounted righteous. (God had not yet changed Abram's name to Abraham, but I have been using them interchangeably.) Abram finally believed that he was the father of many nations, even though he had no children.

The identity seed had penetrated, and I am sure that he now thought that all systems were go for both him and Sarai. Because God decreed it, a baby was on its way. You and I tend to do that—but not so fast.

God's promises are never put on a fast track. However, it is reasonable to assume that when you sense God's 'yes,' you might think it will happen soon and that you can make it happen because God promised. But as you continue your walk of faith, you will discover that what you think should happen doesn't, and the purpose to which God has called you He must accomplish in and through you.

Abram's initial faith under the stars, though real, was not substantial enough to support the structure God was building, so Abram would have to dig deeper to develop a faith foundation that would. That foundation is called hope, which is the full assurance that what God has purposed will be done, regardless of the circumstances and, most of the time, in spite of them.

The seed of faith must develop a root system. The glimmer of stars, that Abraham beheld without, had to grow brighter within to chase away all doubt. The moment of believing had to become continuous moments of believing, or a hoping against hope, or rejoicing in hope, which holds you through the times when nothing seems to be happening.

But while nothing was happening, Abram bungled the hope stage as he did the faith stage. Unbeknownst to him, Abram was an un-hoping hopeful. He tried really hard to believe and to show his faith by his deeds. Abram tried his best to make it happen with Sarai. But, when nothing happened, they made plans to do God's will the best way they could.

Their best, though, was to create Ishmael who Abram thought was God's plan. Even when God met Abram to tell him that Ishmael was not the answer, Abram dismissed God and laughed because he had all the son that he could imagine. God's fulfillment stood before him as a strapping young man, or so he thought.

So, it should not surprise you, nor should you beat yourself up, when you discover that what you have created is your own Ishmael. Discovering that you have been wrong should be an encouragement because you are in good company. You have Abram as your example because you too learn by trial and error. It's that developmental darkness thing. You just need to keep your heart open and soft. His story should encourage you in your own cluelessness and failings.

God's response should also temper your reactions toward the Ishmaels of others. Ishmael was not a problem for God. God even blessed Abram's mess. As shown in God's kindness and directness toward Abram, God also knows and has your situation well in hand. And when He is ready, He will step in, if you can recognize His intervention.

God also knows the challenges that walking in faith creates because you are naturally wired to live by what you see. Your sight is limited though. It can't see beyond the horizon of your own abilities and resources, nor can it see around your circumstances.

Faith, however, sees beyond the natural and lives in the same faith space as God, for He too lives by faith. Without faith, you cannot please God nor be like Him, and without hoping, you will trip over your own abilities as Abram did.

The hope stage is challenging because you live in two realities, the first being God's glowing promises and the second being your limited resources and abilities coupled with the situation you find yourself in. This is the conundrum called "you," that is, hoping for a better future without any encouragement which you would hope comes from your surroundings. You are often left alone with your dreams and, in time, find that your dreams have left you as well.

You were created to soar, yet you seem to have one foot tied to a peg. And at times, what God has said about you can even seem to mock you, if you have dared to believe more about yourself because life does not agree.

The "more about yourself" is your existence "in Christ." "In Christ" is an expansive spatial reality that can only be accessed and experienced through faith because it touches the eternal. This is the "unbelievable" part of you.

It's so unbelievable that you cannot even begin to fathom the person God imagined—the height, the depth, the length, and the width. You have been given permission, however, to believe into this new creation because God has created it and has invited you in.

Only Christians, by the way, live in two realities (those outside of Christ have only the natural) and therefore have the choice either to believe the "unbeliev-able" you or the "believable" one. And, as Jesus said, "according to your faith. . ."

Your natural ability is a hindrance in the hope stage because you think that you can live the Christian life and do God's will. God has given you strengths and corresponding weaknesses to navigate life, and over the years, you have developed them, and they have, to some extent, served you well.

The problem is that these were given to augment your spirit and not to be the driving force. I am sure that you know some with strong personalities who use their charisma and their natural giftings to get their way, even in the church. But even if you don't have "charisma", I am describing you as well because you also confuse your natural giftings and strengths with that which is of the Spirit. It is easy to conflate the two.

Your spirit, which is vitally connected to the Spirit of God, is to call the shots. When you became a Christian, it was your spirit that was born from above. Your spirit became new. But your old soulish understanding and behavior still hang around and can drown out your spirit. It takes time to learn the difference between walking in the flesh, or in your own natural abilities, and walking in the spirit.

Now don't get me wrong, the only way that you will learn how to walk in the Spirit is to plow ahead until you crash and burn like Peter and Paul and Abraham. You must come to the end of your own abilities before you begin to realize that life in Christ is not building up sweat equity. Only when you come to the end of your own efforts will you discover the beginning of God's.

There was a time when Abram could still plow ahead, but not in Sarai. So, knowing God's will, they decided that they could make it happen with Hagar, Sarai's servant. In fact, they would not have even thought about impregnating Hagar without desiring to see God's will being done.

While they were right about the what, they were clueless about the how. To be kind, they didn't know the how and were doing their best to please God. They didn't know, at this time, that God's will was to be done in God's way, through His power, and in His time. And so, Ishmael was born.

I think that, in this performance-based Christian culture which desires God's will to be done, it is easy to confuse God's ways with your own. "God has willed that His kingdom come, so, by God, we will make it come, come hell or high water," is not the stance that God desires. That is adolescent thinking.

And while plans and conferences and programs are good (Abram still had to have intercourse with Sarai), dependence upon God and waiting for both the willing and the doing is paramount. Only when Jacob walked with a limp did he become Israel or "one having power with God". Declaring your own inability and ignorance daily, even in the things that you think you know, opens the door for God to perform His will through you.

As with Abraham, however, God's best can be dismissed because that godly thing, for which you have worked so hard, is working. But hopefully, you are willing to change your thinking in your success. And hopefully, in your failure, you can accept it as a door into the realm of the Spirit.

Both are difficult things to do as witnessed in Genesis 17 where God unveiled His thoughts on His promise to Abram. Abram was not willing, at first, either to believe or to give up what he had. But God's desired outcome will never be produced by natural means.

The work of God has always been based on believing the promise through thick and thin. God was establishing in Abraham's narrative, the "by grace, through faith" principle which Paul would later codify. Abraham's narrative, in fact, is the primer on what faith looks like and how it works. His was a simple faith that matured and became an unshakeable faith, called hope, which then became the foundation for everything God was going to do.

Paul, in Romans 4, describes the practical steps Abraham took in response to God's promise in light of his impotence and the impossible circumstances he faced. Paul paints the picture of a hoping hopeful. And to remind you, Paul attributed the phrase, "accounted to him as righteousness," to this moment of Abraham's life and not when it was first inserted in the Scriptures. He was certifying and declaring the importance of the hope stage.

Paul took liberty, in Romans, to describe how Abraham grappled with these two realities because the Genesis account is silent on what was going on inside of Abraham. Paul must have read his own heart which faced its own impossibilities and rightly assumed that this was how Abraham had triumphed over his.

In taking liberty by transposing Genesis 15's stamp of approval, "it was accounted to him as righteousness," to this event which occurred over a decade later, Paul declared that the hope stage was not only a continuation of Abraham's faith journey, but a critical step toward the fulfillment of finally being the person God imagined or being right with God, with himself, and with his place in the world.

Hoping against hope is part of the faith process and one that must be successfully navigated. I will expand on Abraham's and your part in the next chapter, but for now, I want to look at God's part in creating hope in Abram because you too must hear what Abram heard. Not only does faith come by hearing a word spoken by God, hope also comes by hearing as well. So, God spoke. And so, God speaks.

The first thing God did was change Abram's name. I will leave this for last because the other part of this story is changing Sarai's name as well. But changing Abram's name was not sufficient of itself.

What was sufficient for Abram, though, was God's name. God did not change His name for Abram, but He revealed Himself in a new way—as God Almighty. To that point, Abram knew God as the relatable promise-giver and as the covenant-keeping God. But, for Abram to become Abraham, a new understanding of God was required. When it was not in Abram and Sarai to produce a thing, God said, "Oh, but I can."

This is the first time that God revealed Himself as God Almighty, the God who does the impossible. We sing about the God of angel armies, but, if we are honest, it has little impact because God, in our thinking, is directing his armies to other places in the world. Here though, God tied His almighty-ness directly to Abraham's un-mighty-ness.

Have you looked at your life through the lens of "God Almighty"? Has your faith laid hold of the One who raised and raises the dead? The implication is that you must be dead to see the operation of God. Ezekiel's dry bones are not an exception to the rule. Dry, dead bones are the rule.

In his second letter to Timothy, Paul reminded Timothy, who had all but given up hope, that according to Paul's good news, Jesus was raised from among the dead. But what did that have to do with Timothy's situation? Everything.

"Timothy, you are in the best place to see God move because Jesus' death, burial, and resurrection were not a one-off. It is God's way of carrying out all that He does. Death always precedes life, so the deader the better. Therefore Timothy, stir up the gift of faith that I imparted to you. God is about to break out!"

Then God piles on by pointing to Himself and saying, "I will," multiple times. The Almighty said, "I will make. I will establish. I will multiply. I will make you fruitful. I will make nations of you. I WILL. I WILL. I WILL."

These "I wills" have resided in God's heart from eternity and have found their fullest expression in the New Covenant that Jesus came, once and for all time, to establish. The New Covenant, which both Jeremiah and the writer to the Hebrews declare, is a string of God's "I wills".

God's "wills" and "cans" have overpowered yours, and the sooner you are convinced of this, the sooner you will enter into rest or into the land of promise that God has given you. You have to push out your "I can't," your "not sure," and your "It'll never happen" with "the One who promises, who is the Almighty, can and will and has."

The next thing God did, before He dropped a bomb on Abraham by telling him that Sarai was going to be the mother, was to say something strange. God told Abram that his part in keeping the covenant was to be circumcised and that circumcision was to be a sign for all his children to countless generations. Circumcision was to be the mark that identifies all those who would walk in faith, both male and female.

I am sure that you know that circumcision is the removal of the outer skin of the male's reproductive organ. As cringy as that sounds, God was forcing Abraham to fully acknowledge his total inability to produce what God desired. Abraham had to hold, in light of the promise, his flaccid appendage (sorry to be graphic) that was lifeless, and cut away the unbelieving part to expose the believing part.

Paul wrote of this moment and the moments that followed: "And without being weakened in faith he considered his own body (that cringy part) which was now as good as dead." Being fully aware of his own inability, Abraham faced his impotence with a resounding, "I can do all things through him who strengthens me."

There will come a time (and maybe it already has) when you too will be confronted with your own impotence. At that moment, God is calling you to walk in Abraham's steps, to look at that thing and say, "Arise".

There is a tendency, though, to keep your unbelief hidden behind platitudes, head nods, or self-deprecation. But, just as Abraham was told to remove the outer skin, you too will need to expose your unbelief.

Paul learned to embrace his weakness because he saw the connection between the awareness of need and God's power. This helps you understand Paul's seemingly incongruous responses to adversity. Singing, while in shackles, was not just about gutting it out and praising God because God is God, and you're not.

Paul knew that God was about to do something because he had learned that God's power flowed through weakness. In Paul's straits, he found a wideness. While chained, God was about to unleash His life and power and freedom in that jail through Paul, so he sang in anticipation. Like Abraham, he grew stronger in faith by giving glory to God.

Paul went so far as to say, in Philippians, that "YOU are the circumcision," that is, your life is defined by your weakness and need. In a Christian culture that celebrates strengths, weakness must become the message. Paul wrote that a part of being the circumcision means having no confidence in the flesh.

Having no confidence in the flesh assumes that you have tried it and have found that you have no power to live the life to which God has called. It means that your natural abilities and gifts have given way to the leading of the spirit. Proverbs describes this life as "trusting in the Lord with all your heart and not leaning on your own understanding".

Then God changed both Abram's and Sarai's names. In the Bible, names are significant. They identify or describe the essence of that person or thing, so changing a name, as He did with Abraham and Sarah and Peter, speaks of a change of identity. Knowing and believing your name, or your identity, allows for a couple of things.

It lets others know who you are, but more importantly, it tells you who you are and helps you carve out your space in the world. Every part of you is stuffed into your name. And whether you know it or not, you always live up or down to your name, or who you believe yourself to be, because there is a not-so-secret law that says you are the person you believe yourself to be. Proverbs puts it this way, "As one thinks within themself, so he is." (NASB)

So, when God renamed Abram and Sarai, it was a big deal. Their destiny changed because their identity changed, and with that, their ability changed as well. It didn't matter what their bodies said because God had changed their names to match His. They were now just like Him, a Father, and not just any father, but a father just like Him—amazingly and exponentially reproductive. When He calls you a son, this is what the Father is saying about you. Think about that.

God changed their names in the most remarkable of ways. He added the same single letter to each of their names. But what a difference it made. That letter changed their names from "exalted father" to "father of multitudes" and from "my Princess" to "Princess." The implication was that Sarah now belonged to the world and not just to Abraham. It gave each global significance that reached far beyond their immediate family and years.

But even more remarkable, that letter, which God inserted into their names, was the fifth letter of the Hebrew alphabet. It is the letter *hei*. Without getting too geeky, *hei* stands for divine breath. The Hebrew word for Yahweh has four letters, with two being *hei*. God's breath is pretty important to Him.

God inserted Himself by breathing Himself into the core of their being. This is Jesus-talk. Speaking to His Father, Jesus said, "I in them and You in me, that they may be perfectly perfect as they become one or whole (with each other, with themselves, and with God)." TCA

Neither Abraham nor Sarah became different people. They looked the same. They talked the same. Their personality didn't change. They did, however, become the God-version of themselves. They now had the ability to become the ones God imagined and to be that on steroids.

Just like Adam, God breathed the breath of life into them, and the Adamic mandate to be fruitful, become great, and fill now became possible. As with Jesus' disciples, God breathed His Spirit in Abraham and Sarah, and Abraham and Sarah could now make disciples of all nations. God was in them in a way that practically affected everything.

Their weakened bodies now came in line with the Almighty. Abraham now began to know himself as the father of many nations. He, who had no ability to perform, found the ability by hoping against hope. Because believing trumps performing, he and Sarah were able to perform.

Mind you, I am not talking about belief-ism where you try hard to believe for specific things. Nor am I talking about shamanism where your believing makes it happen. I am talking about a faith that comes from hearing something special from God which then produces rest, before becoming actual. This is part of the faith journey that Abraham's story details.

God has changed your name from "having fallen short of the glory of God and missing the mark" to "having been fully restored to sonship and to the fullness of glory, by the freedom purchased by Jesus". He has done this by inserting Himself in your life, so the life that you now live in this tangible world, you can live by the faith of the Son of God who loves you and has given His life for you.

This is the hope stage of which Paul wrote, "Hope that is seen is not hope. For who hopes for what he sees? But if we hope for what we do not see, we wait for it with patience." You, too, must follow Abraham's footsteps and learn to live in anticipation of the promise while everything around you says, "No."

A practical side of changing Abraham and Sarah's name is that they had to tell each other every day whom they were becoming, and not whom they seemed to be. I am sure, for a while, they caught themselves and had to correct each other. "Oh, Abram!" "Princess, remember? That is not who I am." "Sorry, father of many nations."

There will be times, especially in close relationships, when you will hear the "always" or "never" word. "You are always like this" or "You never do that". On the outside, you must do what you can to ameliorate the situation, but on the inside, you will need to reject that name and affirm who you are.

From that moment on, Abraham and Sarah stopped responding to their old name and began calling each other by His until it became second nature. God was creating heaven's faith atmosphere through their speaking the truth about themselves and by their believing it.

As they named or called each other by God's naming, their biology began to work. And as you do this, the natural will also yield to this spiritual reality. Calling someone beautiful, who thinks they're not, will open their heart to the beauty God has created and will help them flower. And calling someone else beautiful will also open your own heart to your own beauty.

Telling someone how important they are and highlighting the significance of the things they do, no matter how small, will infuse them with purpose as they continue doing things that don't seem to matter. (Isn't life comprised of daily, mundane, and seemingly insignificant repetitive taskses?") Affirming others will also affirm you.

You have the ability and responsibility, by speaking the truth in love, to lift heads and help others into their God-given destiny. This is one reason Jude called on his friends to keep themselves and each other "in the love of God" because they are loved, significant, and safe.

You too are to call those things, which are not, into existence. When you look at your spouse, your children, your church, your life, the temptation is to express what you see. God doesn't, and He has called you to come up to His level.

Because God has changed both your name and theirs, because He is God Almighty, because His covenant is not based on your ability to keep it, but on His, and more than that, because you are the "circumcision" or because you self-identify as impotent, you, like your father Abraham, can become unbelievably productive because of this word— "So shall YOUR offspring be."

Questions

1. Have you experienced a moment where you sensed God's promise or "yes" about your identity or purpose, only to face delays or challenges that made it seem impossible? * How does understanding that trials often follow God's promises, as seen in Abram's journey, change your perspective on these delays or circumstances? * What can you do to keep your heart open and soft when your efforts produce an "Ishmael"?

2. What does it mean to you to shift from a single moment of believing God's promise to continuous moments of believing, or "hoping against hope"? * Where are you in this hope stage—are you striving to make God's will happen (an un-hoping hopeful), feeling discouraged, or resting in an inner assurance that God's purpose is already done?

3. The chapter describes living in two realities—God's eternal promises and your limited natural circumstances. How does this tension impact your understanding of your identity "in Christ"? * In what areas of your life are you relying on natural abilities or strengths, and how can you surrender these to walk in the Spirit?

4. God revealed Himself to Abram as "God Almighty" and used four actions (revealing His name, declaring "I will," requiring circumcision, and changing names) to create hope. Which of these actions resonates most with you in an area where you struggle to believe your "unbelievable" identity in Christ?

5. Circumcision symbolized Abram's acknowledgment of his inability to fulfill God's promise on his own. What abilities, giftings, or past successes in your life are no longer producing results, and how can you acknowledge your weakness in these areas as a step toward God's power? * Can you hold this limitation in your mind, declare your dependence on God, and trust Him to "arise" in your situation?

Abraham-The Hope Stage in the New Testament

T he second soil in the Parable of the Sower represents the hope stage. Since Jesus added, "Those with ears, listen", He is alerting you to specific stages in the life of the seed of which you need to be aware. The word sown is full of life, so the Sower's parable is anything but fatalistic because Jesus is anything but.

Jesus does not believe in fatalism. He believes in the power of the seed to fully flower and is hopeful every time a seed leaves His mouth. But to become fruitful, you will need to participate in the process by identifying these seasons in your life and addressing them successfully as Abraham did.

This stage follows on the heels of your initial believing who God says that you are. There is a moment when the light turns on. This is the faith stage. Something spiritual has happened. God has made His thoughts about you known, and you have finally sensed assurances that your life matters, that things will work out, and you believe.

The light has turned on and there is an inner knowing that you know. But, as with Abraham, what God desires to do in your life is so substantial that your initial believing must go deeper. The seed needs to develop a root structure, and since its roots dictate the size of the plant, the deeper, the better.

For Jesus, the hope stage followed hearing His Father's words. "You are my beloved Son in whom I am well pleased." With this ringing in His ears, the Spirit then drove Him into the wilderness where the sun DID come out. All external evidence of His belovedness withered.

All that Jesus had were the words that His Father had spoken to him. So, He let them go deep as He buried Himself in Deuteronomy. So, when the devil said, "If you are," Jesus dispatched him with a word or two and by saying, "Of course I am. Go away."

This stage consists of three things: the seed, soil that is not fully tilled, and an adversarial sun. The seed is a word or promise that you have sensed. (Again, if you have heard nothing else, God has told you, in Christ, that you are both His and His beloved.) You are the soil, and the sun is your situation or circumstances.

Abraham, to become the person God imagined, had to protect the word spoken to him through this stage by believing it more than his experience. You too will face "it doesn't seem so" and "this can never happen" and will need to figure out what to do with God's promises.

The soil in this stage has loosened dirt which allows for some growth. You have believed, but there are still pockets of unbelief or possibly cluelessness, which do not allow the seed of His word to establish its root system.

This soil is also littered with the mindset that you can, in your own strength, do what God will only do in His. These rocks remain from the first soil's hardened surface and haven't been completely removed because these assumptions and attitudes go deep.

If you are honest, there are things about God and yourself that haven't yet rooted. There might have been moments when you tell yourself, "God is my supplier," but when the sun comes out and dries up whatever resources you might have, you freak out and let go of the faith you once held.

There are things that you have believed about yourself that can easily wither because the sun has parched the ground. The things that have worked in your past, stop working. You still lose your temper. Your gifts aren't recognized. The dream that you have held out for yourself is no longer in your thinking.

The challenge is being able to recognize these hard patches in your life and see them for what they are—part of your faith journey. Many things resist the seed. Some seed-resistors are without. Most, however, are within. Grace is so foreign to your thinking that it might take years before you begin to believe it.

You are to look at these rocks, not as immovable objects but like Joshua and Caleb viewed their giants. While the rest of the spies saw the giants as a padlocked door to the dining room, Joshua and Caleb saw them as the banquet feast.

This shift in thinking, this faith-sight, gave Joshua and Caleb the freedom to go forward. The rest of Israel were fatalistic and found that to be fatal. So, when you discover seed-resistors within, you are to do the hard work of bringing those rocks to the surface to remove them.

The scary thing about this season is just because you have initially believed does not mean that what God has purposed for you will become a reality. Paul wrote of this stage, "that Abraham MIGHT become". Might is a scary word because it implies uncertainty.

Both an initial, "believing-faith", coupled with an enduring "hoping-faith", are required. Sadly, the children of Israel discovered the scary part of this truth as they died in the wilderness. This necessitates that you deal with the rocks as you endure the sun.

Your problem, though, is not the sun or your circumstances however relentless they may seem. The sun is your friend because it forces your faith roots down to find God in a real, more desperate, sort of way. When your circumstances seem to resist you, James' "count it all joy" thing needs to be activated in order to allow patience to have its perfect work.

The plant, at this stage, is weak. You are stronger than the word as heretical as that sounds. You might think twice before trying to wrestle and pin down an oak tree, but taking on a seedling? Ten out of ten times, you win.

So, the challenge comes after you sense something from God, whether it is a promise, an assurance, or a presence. God has come to insert Himself into your life. And when that happens, the sun will inevitably come out to test you and reveal your doubts and strivings.

Mark wrote, "When trouble or persecution comes BECAUSE OF THE WORD, they quickly fall away." The cause of your trouble sometimes is that you HAVE believed something of God. The word, believed by you, invites trouble. If misinterpreted, though, instead of developing a deeper root system, your faith will wither as your heart hardens.

And so, it happened in Abraham's life. As the sun slowly parched the ground and there were no children, his waiting turned into self-effort. His self-effort seemed successful, and he believed that the son he produced was of God. But only after Abraham had nothing left in the tank did God show up.

Paul, in Romans 4, highlights this stage in Abraham's life. As I mentioned in the last chapter, Paul seemingly misapplied the phrase, "it was accounted to him as righteousness" to this part of Abraham's life. The Genesis account has that phrase being declared under the stars and not after Ishmael was born.

But Paul rightly inserted this phrase here because Abraham's faith journey encompassed more than his initial believing. Hoping against hope is an important part of the journey into becoming the person God imagined and describes a more mature faith.

The phrase, "It was accounted to him as righteousness", is one of the most important phrases in the Bible because it describes the fullness of God's heart toward all of humanity and His desire for you. You were wired wrong in the fall, but Jesus, in His death, burial, and resurrection rewired you in all of His rightness.

Righteousness is code for you becoming the person God imagined. It's what a saved you looks like—one who is whole and giving full expression to the person whom God made. Right, as it relates to God, to yourself, to others, and to your world.

It is the opposite of you being messed up, clueless, and having your life implode. It is the difference between a shriveled plant and one with voluminous growth. It is the difference between being as bold as a lion or skittish as a deer.

It is a glorified you. Being righteous is you, knowing who you are and living that out calmly in the face of nay-sayers and, like Jesus, who was stripped of all the trappings of deity and humanity, giving up your life for others.

Righteousness is not a dry, pedantic religious term. It pulsates with life and affects everything it touches. Both Paul and James realized this because this "accounted as righteous" phrase was used to describe the entirety of Abraham's life. You will see shortly how James used this phrase to describe the culmination of God's work in Abraham, but here in Romans 4, Paul puts on a master class on how to grow beyond an initial believing and master the hope stage.

The hope stage has Abraham persuading his own heart before God. As I have said, the Genesis account is silent as to how Abraham did that. It is left to your imagination as it was to Paul, who, writing under the inspiration of the Holy Spirit, used his.

Paul, who successfully navigated the hope stage with its own impossibilities, explained the process that Abraham went through by describing his own. And hopefully, you will also be able to explain the process to others because you too have discovered God's possibilities amid your own impossibilities.

A couple of things stand out in Paul's understanding of Abraham's response to God, concerning Abraham's new identity as he faced his own inabilities and Sarah's barrenness in light of God's promise. Abraham did not accept the status quo, even though he had no ability to change it. But now, knowing God as the Almighty, he began to live on a higher plane.

To do that, Abraham let the glimpse that God gave him of who He was to fill his prayers and thoughts. As he went about life, doing the things he needed to do, what was going on within, intentionally and in wonder and awe and worship, was, "My God is the Almighty! I have no ability to accomplish what God has called me to, but that doesn't matter. He does."

Paul put it this way— "He believed in the God who raises the dead and calls into existence things that are non-existent." Things that don't exist are no problem for God because all it takes is a word. If He speaks, it is done.

God spoke a creative word to Abraham who now knew that he had nothing to contribute to the outcome except his believing. So, Abraham's faith made him more right than he was under the stars because his faith had morphed into hope and God's promise pushed out any question.

He WAS the father whom God said that he was, even with his impotence and Sarah's inability to conceive because God said it. Abraham believed that "it was finished." A large component of hope is a deep-seated knowing that what God has purposed for your life is already done and that you are walking into it.

Like Abraham, living in the reality of "it is finished" is "hoping against hope". "It is finished", by the way, is the gospel. You will never begin to walk into your "future you" unless you believe that your "future you" is a present reality, even if your present reality is a mess.

As Paul wrote, "Already justified. Already sanctified. ALREADY GLORI-FIED." Past, present, and future. Already done. Yes, it won't look that way, but "hope that is seen is not hope".

This is the atmosphere in which God lives, and He has invited you to breathe the same air that He breathes. God has spoken to you, in Christ, that you are His beloved. Like Abraham and Sarah, you need to disbelieve the old version of yourself, what you know of natural processes, and then believe in God Almighty and "the exceeding greatness of His power working IN you" to make this real in you.

But, like Abraham, you are also not to deny physical realities. Paul wrote that Abraham carefully considered and clearly perceived his own impotence. He and Sarah embraced their weakness, as Paul embraced his. They acknowledged their own inability and, because of that, came to know God's grace. And when you begin to see the connection between your weaknesses and God's grace, you will as well.

Abraham embraced his new identity as "the son of His love who is just like God—a father to nations," and so he BECAME. Paul wrote that Abraham's becoming was tied to his believing through thick and thin. "He believed THAT he might become."

Abraham was required to have some skin in the game (that is not a cir-cumcision reference, though it absolutely is). Your circumcision also cuts deep because it addresses who you believe yourself to be, which is that sense of self that you protect at all costs. For Abraham, it might have been a simple snip. For you, however, it is a constant disbelieving of what you see and a daily believing into what you have heard.

God's will does not happen in a vacuum. Sometimes, God will step in "just because" (He IS full of mercy, and He is God), but most of the time some action is required on your part. That action is believing into the future which Paul calls "the work of faith". Hoping against hope is hard work because you must acknowledge very real physical realities while you reach out for less tangible, spiritual ones.

It could be your marriage on the rocks. It could be a wayward child. It could be the dream of a ministry that has evaporated. It could be a hurt so deep that you can't see a way out. Whatever it looks like, it feels like death with no apparent remedy.

(Don't hear what I am not saying though. The situation might not change, but what's important is that you do. What you need to determine is, "Has God said something?" If He has whispered a word to you, hold on to it because you are in Abraham's hope stage. If you haven't heard anything, still let your roots down into the eternity of His faithful love because the only way that the situation might right itself is when you change.)

Initially, I am sure that Abraham had to be very intentional about giving glory to God. Learning the faith language is no different than learning any other language as an adult. At first, it will be uncomfortable, and you will feel self-conscious. But as you continue, this language will flow, and your hard work of putting God's words in your mouth will become your new language.

So, Abraham "grew strong in faith, giving glory to God." Paul goes on to write that Abraham became fully convinced that God was able to do what He promised. This "fully convinced" was against the backdrop of all the reasons it shouldn't or couldn't happen. This is hoping against hope, that is, despite lacks, in spite of resisting circumstances, you are rejoicing and at rest.

Rejoicing and being at rest is the standard by which you can judge your spot in the faith journey. If you find yourself stressed and anxious or just living, you are falling short of living in "it is finished".

Don't beat yourself up though because you are following Abraham's footsteps who was as clueless as you. But once the light turned on, he changed. Has the light turned on for you? If so, use this awareness as motivation to develop your faith language.

(A little suggestion, if you haven't yet prayed in your spirit's language, ask God to release you and it. Paul said that when you pray in tongues, your spirit (that unadulterated God-part of you) prays and that you build yourself up. And with the amount of energy he expended, Paul was excessive when it came to spirit-praying. By praying in tongues, Paul also prayed, not only to the limit of his own understanding but, from his spirit, prayed to the limit of God's.)

Paul ended this section on the hope stage by saying, "The words 'it was counted to him' were not written for his sake alone, but for yours also. It will be counted to you who believe in him who raised from the dead, Jesus our Lord." Jesus' resurrection from among the dead was yours as well. Paul makes it clear that your faith journey is the same as both Abraham's and Jesus', who is both Abraham's son and his God.

Paul made it clear that being declared righteous is more than regeneration. It is about becoming the person God imagined. You, like Abraham and Jesus, will also need to be raised from the dead, and the deadness that you are to be raised from is your old way of thinking and doing.

But having Isaac, though, was not the end of Abraham's story. You would think that having Isaac would be the pinnacle of Abraham's life. But no. While he had believed into the person God imagined him to be, and while he had hoped against hope to become the father of Isaac, and while he successfully navigated the faith and hope stage, one more stage remained. It is also one that you will face as you walk into your eternal destiny.

As John wrote, Abraham had "come to know and to believe the love that God had for him." Abraham's identity had been cemented. He was now right, and all was right in the world, or so he thought.

James said that this phrase, "It was accounted to him for righteousness" was fulfilled or finalized on Moriah, where he held a knife in his hand and not when he held a baby. Paul wrote, "Now these three remain: faith, hope, and love. But the greatest of these is love." So, let's walk together with Abraham to Moriah, which is the greatest of these.

Questions

1. The hope stage involves a seed (God's promise), soil (you), and the sun (challenging circumstances). Can you identify a specific promise, assurance, or sense from God that you've received? * What circumstances in your life feel like the "sun" parching your faith? * How are you actively holding onto God's word in this season to deepen your spiritual roots?

2. What doubts, self-reliance, or ingrained mindsets (the "rocky patches") are hindering God's promises from taking deeper root in your heart? * How can you shift your perspective to see these challenges as opportunities for growth, like Joshua and Caleb viewed their giants? * What practical steps can you take to remove these obstacles and trust God's possibilities over your limitations?

3. How can you embrace your weaknesses or difficult circumstances as opportunities for God's grace and power to work, as Abraham and Paul did? * Why might the "sun" of trials be a friend in your spiritual growth, and how does this perspective challenge or encourage you? * What specific situation in your life can you surrender to God to transform into a moment of divine strength?

4. The text emphasizes developing a "faith language" by giving glory to God and speaking His promises. What practical habits—such as prayer, worship, or praying in tongues—can you adopt to strengthen your hope and align your thoughts with God's truth? * How can you intentionally practice this language daily, especially when circumstances contradict God's promises?

5. What does it mean to you to live in the reality of "it is finished," believing that God's purpose for you is already complete despite external challenges? * How can you cultivate a deep-seated hope, like Abraham's, that trusts God's promises over visible realities? *Can you embrace the truth that you are already complete in Christ, even amidst your imperfections, and how might this belief shape your daily life?

Abraham-The Love Stage

After these things, God tested Abraham and said to him, "Abraham!'" And he said, "Here I am." He said, "Take your son, your only son Isaac, whom you love, and go to the land of Moriah, and offer him there as a burnt offering on one of the mountains of which I shall tell you." Genesis 22:1-2

You would think that having Isaac would have been the high point of Abraham's life, and the "happily ever after" ending, which we all desire, would have been written. For God, though, it has never been about outward success. It has always been about the imprint of His Son in you, that is, Jesus becoming incarnate once again. It is about you knowing within, regardless of the externals, that you are His beloved because then the outcome glorifies Him, whether it is the cross or the throne.

Through many trials, toils, and snares, he had already come and had come out on top. Abraham's faith had been proven genuine and was found "of greater worth than gold which perishes". The birth of Isaac resulted in God's praise, glory, and honor.

So, you would think that once you have got your life together, that is, you have figured out who you are, the lane you are to operate in, and that life is working for you without much effort, you would have reached your apex. Trying to make life work is past, and you just are and because of that, you are fully being you, and life is working.

Like Paul, you have come to the place where you don't have to figure out what to say because you no longer try to put together messages. You have become the message. Paul said that, while in Corinth for 18 months, he had only one message which he proclaimed.

Think about that. Paul preached and taught only one subject for a year and a half, and unlike today, he spoke daily and for more than 30 minutes at a time, yet he didn't run out of things to say and neither did his audience tire of him. He interpreted Christ and the cross through the lens of both the Scriptures

AND his own heart because Christ and the cross had become transliterated in him. And so, the message of Christ and the cross kept expanding in him and resonating with others.

But no, "after these things . . ." This Genesis 22 passage has been much debated. Why would a God who abhors murder ask His friend to kill his own son? What does this say about God and what implications does this have for you? Are you called to blindly obey? Are you going to be asked for your Isaac or that thing that God has given and which you love and have embodied?

And what sort of test was this? Is God so demanding that He insists on being worshipped to the point of being a spoilsport? When you lose a child, a job, or a relationship, is this God "testing" you? What was the purpose of Abraham's test?

Let me first say that God is worthy of worship whether, like Abraham, God is asking something back, or as with Job, Satan is orchestrating your seeming demise. It is always better to bless Him than curse. And as we have seen with Adam and Jesus, and now with Abraham, life is a test which includes specific times when the test is pivotal.

I am not going to use this space to try to defend God or explain your testing. All I know is that God loves you as much as He loves Abraham. The Father proved His love for you on His own Moriah where He allowed the knife to come down on the Son whom He loved and who not only consumes His life but gives His life definition and meaning. (God is not a Father without having a Son.)

And Jesus, who also carried the wood for the burnt offering and willingly laid Himself on the altar, interpreted this moment for His followers, "No greater love is this than a man laying down his life for his friends."

Doubtless, though, you ARE tested from day one on the things you begin to believe. Is God good? Life will test you on that. Are you the son of His love? Your own thoughts will affirm or deny that.

Do your missteps change His attitude toward you? Does He care for you so much that you don't have to worry? Hopefully, you can, more and more, pass these tests because God tests you toward Himself, while the devil tempts you toward himself.

This, however, was not a regular run-of-the-mill test for Abraham. Yours might be of the kindergarten variety. Abraham, however, had passed grade school, high school, and college. Little did he know that he was completing his

PhD program. The thesis on righteousness was written, and he was now being asked to stand and give an oral defense of his dissertation.

"Take your son, your only son, whom you love, and offer him up." Though this was the final test for Abraham, it must be seen in context and as a continuation of his others. From the beginning, Abraham's tests were centered around his identity and here, on the mount, all of his book knowledge had to give way to heart knowledge. Was God's perception of Abraham transliterated in him? Would Abraham know himself to be the father of multitudes even without a child?

It might be decades before you will face a test like this because you first need to pass the faith and hope classes. And you might never be tested this way if you remain uncertain of His goodness or why God created you. If you haven't come to the end of yourself and learned to hope against hope like Abraham did, Moriah won't be in your future.

The first test came about thirty years earlier when God told Abraham to leave where he was and sacrifice his familial and cultural attachments. While promises were attached to this command, Abraham obeyed out of fear because the God who appeared to him was the "God of glory", as Stephen proclaimed. He passed this test because what else could he do..

Throughout the Scriptures, when people encountered the glory of God, they experienced an abject terror. So, if the "glory of God" causes knee-shakings and heart palpitations, what do you think encountering the "God of glory" would do? That encounter had to have scared the wits out of him. Abraham had no choice. Come hell or high water, family or not, he was leaving.

In Ur, God was not yet a close friend, so the "fear" which motivated Abraham to obey was not the same fear which beckoned him now. This "fear" was an awe and worship which drew Abraham into the embrace of a Friend who walked together with him toward Moriah.

In fact, it is in this account that the word, "worship", is first used in the Scriptures. Abraham used this word to describe to Isaac, and to those who accompanied him, what their journey was about. It is the same heart attitude that Jesus had as He walked toward His Moriah.

Drawing on all his past experiences with God, Abraham knew that God had something up His sleeve, so he was filled with anticipation. The writer of Hebrews said that one of those expectations was Isaac's resurrection. Abraham knew God as a friend, so while he couldn't figure out what was in God's mind, he knew His heart.

But maybe he did know God's mind. Jesus said that Abraham saw His day and was glad. Maybe Abraham, like Jesus, figured out the principle of the cross before he went to his cross, that is, he understood that "unless a kernel of wheat falls into the ground, it remains alone." Maybe he knew that Isaac needed to be planted before the unbelievable fruitfulness that God promised would happen and that this was the time.

While his first obedience was imperfect, this time it was astoundingly perfect. In Ur, Abraham didn't completely leave his family as he was told. They came with him just like the baggage that you have accumulated over the years goes along with you for the ride.

This time, however, he got up early the next morning to do the deed. God, mind you, left the scheduling to Abraham. He just said, "Go", but Abraham couldn't leave soon enough. So, Abraham, took his only son, the son he loved.

Abraham's test consisted of two things. The first was his identity because God said, "Take your only son" with an emphasis on "only". And then, Abraham's love was tested, that is, the test centered on whom he loved most.

Abraham was told to take his only son. There was no "plan B" for Abraham. His identity was wrapped up in Isaac. His future, his significance, and his ministry revolved around his son. As I just said of the Heavenly Father, you can't be a father through whose children everything will be blessed unless you have a child.

Or can you? While the evidence of who you are is manifest in the natural, physical evidence is not the proof. The proof is the inner sense that is brought about by a witness of the Spirit. Testing comes to make that inner sense rock solid to the end that the word becomes flesh in you. And when it is rock solid, God can build as big of an edifice as He wants.

And when this settles in your heart, as it did in Abraham's, you too will live with an open hand because you will have found your existence in God, not in externals. Do you know the difference between living with an open hand and a closed one?

An open hand gives freedom to that thing which is yours to leave. Isn't this a part of the definition of love? And isn't this how God holds you? Yes, He has you firmly in hand in one sense, but, in another sense, He has truly set you free. You have complete freedom to leave but, when all is said and done, you don't want to. This is the essence of love. Marriage, by the way, works best this way.

An open hand also gives freedom for others to take what you think is yours. When John the Baptist was told that many of his disciples were leaving to follow

Jesus, he said that they weren't his anyway: "A person cannot receive even one thing unless it is given him from heaven." Since you are not defined by things and since everything you possess is God's, you needn't get stressed when things leave.

I have often wondered how many men and women of God have lost their way, and their ministry, because they did not know about Moriah. Instead of freely giving back what God had given and, in doing so, find fulfillment and real power in their ministry, they lost what they sought to hold on to.

"Take YOUR son, that God-given thing that you have also worked so hard for, and give it up" is difficult because you, by default, are territorial and therefore live with a clenched fist. But Abraham's hand was open because he knew that externals did not define him. And because of that, God could multiply both him and the thing which he freely gave up, exponentially.

You know that you are holding onto things, even God-given things, when they are threatened. All sorts of lovely emotions pop out. Let someone invade your space and take note of your reactions. You might think that you are protecting that thing, but, in reality, it is controlling you.

In so doing, you negate "Jesus is Lord." Abraham, in leaving, declared that God controlled him and all that he had. What a stress-free way to live! But it does require faith-sight, coupled with a reckless abandon. So, when God asked back from Abraham what He had given him, there wasn't a second thought because he was living with an open hand.

The other test was a test of love. Abraham's relationship with Isaac was second to none (sorry, Sarah). God had given Isaac to him as a treasure to protect and as a sword to sharpen. God has also put things in your orbit to enjoy and nurture. The problem is when you begin orbiting around them.

So, "Take the son whom you love." God might have been concerned that Abraham was beginning to orbit a little around Isaac. While you are called to love and care for that which God has put in your life, you are not to have those things define you. And without Moriah moments, you can center your life around things, and even God-given things, and not God.

So, "You take the son whom you love." Whether it is your job, your ministry, your family and friends, your free time, or your "not-so-free" time, whether it is your plans or resources, Jesus asks, "Do you love Me more than these?" and "What have you centered your life around?" These are the questions which underly life because every test is a test of love.

For a number of years, I had seen the Moriah principle in Abraham's life but also knew that I hadn't yet experienced it. I had walked the path Abraham blazed because I too began as an unbelieving believer until I heard God say, "You are the son of my love. Look at the stars to gauge your significance."

Then I learned to walk by faith and to hope against hope while God brought into being what I couldn't produce on my own. I knew Moriah awaited but didn't know what it looked like until the day God asked back from me that thing that gave my life meaning and joy.

I didn't hear a voice, but I did say, "Here I am" because moments, like these, arrest your attention. The threat of loss was real, and I thought, "I don't think that this is how You want it to end, but if it is, I give the dream I have had for my life back to You." When that thing wasn't taken, it hit me a few days later that this was Moriah, and I said, "Wow. Ok, now, with blessing, You will bless me." And He has.

So, "'By myself I have sworn, declares the LORD, because you have done this and have not withheld your son, your only son, I will surely bless you, and I will surely multiply your offspring as the stars of heaven and as the sand that is on the seashore. And your offspring shall possess the gate of his enemies, and in your offspring shall all the nations of the earth be blessed, because you have obeyed my voice.'"

God's "I will" promises became, for Abraham, "I surely will" statements of fact. Because Abraham embodied his identity and didn't let his son become his god, God effused. The potential became actual. The seed flowered. This, as we will see in the next chapter, was the culmination of his journey into "it was accounted to him as righteousness".

Adam's mandate to be fruitful, become great, and fill the earth found its home in Abraham. This was the path Adam was to walk if he had continued in faith. But God was not to be denied, nor will He be denied in this generation.

He found, in Abraham, both the father of faith whom Adam was created to be and the one in whom all the earth would now be blessed. And hopefully, God will find you, as well, walking in the steps of Abraham so that all of your world will be blessed because of you.

Abraham's path of faith, hope, and love became the roadmap for all who would follow his steps to become the person God imagined. And while that person is beyond your most far-flung imagination, like Abraham, your life will seem to you most unremarkable because you are wrapped in plain paper.

Reading over Abraham's life, I can't help but think of how remarkably unremarkable it was. What did he really do? Abraham lived his life, did some traveling, built a business, and had a son. The real story centered around his encounters with God, what went on inside of him, and how he responded. Abraham just went forward, taking baby steps, and doing his thing.

I liken life to piloting a boat. The wake that is created behind you is not yours to see. Your gaze is to be ahead, but, like Abraham, the wake you leave behind is immeasurable. It continues to expand as you continue on your way, even into eternity.

So, "Abraham returned to his young men, and they arose and went together to Beersheba. And Abraham lived at Beersheba." Beersheba has two meanings—"the well of seven" and "the well of the oath." Seven in the Scriptures means completeness, wholeness, and perfection.

Abraham, like God did on the seventh day, could rest because the journey into becoming the person God imagined was now complete. Abraham embodied fatherhood. He was like God. The likeness now aligned with the image.

He lived life on the highest plane because God now was incarnate in him. "When you have seen me, you have seen the Father", was Abraham's testimony. This is the good news foretold to Abraham and is the same good news being proclaimed to you. A Son becomes a father by becoming like their father, and. you, as a son, were created to reflect and embody the Father.

And then, Abraham continued to live in the promise. Beersheba means "well of the oath or promise". He lived in and drank from the unfathomable well of God's promise. He had learned to walk in the Spirit which means that "by grace, through faith" was a living reality for Abraham.

If you remember the chapter on transliteration, righteousness, and grace now had internal definitions and resonance for Abraham, so he didn't need to try to be a father. Nor did he need to defend his fatherhood. He just was and knew it, and from that place, he lived.

But while he knew himself to be the father of nations, Abraham still was "not yet". Millennia (and possibly millennia to come) still needed to pass before the promise would be fulfilled. But for Abraham, he lived the rest of his remarkably unremarkable life in Beersheba, doing what he now could do best in the power of the Spirit. He continued to give expression to the person God imagined. He kept fathering and becoming more and more fruitful.

Questions

1. How has this book helped you see your identity as God's beloved, rooted in His love rather than external achievements or possessions? * Can you identify moments in your life where you've struggled to internalize this truth? * How might viewing life's tests as opportunities to solidify your identity as a son or daughter of God change your perspective on current challenges?

2. Are there God-given blessings—relationships, roles, or dreams—that you might be holding onto too tightly? * How can you cultivate an open-handed faith, trusting God to provide even if these blessings are altered or removed? * What steps can you take to ensure your life orbits around God rather than these gifts?

3. Have you experienced a "Moriah moment" where you felt called to release something deeply valued, such as a dream, relationship, or role? * How did you respond, and what did this reveal about your trust in God's goodness? * How has this experience shaped your understanding of love and surrender in your relationship with God?

4. Reflecting on Abraham's journey, what past experiences of God's faithfulness in your life can you draw upon to fuel hope in your current challenges? * How can you actively wait on God, as Abraham did, trusting His promises even when the outcome is unclear? * What practices help you maintain faith and hope in difficult seasons?

5. Abraham's life appeared unremarkable on the surface, yet his faithfulness led to immeasurable impact. Can you embrace the idea that your seemingly ordinary life holds extraordinary significance in God's plan? * How do you reconcile the tension between feeling unremarkable and believing in your God-given destiny to bless your world? * What is one practical way you can live out this calling daily?

Abraham-The Love Stage in the New Testament

In the Parable of the Sower, the soil type before 30, 60, or 100-fold fruitfulness, housed weeds. Weeds suck the life out of the soil, grow around the good plants, and choke them. If your garden is overgrown, don't expect a harvest.

Weeds speak of carelessness. It is allowing other things to fill the space that was designed to house God and God-sown seeds. What began as an intentional effort to plan and plant can be left unattended once the plants are established.

If you are the soil, you then, as its gardener, need to protect it. You need to see the value of your own soul, the importance of the word that God has spoken to you, how that word and your soul work together, and then love them in such a way that both flourish.

Weeds can also speak of cluelessness. You can misidentify the things in your life and focus on them more than the things of God, or even God Himself. Jesus rebuked the Pharisees for elevating His word over Him.

Wheat looks a lot like tares, and tares, like wheat. So, if you aren't aware, you can let other things, even things that God has given, choke you. Isaac could have become a weed. He didn't, but Ishmael did and had to be painfully yanked.

How many legitimate areas of responsibility become the turf that you defend at all costs to your own hurt and others? If you have been a churchgoer for any amount of time, you have seen this at work. Watch someone inadvertently touch another's ministry and see what happens. "This is my job, my ministry." Feelings are hurt. Words are said.

"As for what was sown among thorns, this is the one who hears the word, but the cares of the world and the deceitfulness of riches choke the word, and it proves unfruitful." God-given things become cares and burdens when you center your life around them. You can also become anxious when you think that you might lose them.

If you center your life around things and let them define you, it's not going to go well for you. God-given things become deceitful riches when you find your worth and significance in them, when you value them more than God, and when you hold on to them more tightly than you ought.

This is the love test. Weedy soil will prove to be unfruitful. But the soil of Abraham's heart was tested on Moriah, and because he passed the test, he became fruitful. Un-weedy-ness which allows for a harvest finds its definition in Abraham's narrative and especially is discovered on the Mount.

Obviously, you are tested often, with the question being, "Do you love me more than these?" Sometimes you pass, and sometimes you fail. But this test for Abraham was different. It was his sort of "coming of age" test at 113 years old.

Once you have seen God fulfill His good will in you, once you know who you are, and once you are being and acting from the place, you will be asked to give your Isaac back. The questions that need to be answered are "Has what God shown you become internalized?" and "Do you love Me more than these?" If it has, you will get up early in the morning to go to Moriah. If not, you will drag your feet.

You succeed or fail depending on who or what is orbiting around whom. God has set up the entire creation as "wheels within wheels". Everything orbits something else. The universe, from atoms to solar systems, effortlessly exists this way.

God has created you to orbit around Him with the things that He has given to orbit around you. But when those things become your center, your world gets out of whack and the effort needed to hold everything in place becomes exhausting.

When you sense anxiety or when you find yourself stressed or angry, check your orbit-meter because emotions like these indicate that you are not rightly aligned with God and things are not rightly aligned with you. Or to use Biblical language, you are not right or righteous.

But Isaac was in his proper orbit. He was the son whom Abraham loved for sure, but Abraham's love was not possessive. God knew this. He said to Himself years earlier, "Abraham WILL command his children and his household after him to keep the way of the LORD." Even though, God knew that Abraham was rock solid, the test still came.

But why? I don't think that God was concerned about the outcome, nor is God into blind obedience. The test came as the culmination of all that

Abraham learned. Moriah was to be God's stamp of approval to show anyone who cared to look that wholeness or righteousness is possible and that God's way to a right sense of self is best.

Abraham became the father of the "by grace, through faith" principle because he passed the test. He became the father of all those who have fallen short of God's glory and who have been, and are being, restored to that same glory from which they fell. He became the father of those, who, despite their circumstances and inabilities, become exceedingly fruitful.

This means that how Abraham tended his garden is the pattern for his children to follow. The final love test precedes exceeding fruitfulness. Pulling weeds guarantees a harvest because it allows the plant to do its thing. Correctly addressing this stage and passing this test proves to you that, not only is God's way the best, but that your end will be the same as Abraham's, which was defined by the number of stars and all the grains of sand.

The test proved to Abraham that God's wisdom and way is more informed than any man-made or demon-inspired philosophy and that His power to make broken things whole, and insignificant things great, has no equal. The test proved that the faith walk works.

Job also teaches us that God had something to prove to the powers in the heavens. Paul agreed when he wrote, "Through the church, the manifold wisdom of God might now be known to the rulers and authorities in the heavenly places," that is, through the weakness of weaklings, the power of the evil cabal is broken.

If you were a betting person, I don't think that you would lay odds against the rulers and authorities in the heavens, especially with their opponents being the likes of you and me. But God takes that bet every time because He knows what He can do through weakness.

The test also came to prove to Abraham that you can't outgive God. You give Him your best and all heaven breaks loose. It came to prove to Abraham that you cannot outsmart God. You say "yes" just because you love Him, and you walk away amazed at His upside-down logic. It came, once and for all, to prove to Abraham that God had nothing but Abraham's best in mind.

And can you imagine Abraham's and Isaac's walk home? While they were close before, Abraham and Isaac's relationship went to another level. What an experience they had together! What discussions were formed around their time! What memories were created!

And, by the way, God had something to prove to Isaac. I'm not sure whether Isaac had encountered the God of his father before this moment or only believed because of his father, but from this moment on, I doubt that Isaac ever doubted again. Both walked confidently because God proved to them that He was real and really, really good. All because of this test.

So, you will need to attend to your weeds every day, just as you have to hold on to what God has said when the sun comes out, and just as you will need to say, "yes", when God speaks to you, and not let His word fall to the ground. What you do each day determines what you will do on THAT day.

The reason Moriah turned out the way it did is because Abraham gave Isaac over to the Lord every day, and Isaac surrendered his life to his father every day as well. Martyrs can joyfully give up their life on the evil day because they joyfully give up their lives when they wake up each morning.

Jesus said as much when He said, "If you are faithful in the little things, you WILL be faithful in the bigger things." (TCA) So, little tests come to ready you for the big test which comes to prove to you, to those around you, and to the powers that be that you know, from the deepest place, that you are God's beloved in whom He is well pleased.

Abraham never doubted his sonship or his purpose ever again. He just kept fathering. So, according to the Parable of the Sower, fruitfulness in your life, or you, becoming fully and effectively you, is determined by successfully navigating these stages of faith, hope, and love.

You, producing 30, 60, or 100-fold is the gospel or the good news of the garden. Conversely, the bad news is that your garden is overgrown with weeds. No crops. No beauty. No return on investment. The gospel is the good news of you growing into the person God imagined. The good news of Jesus is the good news of you becoming fully you. This glorifies God the most. Jesus agreed by saying, "By this my Father is glorified, that you bear much fruit and so prove to be my disciples."

Only being caught up in the Trinitarian relationship allows you to think this way. That is why you need to rethink how you think about God and get it aligned with John's and Paul's understanding. If you perceive God's holiness as primarily moral, you will find the thought of God embracing an "amazing you" hard to receive because you will never measure up to that sort of perfection.

But as you come to see that holy means "other", or so unbelievably different than anything you could ever imagine, you will begin to perceive God and His holiness in a new light. His Image will reflect Jesus and Jesus' relationship with

His Father more perfectly. You will see Him as He is—a relational, ever-including, and symbiotic Trinity, who is and was, and who evermore is continually drawing all into their Trinitarian embrace.

God is the Trinitarian relationship who desires all to be included in His sphere of love. And, as you begin to glimpse this, you will begin to discover the God whom you could never have imagined, and the "you" imagined before time.

So, the seed believed and received, the plant taking root and developing a root structure, and you pulling weeds guarantees fruitfulness. Receiving and believing God's estimation of yourself, holding on to it while living among nay-sayers (including yourself), and dealing with the distractions that try to define you will result in a sense of self that will glorify God.

I have also traced these three same stages in the New Testament's application of "it was accounted to him as righteousness". Scriptures interpret Scriptures. Not only did Jesus describe the life of faith in the Sower's parable, Paul and James did as well by referencing this phrase. So, from the mouth of two or three witnesses, as the Bible says, let everything be established.

As I have mentioned, this phrase was only spoken one time in Genesis when Abraham first believed something about himself. But the New Testament writers insert this phrase at other points of his life to explain that believing into who you are is a journey.

Righteousness, according to Abraham's life and as interpreted by Paul and James, is NOT just about being right with God. This is a given if you have surrendered your life to the Lordship of Jesus. Righteousness is becoming right with yourself.

It's you, fulfilling the Adamic and Abrahamic mandate of becoming fruitful, becoming great, and filling your God-given space with the "you" whom He created. It's you, growing into the likeness of the Image of God. It's you, knowing who you are, being satisfied, impactful, and at rest.

So, both Paul and James laid out the path which they discovered in Abraham's life. First, Abraham ended his disagreement under the stars with God's assessment of himself and believed, "So shall your offspring be", and therefore, "it was counted to him as righteousness". The years of being an unbelieving believer ended. Paul intimates this in Galatians where this phrase is tied to the immediacies of the gifts of the Spirit. Once you believe, God considers it done, even while God continues to work.

Paul then points past Abraham's initial believing because he uses this same phrase in Romans 4 to talk about the long process that Abraham went through to come to the end of his own ability and to hope against hope. This stage was marked by Abraham's effort to "do" God's will. Doing, however, is important because only as you exert effort will you come to the place where you realize that what God has called you to do is impossible.

So, don't be surprised when your "doings" come up empty or, possibly worse, when you find success and create your own Ishmael like Abraham. Misinterpreting one's failure has been a large reason some have left the faith. Being successful, though, can been a reason for some to believe their own press, even while their world is collapsing. Being aware of this necessary stage can put you in a good place to learn how to get back into the game and wait for Him.

You CAN avoid some pitfalls by learning from the meta-story of Abraham. "They who wait for the LORD shall renew their strength; they shall mount up with wings like eagles; they shall run and not be weary; they shall walk and not faint". You CAN learn to actively wait just like Abraham did, and, with this understanding, possibly learn sooner than he did.

But then you will be invited to Moriah where all that God has done in you will find its fulfillment. James wrote that "the Scripture was FULFILLED that says, 'Abraham believed God, and it was counted to him as righteousness'—and he was called a friend of God." On Moriah with a knife in his hand, Abraham became the "father of many nations".

"Fulfilled" means that the bow has been put on the package and what was first intended is now complete. God's purpose for Abraham was realized. Abraham was perfected because he embraced his identity. He didn't need externals to confirm who he was. He knew himself to be the person whom God imagined before time, with or without Isaac. "I am who I am", was Abraham's understanding of himself, regardless of externals.

James also says that God's purpose in testing was to grow their relationship and that their relationship would be defined as friendship. The last stage of your journey is the love stage because there is no greater or more satisfying love than friendship. Isn't the goal of marriage to have the passion of the bedroom morph into long walks together, hand in hand?

You become friends when the space between becomes smaller and smaller. You become friends because of shared history, shared interests, enjoying each other's company, having mutual respect and trust, liking each other, comfortability and conformability, and completing each other. You can befriend anyone, but you can't be, and aren't, friends with everyone. This is the hand of friendship God is extending to you because He wants those long walks together.

Friendship only satisfies and works between equals who don't think of themselves as better or worse, or on a higher or lower level. They just are. They together are the blending of two unique people, who become a single living, breathing entity. This is the essence of the Trinitarian relationship—the Father and Son, in the atmosphere of the Spirit, uniquely different yet one.

And it is into this friendship or fellowship that you have been invited. For the last time, hear my plea—"Behold your God!" Lean into an understanding of this God who lives in a delightful, engaging, purposeful, and playful relationship that is called agape', and pursue the Presence who pursues you.

You are "in Christ" which means that the relationship Father and Son experience in the atmosphere of the Spirit is, in every way and in the fullest measure, yours, and this should define you. But this sense won't be yours in experience unless you begin to embrace the God of all grace and reject any other version, regardless of how sovereign and holy it seems, and then embrace the glorified you, however powerless and messed up you seem. In so doing, you will discover the Sovereign and Holy One.

God called Abraham a friend, and not just because he obeyed. Obedience is a part of it though because Jesus did say that obedience is one measure of friendship. A dog, however, obeys as well, especially if you have a treat or a remoter for a shock collar in your hand. Hopefully, a buzzer or treat-type of obedience is not your mindset.

Abraham's obedience was not coerced. He was willing and more than willing. So, how can this even be called obedience? Isn't it just better to call it adoration and worship? Wouldn't you just call it love or friendship?

Friends are secure in who they are and in their relationship. Abraham knew that he could ask God for anything, even bringing the number of the righteous down to 10 to stave off judgment. And he knew that God would only ask good of him.

Moriah foreshadowed the greatest display of God's nature on this side of eternity. The relationship of Father and the Son that played out on the cross was first demonstrated on Moriah, where Abraham's love for God surpassed his love for the gift God had given Him. And because of their friendship, the sands of the sea and the stars of heaven, together, don't come close to the greatness of Abraham. And as God spoke to Abraham, "So shall YOUR seed be", so He speaks to you.

This friendship and certainty that Abraham had about God and that God had about Abraham was revealed on Moriah and was rooted in Abraham's sense of self. He began his journey not knowing who he was, but he left Moriah knowing, without the need to say a word, that he had now become the person God imagined. The image of God was completely revealed and perfected in Abraham. Abraham's rightness was complete and has become the definition of righteousness for all.

This will also be your experience as well, as you continue your journey with him on the path of faith, hope, and love. This is the journey from brokenness to wholeness, from being unright to being righted, from glory to glory, and from sinnership to sonship. It is now time for you to follow the breadcrumbs.

Questions

1. How has this book reshaped your view of God as a Trinitarian relationship of mutual love, inclusion, and delight? * In what ways does this differ from your previous perceptions of God's nature? * Which aspects of the Trinity's relational dynamic challenge you, and what might you begin to embrace as you rethink God's character?

2. Has your perception of yourself as deeply loved, inherently significant, and secure in God's care evolved through reading this book? * How would you describe your sense of self before and after engaging with these ideas? * Can you see yourself reflected in the journeys of Adam, Peter, or Abraham, and are you beginning to believe the "good news" of your own worth? * What steps are you taking to internalize this truth?

3. Do you now see yourself as created in God's image with the potential to grow into His likeness, reflecting your inherent worth and divine purpose? * How does this understanding influence your view of your current circumstances as God's "garden" for growth? * Are you beginning to embrace this identity, and how might this shape your ongoing journey of wonder and worship?

4. Has your definition of righteousness shifted from a focus on moral perfection to an identity rooted in being right with God and yourself? * How does Abraham's story illustrate this concept of righteousness as becoming the person God imagined? * Are you embracing both the good news of God's grace and the good news of your own purpose—that through you, your world can be blessed? * What challenges remain in fully accepting this truth?

5. How has this book clarified the process of becoming who God created you to be, through faith, hope, and love? * Do you recognize the stages of believing God's estimation of you, holding fast amidst challenges, and surrendering to God's love as illustrated by Abraham's journey to Moriah? * How are you navigating distractions or "weeds" in your life, and what practices are you adopting to align your "orbit" with God's purpose for you?

6. What is one key insight, truth, or practice you are taking away from From Sinnership to Sonship that will shape your spiritual journey moving forward? * Are there chapters of this book that you will want to reread?

Afterword

Well, there you have it. Have you seen it? Has there been a shift in your thinking? If you remember, I began this book by saying once you have seen it, it cannot be unseen. And the "it" is the amazingly good news of you and your sonship. Have you sensed your heart open up like the sunflower on the front cover?

When I began this book, I also said that I was going to push some boundaries with the hope that you begin to discover a God whom you could never have imagined and the "you" imagined before time. How did I do?

And not so much on the boundary-pushing part because I knew that I was going to do that. I needed to push out the sides of your box because the one you have put God in is way too small, as is the box you have put yourself in. God is always outside of your box, no matter how big you think He is.

So, how DID I do? Have you finished this book with questions? I hope so. Questions are so much better than answers if your heart is open to the Holy Spirit because questions always lead you to better questions. Questions are the breadcrumbs that you are to follow. The breadcrumbs that the Holy Spirit scatters, however, are not heady theological or eschatological stuff.

So, don't waste your time trying to figure out how many angels dance on the head of a pin or whether the anti-christ is hiding in Turkey or the Ukraine. The breadcrumbs He scatters are about God and about YOU, and as you follow, you will discover God and when you discover Him, you will discover yourself as well. He, as your Father, and you, His son.

So, are you beginning to rethink your perception of God and yourself? Were you able to see yourself in the stories of Adam, Peter, and Abraham? Have you dared to believe yourself to be a son in all its heretical implications? Have you stopped to worship and wonder, as you have glimpsed yourself in the light of the glory of God in the face of Jesus Christ?

Are you beginning to consider that the fulness of God's heart toward you is embarrassingly true, that is, you are more loved and valued than you can imagine, more significant and important than all the celebrities and influencers in the world, and that you are safe enough to take risks by loving others and Him? Have you seen that the best place for you to become the person God imagined is right where you are and with those around you? If you have, I will have done my job.

Some reading this, however, have had a hard time because it seems that I have softened the hard edge of truth. I get it. As I said in the beginning, "Grace creates such a disturbance and is so foreign that it takes time to figure out."

Sometimes, however, hardened theological positions need to be softened. Jesus softened the Scriptures all the time, especially with those who were already soft. He hardened the Scriptures, however, with those who were hard. If you have found resistance to this amazing news, maybe you need to check the condition of your heart. Just saying.

Did you come away with the thought that this cannot be true? Good. The good news of Jesus Christ is so good, it is unbelievably true. Again, as I wrote in the introduction, for you to begin to comprehend the love of God and his heart toward you, many "grace bombs" would need to find their target. Have they?

Even if what I have written is my own fantasy, doesn't your heart long to know a God like this and to know yourself in this manner? Jesus DID say, "According to your faith, or what you believe, be it unto you." But if you were moved by what I wrote about God and about yourself, then you are experiencing the witness of the Spirit and are on your way.

If so, you are now to hold onto that seed, regardless of how you feel, regardless of your ability, and regardless of what your circumstances say because God is watching over His word to fulfill it. Remember, Abraham's initial believing into God's assessment of himself BEGAN his journey into greatness.

If you continue to follow in his footsteps, you will discover an identity that will morph into a greatness, which will exceed all of the stars in the universe and all of the sand by the sea, combined. This is your destiny if you continue believing because God has called you, "Son".

There are still a couple pieces of unfinished business that I need to take care of that will not happen in this book because it is long enough. I alluded to how Paul turned the four spheres of death, which poisoned humanity when Adam sinned, on their head. Paul, in Ephesians 5, tells you how you can participate in redeeming the four spheres of your life which Jesus has already redeemed on the cross. This requires another chapter.

I also want to lay out more fully Jude's understanding of "the faith once for all time delivered into the hand of the saints", and how to keep yourself in the love of God. That faith, that believing, which will keep you going forward, is not some objective truths, but is God's love for you, embraced by you.

And I said that I wanted to give you my understanding of what happened on the cross and in the grave, by examining the three-fold sacrifice on the Day of Atonement. The cross was NOT about God being angry with sinners and punishing Jesus because Paul plainly states that the Father was IN Christ, reconciling the world to Himself. His wrath was poured out upon those things that have kept Him from enjoying you when Jesus became sin, and the Day of Atonement testifies to that.

I have put these three chapters on my website. You will find them helpful. You will find these chapters on www.tomanderson.in. You can also order multiple copies of this book, on the website at a discount, if you want to use this for group discussions. This book might be best read and considered in a group.

Additionally, I said, in the introduction, my hope is that this book would become part of a larger family conversation. So, there is also a "connect with me" feature on the site, and, as long as the Lord has me around, I would love to continue a conversation with you.

The only thing that I ask is that you identify yourself (isn't that the rage now?) as one of the three categories which I laid out in the chapter "The Trinity and Your Sense of Self". Do you come from an "Outer Court", a "Holy Place" or "Holy of Holies" understanding of God and yourself? Does your understanding of God, and of yourself, begin in the fall, in creation, or in Eternity?

I am asking this to determine whether you have any self-awareness. Are you a seeker or have you set up shop in your own box? I really don't have the time, nor the desire, to argue with those who just want to argue. My intent is to invite discussion as the Lord did through Isaiah. "'Come now, let us reason together,' says the LORD."

God's premise, God's thought process, God's deep desire is that you come around to His way of thinking through dialogue. His upside-down logic is "Though your sins are like scarlet, they shall be as white as snow; though they are red like crimson, they shall become like wool." And this sure sounds to me like a restatement of the title of this book. *From Sinnership to Sonship: The Story of Becoming.*

Acknowledgments

How can I not thank Nancy, my wife of over 50 years? I can't, so thank you, sweetie. Our marriage has been the backdrop for this book. We have walked this path together and have heard God say, "So shall your seed be", and have seen God work in us what we could never have done by ourselves. This story is not mine, but ours.

To Jason Varner, a theological nerd whose heart is bigger than his head. Thanks for your willingness, in the busy-ness of your life, to take on the project of writing the forward and putting my ramblings into a larger framework. Thanks for your friendship, and for writing the forward.

And I want to thank my friend of over 40 years, Jim Stockwell, who told me that he was praying that I would write another book after I had determined NOT to write. I am glad that his encouragement prompted me to put on paper what has been residing in my heart for years. This story has also been his.

And to Bill Jeynes who has told me often that he is my biggest fan and encourager (outside of my wife). I am amazed at your friendship. Again, thanks!

Also by Tom Anderson

Ephesians and All that Jazz. Riffing with Paul.

Ephesians and All that Jazz is my rendition of Paul's book. I took liberty to write it in Paul's voice and pull back the curtain on what went on in his heart. The process transformed me. The eyes of my heart WERE opened to truths that had been obscure. The relationship of Trinitarian God took center stage and began to inform me of who I was. Also, the Pauline prayers came alive, as did grace, "entrenched behaviors", being filled with Spirit, and spiritual warfare. You will find these enlightening as well, as it shifts your thinking. It was published in 2020 by Resource Publications, a division of Wipf and Stock.

Praise for *Ephesians and All that Jazz*

Tom's book was thoroughly delightful! I smiled and even laughed out loud while reading it. It is energetic, engaging, and playful. It has a rhythm to it that is all its own. I have no doubt that it will delight others just as it did me.
Summer Lacy. Author of "His Word Alone"

Tom's rendition of Ephesian is an amazing and delightful book. You must read the first two chapters. These chapters alone are worth a hundred times the price of the book. By the end of the book, the reader will feel like he knows Tom. Whether you are thinking of a book for yourself, an unbeliever, or a believer, this book is for you. On top of that, this book will draw you into the Word of God in a fresh way.
William Jeynes. PhD. Professor at U of C

This is a fascinating book. I enjoyed reading it.
Randy Brown. www.biblebuyingguild.com

Available on Amazon and other sites.